Developing
New Products
With TQM

Other Quality Control Books from McGraw-Hill

Developing New Products With TQM

Charles D. Gevirtz, P.E., C.Q.E.

McGraw-Hill, Inc.

New York   San Francisco   Washington, D.C.   Auckland   Bogotá
Caracas   Lisbon   London   Madrid   Mexico City   Milan
Montreal   New Delhi   San Juan   Singapore
Sydney   Tokyo   Toronto

Library of Congress Cataloging-in-Publication Data

Gevirtz, Charles D.
      Developing new products with TQM / Charles D. Gevirtz.
            p.   cm.
      Includes bibliographical references and index.
      ISBN 0-07-023573-2
      1. Total quality management.   2. New products—Management.
      3. Industrial engineering. I. Title.
      HD62.15.G48   1994
      658.5′62—dc20   93-21915
                                                                  CIP

1 2 3 4 5 6 7 8 9 0   DOC/DOC   9 8 7 6 5 4 3

ISBN 0-07-023573-2

*The sponsoring editor for this book was Hal B. Crawford, the editing
supervisor was Joseph Bertuna, and the production supervisor was
Pamela A. Pelton. It was set in Century Schoolbook by McGraw-Hill's
Professional Book Group composition unit.*

Printed and bound by R. R. Donnelley & Sons Company.

To my parents Jane and Norman for their love and caring. To my brother and sisters Felicia, Ivan, and Karen.

And to the memory of Cornell and Chuck Amster, Ben, Buddy and Richard Bader, Gene Dwyer, Manny Fisher, Louis and Helen Gevirtz, Tony Kern, Manny Rosenwasser, Fanny and George Schwartz, Steven Stark, and finally to Brenda, Marley, Max, and T.C. Gevirtz.

Contents

Preface

International competition has raised the performance requirements of new products in order for them to remain successful in the marketplace. A company must strive for top performance in all operating aspects in order to compete in this environment. The total quality management (TQM) techniques described in this book outline a system as well as the methods and skills that will enable an organization to succeed in the face of its competitors. In May 1991 in GAO/NSIAD-91-190 "Management Practices: U.S. Companies Improve Performance Through Quality Efforts," the U.S. General Accounting Office reported that

> Companies that adopted quality management practices experienced an overall improvement in corporate performance. In nearly all cases, companies that used Total Quality Management practices achieved better employee relations, higher productivity, greater customer satisfaction, increased market share, and improved profitability.... However, none of these companies reaped those benefits immediately. Allowing sufficient time for results to be achieved was as important as initiating a quality management program.

Developing New Products With TQM integrates key management disciplines so that, working together, a cohesive product development process may be begun. TQM will enable its practitioners to rapidly develop new products in a systematic, customer-oriented manner. The products will appeal to their customers and lead to long-term customer satisfaction which improves profitability. The methods and techniques outlined are designed not only to share the latest techniques used in a particular discipline with managers and employees, but also to introduce techniques used in other disciplines. This will give these people a better understanding of the issues facing their counterparts and, as a result, enable them to work with those in other functional areas more effectively. The book discusses both fundamental and advanced methods in marketing, engineering, manufacturing, accounting, purchasing, quality assurance, program management, and supplier involvement. The book walks readers through these methods, many of which are illustrated with practical, real-world examples, and has over 100 figures to better help the reader understand the concepts discussed. This enables readers to gain a thorough understanding of the methods. The book discusses in a logical manner the topics that can be pragmatically implemented in a manufacturing company.

This book can be used by professionals, executives, and managers working in manufacturing industries including the following disciplines: program management, marketing, manufacturing, engineering, quality assurance, purchasing, finance, accounting, and general management. Other people who will benefit are both university students and professors of industrial engineering, operations research, business administration, marketing, business technology, and program management.

There will be times when some sections are somewhat technical. The non technically oriented reader should at least review such sections to gain an appreciation of the issues involved. It is important to include these sections. Many management books make references to these technical issues but do not go into detail to explain how to implement or perform such tasks. This book discusses how to implement or perform systems and techniques such as lean production, SPC, activity-based cost accounting, design reviews, failure mode and effects analysis, design verification and reliability testing, value engineering, reducing product development time, etc. Some companies have tried to implement a total quality management system by primarily addressing the people issues while ignoring the technical and system issues or addressing technical training while ignoring people skills and the reward systems. They found that their products still took too long to develop, had higher than expected manufacturing costs, and were judged by their customers to be of inferior quality. This occurred because they did not address both the fundamental technical and people changes needed to make the TQM system successful. Therefore, it is imperative for corporate management to approach TQM from both a people and a technical aspect. This book will explain such methods so that corporate managers who are serious about improving their systems and methods can rapidly develop new products that are successful in the marketplace.

Charles D. Gevirtz

Acknowledgments

I would like to thank my original mentors, Jim Prestel and Tom Golec, two outstanding engineers, for teaching me engineering fundamentals. I would like to thank Tom Johnston's excellent quality organization from Chrysler Corp. for training me in Preventative Quality Assurance Methodology, including: Russ Jacobs, Tom Calkins, Bob Roush, Mel Cameron, Jim Timlin, Peter Greinert, Mike Warren, Jerry Fani, Mike Thornbury, Don Plezia, Rich Yandora, Gene Prizgent, Terry Merrick, and the others whom I worked with. I would like to thank Kaye Larkin, Ron Griem, Gary Taylor, Rick Dietz, Jim Diffy, and the other fine quality personnel of the Trenton Engine plant who taught the practical methods for developing quality system. I would also like to thank Maurice Wayne, who is one the most outstanding Total Quality Professional that I have ever worked with, for sharing with me the latest developments in Total Quality Management.

I would like to thank the following individuals for assisting me with my book and providing constructive criticism: Cindy Spiegel, Jake Prosper, Rodger Sterling, John Martin, Richard Richardson, Dick Bradyhouse, Kerri Miller, Marc Rachman, Oliver Campbell, Bruce Harris, John Foster, Mike Burke, Tom Golec, Tom Price, Mike Thornbury, Mel Cameron, Bruce Webster, Mike Handley, Rich Rusinowski, Dennis LeFaize, and Christa Cohen.

I would also like to thank the following organizations for their assistance with this book:

American Society for Quality Control, American Telephone & Telegraph, Amoco Chemical Company, Brighton Tool & Die, Champion Laboratories, Inc., Chrysler Corporation, CP Research, Dirksen Screw Products, General Motors Research Labs, H & W Screw Products, International Labor Organization, Jefferson Rubber Works Inc., The Molding Company (a Division of Premix Inc.), NSK Corporation of America, Productivity Press, Reinze Wisconsin Gasket, SKF Bearing Industries, Specialty Forming, Inc., Technical Assistance Research

Programs (TARP), Technimark Inc., Warren Division of Black & Decker.

The Importance of Preventative Total Quality and Overview of the Planning Process

"Plan and prepare; don't react and despair."
CHARLES GEVIRTZ

Introduction

This book introduces ways of improving the product development process. The book discusses the various responsibilities of the key functions including marketing, engineering, manufacturing, quality, and purchasing. Some of the formal planning and analysis techniques that these functions should use will be explained, along with demonstrations showing how to apply them.

Frequently, management books point out differences in techniques used by successful companies and those used by less successful ones. This book will explain some of those techniques and demonstrate how to apply them. Finally, the reader will gain a better understanding and appreciation for the issues, methodology, and processes that are used by several key organizational disciplines.

The principles discussed can be applied in such diverse manufacturing industries including industrial, transportation, consumer, health and beauty, and food and beverage products. However, other enterprises, such as restaurants and hotels can also benefit by applying the principles discussed. The methods discussed are general, so changes will be needed for specific industries and applications.

The nontechnical reader may prefer to skim the more technical sections in the book to obtain a better overall understanding of the process, while the technical reader can study and review those sections in more detail. One can review these methods and see how they can be adapted to their specific industries.

This book will show many examples of what is being discussed throughout the book. Wherever possible, real-world examples have been included.

Project Team Organization

The method describes a teamwork-oriented project management approach which improves the project's prospects for success and discusses preventative planning techniques. Traditionally, department functions serve to protect their own purposes: marketing is concerned with maximizing sales; purchasing with obtaining the lowest price; engineering with the most technically advanced and reliable design; manufacturing with assuring that the product is as easy as possible to manufacture in high volumes; and quality wants the product to meet specifications and not to have customer complaints. Such charters will result in inherent conflicts between departments. Potential conflicts can, however, be reduced if upper management establishes corporate and interdepartmental goals which take priority over department goals. Conflicts can be reduced further by monitoring performance on several indicators including achievement of corporate and interdepartmental as well as department goals. However, there may still be priority conflicts between projects and some projects may be unnecessarily delayed. Therefore, a project team–oriented management approach may be a preferred method.

Reward/recognition system

The reward/recognition system for a project team should include group rewards/recognition for satisfactory team performance as well as individual rewards/recognition where appropriate. Performance reviews should reward teamwork, while individual employee evaluations should be conducted by several managers and colleagues. Such evaluations should be performed in a constructive manner.

Background of TQM

Total quality management (TQM) began in the late 1940s with quality gurus such as Juran, Feigenbaum, and Deming. In 1951 Armand V. Feigenbaum authored the book *Total Quality Control* and that same year Joseph M. Juran edited *Juran's Quality Control Handbook.* TQM caught on more heavily in Japan after this period and led that nation into a transformation from a nation that made shoddy products to a nation that made high-quality products. It has been speculated that this was possible because Japan had lost World War II which resulted in a perceived need to change. At that time, the United States was the world's largest industrial power, and U.S. products were generally regarded as being of high quality. Therefore, they did not perceive a need to change and did not realize that quality standards would improve substantially in upcoming decades. In 1951 the Japanese Union of Scientists and Engineers issued the Deming Prize to a company that demonstrated the most effective implementation of quality policies. This soon became a highly coveted award in Japan.

In 1987 the U.S. government issued the Malcolm Baldrige Award for companies that demonstrated successful implementation of quality assurance programs and systems.

TQM philosophies advocate that all aspects of the company must be well managed and *all* employees well trained with adequate authority to perform their jobs effectively. The Japanese principle of "Kaizan" stresses that all employees should continually search for improvements, no matter how small, everywhere, every day. TQM teaches a philosophy of defect prevention in which a broad interpretation of the term "defect" includes unsatisfactory performance in terms of product, information, or achievement of goals to internal customers and external customers as well as management. TQM also includes a good feedback system so that problem areas can be quickly identified and improved.

Dr. Deming created the "Deming wheel" to demonstrate the *Plan-Do-Check-Act* process for good management. This states that management must *plan,* or develop, goals and plans for improvements and agree to completion dates with their personnel. Next, management is responsible to *do,* or implement, the plan. Then they must *check,* or review, the results on the specified date. Finally, management must *act* by determining what further actions need to be taken. The process then repeats itself. The "check" step in the method was included because Deming realized the importance of management review and audit.

Common Pitfalls with TQM Implementation

Common problems plaguing companies who are embarking on a TQM management philosophy include

1. Management does not devote sufficient resources to training and developing its personnel.
2. Management has insisted that the process is implemented in a manner that employees find acceptable.

3. Upper management does not devote enough time to the issue.

4. Decision-making authority is not delegated to lower levels in the organization.

Avoiding the Pitfalls

The management must also establish a series of preventative quality indicators such as monitoring the number of capable processes on a manufacturing floor, the number of engineering changes that have been issued after initial drawing release, how many tasks were completed after the scheduled completion date, how many tasks had to be revised or redone due to ineffective planning, and so on. However, rather than set numerical goals for improvement, one should monitor improvements and determine how they were achieved. The reasons are that numerical goals may be less aggressive than can actually be achieved once a breakthrough has taken place and that numerical goals have a way of being achieved even if they were not achieved by desirable means. They can frequently be achieved by number manipulation rather than improvements in the process. The methodology by which improvements were reported should be thoroughly investigated to assure that they were achieved in a manner that was consistent with the intent of the goal and did not compromise corporate objectives. An example of such a manipulation would be a plant manager who reports that goals to reduce scrap and improve on time delivery performance have been successfully accomplished. However, a closer investigation reveals that his methodology resulted in an increase in customer complaints. The reason is that many unit components which should have been scrapped were used "as is" and many of the finished products which should have been repaired were shipped to the customer in order to achieve the stated goals. Ultimately this will manifest itself with an increase in customer complaints. However, if the feedback process is slow, the plant manager may be promoted out of his position because of his "remarkable management capabilities."

Upper management needs to spend time discussing TQM implementation and reviewing progress on preventative quality indicators. If they verbally state that "they want total quality and it is their highest priority" or "quality is the most important element in our business," it will not be convincing or supported by their subordinates if they spend the rest of their time reviewing financial reports, developing trade partners, and evaluating new acquisitions among other issues. If total quality is as important to them as they claim, they must spend significant amounts of time discussing it and reviewing progress with their management team.

Management should allow employees to determine how they will achieve the goals that have been established. However, coaching should be encouraged if requested or needed by the employees.

Change is not easy to effect, and there will usually be some growing pains in the process. Change is easier to effect when management and employees perceive a need to change or are involved in a crisis situation. This is sometimes brought about by a competitive threat and seeing a real need to change. Alternately, if management spends time discussing quality, provides training, and is monitoring progress, then these improvements are much more likely to be successful. This is especially true if top management allows a free exchange with subordinates to discuss the difficulties encountered.

Implementing quality successfully into a company's daily operating practices will not be easy. It will take repetition, reinforcement, and monitoring. Frequently, it will require changes in operating practices and decisions. Company personnel will have to make decisions about how to satisfy their customer—from the customer's perspective. This is instead of their own personal preferences or numerical performance goals and corporate operating constraints. It will take a conscious effort on the part of company personnel to make this transformation, but it is required in order to be successful in the marketplace.

The Importance of a Preventative Approach

To successfully introduce new products in a cost-effective manner, resources should be allocated up-front to prevent problems rather than react to problems. Companies will spend more time and money correcting a problem when it occurs than they would have preventing it. It is more expensive to fix problems farther along in a development cycle and/or after a product has been manufactured than it is to prevent them. Figure 1.1 illustrates how a proactive company institutes a majority of engineering changes well before new production start-ups while a reactive company institutes a majority just before and after a new product launch. The area under the curve suggests that more resources are used in the reactive company than in the proactive company. Additionally, it shows that the reactive company has already shipped products with design problems to their customers.

Technical Assistance Research Program (TARP) has found that

1. Between 40 and 50 percent of the customers who are dissatisfied with a product complain. This means that more than half do not (this varies by industry and product). Only about 5 percent of these complaints were made direct to the manufacturer; the rest were to the retailer.[1]

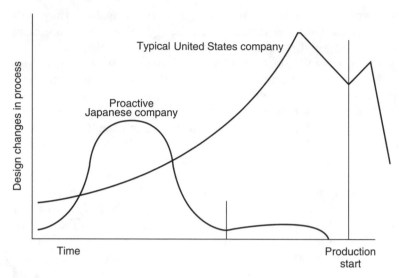

Figure 1.1   An engineering change comparison between a typical United States company and a proactive Japanese company. (*Courtesy of the American Supplier Institute, Dearborn, Mich.*)

2. Ninety-one percent of unhappy customers who did *not* complain will not buy another product from that manufacturer. (This applies to products whose complaint value was more than $100). Sixty-three percent of unsatisfied customers who experienced minor dissatisfaction (the value of the complaint was less than $5) and did not complain would *not* make another purchase of that product.[2]

3. As a rule of thumb, it costs 5 times more to get a new customer than to retain an old one (this can vary significantly with different industries).[3]

4. Generally speaking, the average unhappy customer tells twice as many people about their dissatisfaction with a product than they would if they were satisfied with a product. Also, the more expensive the product, the more people they will tell.[4]

The General Electric Company (GE) found that word-of-mouth advertising had more impact on consumer purchase decisions for their high-ticket goods than media advertisements. Only 29 percent of the consumers found manufacturers' advertising useful when considering the purchase of high-ticket durable goods, while 61 percent found that the opinions of friends were useful.[5] TARP found that the potential negative exposure for a company of making one customer unhappy is approximately 10 people for a low-ticket good (costing less than 5 dollars in the time period 1979–1992) such as a soft drink and 16 people for a high-ticket good (costing over 100 dollars) such as an automobile.[4] Additionally, they lose the positive word-of-mouth advertising that would be experienced from happy customers (which is about 5 people for low-ticket items and 8 for high-ticket goods). Using these numbers, one can conclude that the magnitude of the difference in positive exposure and negative exposure is 16 people for low-ticket item and 25 for a high-ticket good (see Fig. 1.2).

The bad publicity described will not change all people's purchase selections based on their friends' information. However, based on the GE study, it should influence more than half of the people who were in the process of buying such a product, and it will have much more impact than mass media advertising. With all the money spent on advertising, it would be logical to devote more resources and efforts to quality.

The negative effects resulting from poor quality could have a very large expense when one considers the cost to overcome this bad publicity in terms of advertising dollars. Suppose a firm has a profit margin as a percentage of sales of 6 percent, and 2 percent of its sales dollars are spent on advertising. This company is spending 25 percent of its potential profits to generate further sales. Therefore, a firm cannot afford to overlook the effects of positive or negative word-of-mouth advertising that relate to the quality of the products sold. Additionally, companies with a reputation for supplying quality products can frequently charge a premium for their products and enjoy a higher profit margin. It is often less expensive to resolve problems with old customers in order to maintain brand loyalty than to win a new customer.

As a result of this information and other studies, TARP concluded that developing an effective consumer-complaint–handling system will greatly enhance business success through improved sales. The sales improvements result from (1) improved or maintained brand

	Number of people affected	
	Low-ticket product	High-ticket product
The unhappy customer	−1	−1
Number of friends they tell of their dissatisfaction with a product.	−10	−16
Minus: the number of friends to whom they would have made positive comments about the product, if they were satisfied with it.	(5)	(8)
Total	−16	−25

Figure 1.2 The number of potential customers who are the recipients of bad publicity about a product from a dissatisfied customer.

loyalty from customers whose complaints were satisfactorily resolved, (2) positive word-of-mouth advertising, (3) reduced negative word-of-mouth exposure, and (4) having fewer product problems experienced with future customers because the reported sources of dissatisfaction were permanently addressed with product improvements and other corrective measures. A properly developed customer complaint system will make it easy for customers to report issues of dissatisfaction with their products.

A good customer complaint and corrective action system addresses quality problems effectively in a reactive mode. However, this approach should be used in conjunction with a more preventative approach. Many companies are realizing that preventative planning lowers total operating expenditures. These savings result from reduced engineering design and test time, tooling revisions, engineering changes, in-plant rework, and warranty expenditures. Once a defect or design problem gets into the system, the cost to correct the problem increases astronomically, the closer that the defective product has gotten to the customer. This can be summarized by the 1-10-100 rule, which is shown in Fig. 1.3. This rule says that it costs 1 unit to prevent problems, 10 units to correct a situation before it reaches the customer, and 100 to correct a situation after it reaches the customer. The 100 incorporates warranty expenses and corporate resources used to correct the problem including failure investigation, testing, administrative expenses, travel expenses, product liability, and so on. To illustrate this concept, Ricoh Co., Ltd., estimated that it cost them \$590,000 to correct a defect in a copier after it reached customers. It would have cost \$17,000 to correct it before leaving the plant, \$368 to correct it before beginning production, and \$35 dollars to correct it before making the initial components.[6] However, these reported costs do *not* include possible lost sales of future products due to dissatisfied customers.

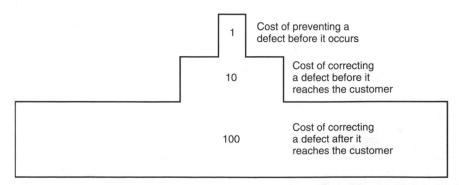

Figure 1.3   The 1-10-100 rule.

A common misunderstanding is that a company can catch all the defects so that their customers will have zero defect products. Juran reports that 100 percent inspection catches approximately 80 percent of the defects (this number varies with the inspection method and product complexity).[7] Companies that are detection-oriented often ship marginal products which result in more customer complaints. Additionally, resources are not utilized efficiently, as was shown in Fig. 1.1 which depicted the number of engineering changes in proactive companies vs. reactive companies. Therefore, to have the best quality and lowest cost, one must focus on the preventative aspects of planning. Figure 1.4 shows some of the system and attitude differences between proactive companies and reactive companies. In order to become more proactive, the corporate culture needs to be changed. This requires a lot of training, repetition, and reinforcement from upper management.

	Prevention versus Detection	
Systems approach:	Up-front involvement with different disciplines: marketing, engineering, manufacturing, quality. (concurrent product development)	Specifying a product; telling the next department affected to make the product as specified
	Documenting procedures and requirements	Operating with verbal instructions
	Manufacturing components to engineering specifications or requesting written deviations.	Manufacturing components and reacting if someone complains
	Utilizing statistical process controls	Reacting when processes manufacture product out of specification
	Zero defects	Acceptable quality levels
Attitudes:	Let's see how we can improve our existing methods.	We've always done it that way, why change?
	Let's address this before it becomes a problem.	If it becomes a problem, we will fix it then.
	Let's try to see how we can make it work.	It will never work!
	It does not meet requirements.	It's good enough for now.

Figure 1.4   Some differences in approaches between prevention and detection-oriented organizations.

Statistical techniques are an effective tool that can be used to help implement a preventative quality approach. In a manufacturing environment, it can be used to determine if the manufacturing process is capable or if something undesirable has changed in the process. Statistical analysis can be used for the purpose of "inspecting to prevent defects" as opposed to "inspecting to detect defects." The distinction is subtle, but the difference between the two approaches can result in substantial savings in terms of scrap and lost production output from machinery.

Independent Quality Department

It is important that everyone in the company have responsibility for quality. However, to assure that the system is working as it is supposed to, an independent quality assurance department that reports to the president of the company should exist. The quality organization's responsibility is to report the status of quality as an audit function, not to be responsible for it. In the world of finance, an independent auditing principle is a requirement for financial reports so that stockholders are not misled by erroneous financial reports into making poor investment decisions. Without such a system, shareholders would frequently assume that their company's earnings are growing and its stock prices are increasing when in fact it's about to be forced to file for bankruptcy. Financial analysts would not give any credence to a company's earning reports that were not independently verified. Another example would be automobile drivers who know that it is safer to drive at a lower speed. They also know that they are required to obey posted speed limits. These laws are frequently violated even with strong law enforcement. If traffic law enforcement did not exist, speeding and other traffic violations would increase, as would traffic accidents. The U.S. Congress General Accounting Office reports how the Executive Branch spends tax dollars so that misuses of money can be identified and corrected.

The independent audit principle also applies to quality. Unfortunately, there is a delay between the time that a product is designed, developed, manufactured, and sold—feedback is slow. Audits reduce exposure to quality problems that exist but would not normally be identified. Audits also help reinforce management priorities and focus on properly practicing and following quality methodologies and the business management systems. By having independent audits of products as well as management systems and procedures, employees will be reminded of the importance of following procedures by assuring a proper system of review and reinforcement. Without an audit system, the customer becomes the inspector and determines whether a product is acceptable. This is a very undesirable, risky, and expensive way for a company to conduct its business affairs. Therefore, if properly established, an independent quality department can be cost-effective.

The audits should be randomly performed. If they are announced in advance, management can prepare for them and present information so that it looks better than actual business practices would normally indicate.

The quality department should prioritize its audits to address issues where, if discrepancies exist, they will have an adverse effect on existing and future products as well as the management system.

Plant quality control managers should report to an independent quality organization or have a matrix reporting structure to this organization in addition to the plant manager. If a matrix reporting structure is used, both the quality assurance and the plant management should be involved in the review process. If the quality department only reports to manufacturing, and a quality-related production or supply problem that is expensive to correct is imminent, quality decisions may take a back seat. The quality manager's concerns will frequently not receive the attention that is deserved.

Lower Decision-Making Authority

Employees must be empowered to make decisions that affect their job. The decision-making authority must be moved down to a lower level. To assure that decisions are well thought out, a committee of persons affected by a decision should be involved and they should report the results of their decisions to their management. The committee should be interdisciplinary when decisions affect other areas of the organization. Employee training is a requirement for this system to work. The employees should be given brief overview training in market research, financial analysis, problem-solving skills, conducting meetings, and engineering research reporting methodology. The training should help employees understand the issues involved when they are presented with finance information, market research, or engineering research results.

Self-Directed Work Teams

On the factory floor the self-empowerment principle applies. Employees should have the responsibility to make recommendations regarding improvements in material handling, ergonomics, manufacturing process, product, productivity, or reducing costs. If the suggestion requires an investment that exceeds a predetermined amount, or if a product or process change is involved, a coordinator will oversee the project. The coordinator will assure that affected departments are involved in the decision-making process. Again, in order for self-empowered work teams to be successful, extensive training is paramount.

The Product Development Cycle

A phased approach is recommended for management of the product development cycle. Breaking down the approach into phases (1) enables the program manager to determine how well the project is progressing according to the schedule, (2) allows for specific times when the management can review the project to determine if it should continue, and (3) provides a sense of urgency for the team to meet the project completion dates at each phase.

Rosenau recommends an eight-phase approach.[8] The eight-phase approach involves a variation of the following phases (he gives the phases different names in his book): idea/concept origination, new technology feasibility study, specification development, design (advanced prototype), development (prototype), pilot lot, production start-up, and postintroduction market follow-up (see Fig. 1.5). The number of phases can vary depending on the product and markets. For certain products and industries, some of these phases are not needed and a variation of the technique should be used.

It is important to involve all employees in the planning process for tasks that will affect their projects. It helps create ownership and a stronger sense of commitment to the project on the part of the employees. It will also allow for them to have a greater appreciation for the other disciplines, priorities, and concerns. The project leader should be a "product champion" who will persevere through all challenges and setbacks to make the project work because of their undying belief and support for the project. This champion should be organized and have good interpersonal skills, the respect of colleagues, and an appreciation for the various challenges facing different disciplines.

Each of these phases is briefly summarized below. The activities to be performed will vary depending on the industry and product line. However, the following information will be the basis for a good starting point. The eight phases should have interdisciplinary involvement. However, for some organizations, the first two phases, idea generation and feasibility studies, may only require marketing, manufacturing, and engineering input.

Activities to be performed at
different phases of a program

The following information is a summary of a well-thought-out product development process. The information and some of the planning tech-

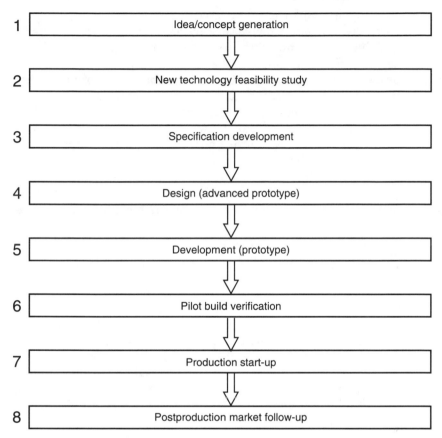

Figure 1.5 An eight-phased approach to product development.

niques are explained and discussed in subsequent chapters. The organizations responsible for performing these tasks are enclosed in square brackets. For example, [Marketing] at the end of an entry means that this task will be performed by marketing. The process assumes that if any issues or problems are discovered after a review, testing, machine trial, or quality verification, appropriate corrective action will be performed to address the issue. After the successful completion of a phase, the next phase will commence.

An overview of the process is outlined below:

1. Idea-concept generation phase
   - Generate new product ideas from customer input, marketing, manufacturing, engineering, or any source of new product ideas. [All Team Members]
   - Show preliminary business potential of the concept. [Marketing, Finance]

2. Feasibility study phase
   - Assess technological feasibility by evaluating, testing, experimenting, and so on, with any new technologies or unproven designs. [Engineering]
   - Assess new manufacturing process feasibility. [Manufacturing]
   - Perform exploratory market research. [Marketing]
   - If it is a new product in a mature industry, review problem history with existing products: warranty, customer complaints or suggestions, plant scrap and rework, process capabilities, etc. [All Team Members]
   - Review new features and opportunities not tried before. [Marketing, Engineering]
   - Assess feasibility of new manufacturing technologies. [Manufacturing]
   - Consider waste disposal and product recycling issues after product has exceeded useful life. [Manufacturing, Engineering]
3. Specification development phase
   - Perform quality function deployment (QFD). [All Team Members]
     a. It is recommended to perform the formal process for mature industries in an area where the competition has a distinct advantage. However, the following information should be gathered wherever possible:
        (1) Identify customer needs and wants. [Marketing]
        (2) Competitive analysis (customer and technical assessment and even processing). [Marketing, Engineering, Manufacturing]
        (3) Evaluate design trade-offs [Engineering]
   - Perform further market research. [Marketing]
   - Assess preliminary cost estimates (only 15 to 20 percent accuracy may be expected at this point). [Manufacturing, Purchasing, Finance]

The final steps of this phase are

   - Develop specifications. [All Team Members]
     a. Identify target markets and customers. [Marketing]
     b. Develop a list of features separated into two categories: *needs* and *wants*. [All Team Members]
     c. Identify application and general performance requirements and field use conditions. [Engineering, Marketing]
   - Develop quantitative technical performance specifications such as durability, reliability, performance, and regulatory test requirements for both field and bench standards. [Engineering]
   - Determine if market potential can justify costs. [Marketing, Finance, Engineering, Manufacturing]

- Develop preliminary product marketing plan. [Marketing]
4. Design or advanced prototype phase
    - Develop a critical path analysis of all projects that have to be performed on the project in great detail. [Project Leader, All Team Members]
    - Address concerns and issues regarding manufacturing environmental wastes and recycling of completed product after its useful life. [Manufacturing, Engineering, Legal]
    - Patent review for infringement or patent filings. [Legal (Engineering and Manufacturing as appropriate)]
    - Review product safety issues and other regulatory requirements. [Engineering, Legal]
    - Perform design failure mode and effects analysis (DFMEA). [Engineering, Manufacturing, Quality]
    - Release preliminary drawings to have several prototype designs (where appropriate) for review. [Engineering]
    - Perform initial design review to assure the product can be manufactured and will meet specifications. Some aspects to consider are briefly summarized below and reviewed in the design review checklist in Fig. 1.6. [All Team Members]
        a. Manufacturability and process capability issues
        b. Use of standard components
        c. Safety issues
        d. Regulatory requirements
        e. Serviceability
        f. Product features
        g. Ability to meet performance, durability, and reliability
        h. Flexibility to utilize in other product applications
        i. Commonization to manufacture with existing equipment, tools, and equipment. [Engineering, Manufacturing, Quality, Marketing, and, as appropriate, Suppliers, Management, and other Technical Specialists]
    - Manufacturing source selection (both internal and external sources). [Purchasing, Engineering, Manufacturing, Quality]
    - Perform process failure mode and effects analysis (PFMEA). [Manufacturing, Quality, Engineering, and, where appropriate, Suppliers]
    - Develop design verification plan and report (DVP&R). [Engineering, Quality]
    - Perform preliminary manufacturing process selection. [Manufacturing]
    - Identify critical characteristics. [Engineering, Manufacturing, Quality]
    - Perform value analysis. [All Team Members or disciplines]

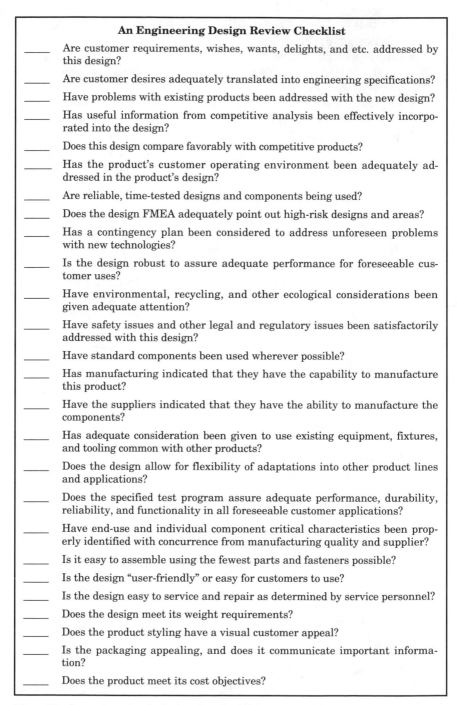

An Engineering Design Review Checklist

_____ Are customer requirements, wishes, wants, delights, and etc. addressed by this design?

_____ Are customer desires adequately translated into engineering specifications?

_____ Have problems with existing products been addressed with the new design?

_____ Has useful information from competitive analysis been effectively incorporated into the design?

_____ Does this design compare favorably with competitive products?

_____ Has the product's customer operating environment been adequately addressed in the product's design?

_____ Are reliable, time-tested designs and components being used?

_____ Does the design FMEA adequately point out high-risk designs and areas?

_____ Has a contingency plan been considered to address unforeseen problems with new technologies?

_____ Is the design robust to assure adequate performance for foreseeable customer uses?

_____ Have environmental, recycling, and other ecological considerations been given adequate attention?

_____ Have safety issues and other legal and regulatory issues been satisfactorily addressed with this design?

_____ Have standard components been used wherever possible?

_____ Has manufacturing indicated that they have the capability to manufacture this product?

_____ Have the suppliers indicated that they have the ability to manufacture the components?

_____ Has adequate consideration been given to use existing equipment, fixtures, and tooling common with other products?

_____ Does the design allow for flexibility of adaptations into other product lines and applications?

_____ Does the specified test program assure adequate performance, durability, reliability, and functionality in all foreseeable customer applications?

_____ Have end-use and individual component critical characteristics been properly identified with concurrence from manufacturing quality and supplier?

_____ Is it easy to assemble using the fewest parts and fasteners possible?

_____ Is the design "user-friendly" or easy for customers to use?

_____ Is the design easy to service and repair as determined by service personnel?

_____ Does the design meet its weight requirements?

_____ Does the product styling have a visual customer appeal?

_____ Is the packaging appealing, and does it communicate important information?

_____ Does the product meet its cost objectives?

Figure 1.6   An engineering design review checklist.

- Review the quality of procured prototype components. [Quality, Engineering, Purchasing (Manufacturing, depending on where prototypes are built)]

The final steps of this phase are

- Build prototypes. [Engineering, (Manufacturing)]
- Test prototypes. [Engineering, Quality]
- Evaluate prototype for conformance to specifications [Engineering, Quality, Marketing, (Manufacturing)]
- Assess service and maintenance issues. [Service, Engineering]
- Perform market research to select the most appealing prototype. [Marketing]
- Team review to select best design for the customer. [All Team Members]
- Freeze specifications. [Engineering Marketing]

5. Development (prototype) phase
   - Select manufacturing processes. [Manufacturing, Suppliers]
   - Revise process failure mode and effects analysis. [Manufacturing, Suppliers]
   - Manufacturing long-lead tooling kick-off. [Manufacturing, Purchasing]
   - Manufacturing process development. [Manufacturing, Supplier, Tooling Equipment Supplier]
     a. Manufacturing process concept approval (utilize tooling and equipment suppliers and manufacturing operators input). [Manufacturing, Equipment, Supplier]
     b. Equipment and gauge drawing release. [Equipment and Gage Sources]
     c. Preliminary trial runs. [Equipment Supplier]
     d. Document tool operation sheets. [Manufacturing]
   - Perform manufacturing process review (see Fig. 1.7) [Independent Manufacturing Group]
   - Perform product development activities. [Engineering, Marketing]
   - Market studies continue. [Marketing, Engineering]

The last items to complete in this phase are

- Build representative prototypes. [Engineering, Manufacturing]
- Perform durability and performance testing. [Engineering, Quality]
- Perform market research tests and communicate the results. [Marketing, Team Members]
- Update DVP&R, FMEAs, etc. [Engineering, Manufacturing, Quality]

- Perform cost analysis (typically within 5 percent accuracy). [Finance, Manufacturing, Purchasing, Engineering]
6. Pilot build
   - Install and perform equipment durability and capability trials. [Manufacturing]
   - Review safety issues on all machinery, tools, and facilities. [Manufacturing, Safety]
   - Perform statistical capability studies, Weibull analysis, chemistry, and lab test verification of all components of the product. [Manufacturing, Quality, Suppliers]
   - Submit initial sample inspection and initial sample lab reports for all components. [Quality, Manufacturing, Supplier]
   - Establish the product's bill of material and associated lead times for material ordering. [Production Control, Purchasing, Engineering]
   - Establish production documentation. [Manufacturing, Quality]
     a. Perishable tooling lists by process
     b. Manufacturing process sheets
     c. Operator's standard operating procedure
     d. Inspection instructions; set-up, receiving, in-process, final [Quality, Manufacturing, Engineering]
     e. Assembly operation description sheets
     f. Train employees on the use of equipment, safety and quality inspections and procedures
     g. Machine and tooling maintenance procedures
     h. Gauge usage instructions
     i. Time motion study sheets
   - Commence manufacturing employee training.

The final tasks of this phase are

- Commence pilot builds. [Manufacturing, Quality, Engineering]
- Document all concerns and assign corrective action responsibilities. [Project Leader, Team Members]
- Complete the development of activity-based cost standards. [Finance/Accounting, Purchasing]
- Review product packaging for
  a. Protection. [Manufacturing, Quality, Engineering]
  b. Appeal. [Marketing]
- Complete durability and performance testing. [Engineering, Quality]
- Update DVP&Rs, FMEAs. [Engineering, Manufacturing, Quality]
- Train or prepare training literature for the sales force about new product. [Marketing, Sales]

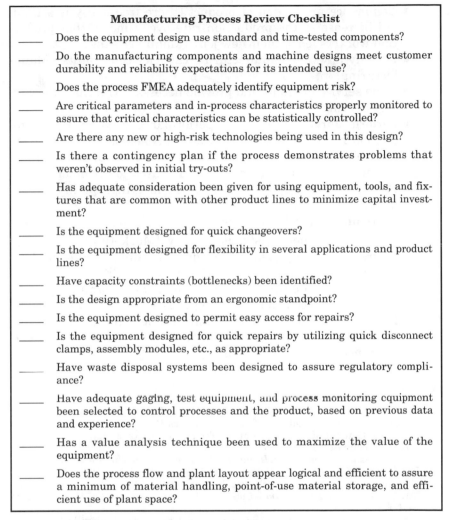

Manufacturing Process Review Checklist

____ Does the equipment design use standard and time-tested components?

____ Do the manufacturing components and machine designs meet customer durability and reliability expectations for its intended use?

____ Does the process FMEA adequately identify equipment risk?

____ Are critical parameters and in-process characteristics properly monitored to assure that critical characteristics can be statistically controlled?

____ Are there any new or high-risk technologies being used in this design?

____ Is there a contingency plan if the process demonstrates problems that weren't observed in initial try-outs?

____ Has adequate consideration been given for using equipment, tools, and fixtures that are common with other product lines to minimize capital investment?

____ Is the equipment designed for quick changeovers?

____ Is the equipment designed for flexibility in several applications and product lines?

____ Have capacity constraints (bottlenecks) been identified?

____ Is the design appropriate from an ergonomic standpoint?

____ Is the equipment designed to permit easy access for repairs?

____ Is the equipment designed for quick repairs by utilizing quick disconnect clamps, assembly modules, etc., as appropriate?

____ Have waste disposal systems been designed to assure regulatory compliance?

____ Have adequate gaging, test equipment, and process monitoring equipment been selected to control processes and the product, based on previous data and experience?

____ Has a value analysis technique been used to maximize the value of the equipment?

____ Does the process flow and plant layout appear logical and efficient to assure a minimum of material handling, point-of-use material storage, and efficient use of plant space?

Figure 1.7   A manufacturing process review checklist.

- Obtain regulatory agency approval. [Engineering, Manufacturing]
- Final (confirmatory) market research. [Marketing]
- Test products with special selected customers. [Engineering, Marketing]
- Identify manufacturing capacity constraints. [Manufacturing]

7. Production start-up
   - Implement marketing and sales plan (advertising, promotions, and sales efforts. [Marketing, Sales]

- Commence production of product (there frequently is a gradual increase in the production rate over time so that production workers learn their new job). [Manufacturing]
- Identify any new manufacturing capacity constraints. [Manufacturing]
- Issue service manuals and provide necessary training. [Service, Engineering]
- Perform durability tests and performance tests on initial production units. [Engineering, Quality] *Note:* Confirmation tests from initial tests must demonstrate that product meets requirements or product cannot be released to customers.
- Finish DVP&Rs; update FMEAs. [Engineering, Quality, Manufacturing]

8. Postproduction market follow-up
- Perform customer satisfaction survey. [Marketing]
- Address warranty issues from data, hotlines, and early trial test units. [Engineering, Manufacturing, Quality]
- Discuss how the product development and planning process could be improved on future programs. [All Team Members]
- Develop plans for continuous improvement in manufacturing, engineering, marketing, warranty, product features, and performance. [All Team Members]

References

1. TARP, *Increasing Customer Satisfaction through Effective Corporate Complaint Handling,* for the U.S. Office of Consumer Affairs in Cooperation with Chevrolet Division of General Motors Corporation, Technical Assistance Research Programs (TARP), Washington, D.C., 1985.
2. TARP, *Consumer Complaint Handling in America: An Update Study part II,* Washington D.C., for the U.S. Department of Consumer Affairs, 1986.
3. TARP, Industry Specific Research, unpublished, 1980–1985.
4. TARP, *Measuring the Grapevine—Consumer Response and Word of Mouth,* Atlanta GA, Coca-Cola, 1981.
5. General Electric Company, *The Information Challenge,* Louisville Kentucky, General Electric Company, 1982.
6. Bemowski, Karen, "The Quality Forum," *Quality Progress,* November 1991, pp. 18–20.
7. Juran, J. M., and Gryna, Frank M., *Juran's Quality Control Handbook,* 4th ed., McGraw-Hill, New York, 1988.
8. Rosenau, Milton D., Jr., *Faster New Product Development—Getting the Right Product to Market Quickly,* AMACOM, New York, 1990.

Bibliography

Chrysler Motors, "Design Review Guidelines," revised January 1988.
Engle, J. F., Knapp, D. A., and Knapp, D. E., *Sources of Influence in the Acceptance of New Products for Self-Modification: Preliminary Findings,* in R. Haas (ed.), American Marketing Association, 1966.

Imai, Masaaki, *Kaizen = (Ky'zen): The Key to Japan's Competitive Success,* Random House Business Division, New York, 1986.

Juran, J. M., "World War II and the Quality Movement," *Quality Progress,* December 1991, pp. 19–24.

Maggio, Stephen P., "General Motors Four Phase Process," Presented at the Advanced Manufacturing Forum, Penn State University, February 22, 1991.

Peters, Thomas J., and Waterman, Robert H., *In Search of Excellence,* Warner Books, New York, 1982.

U.S. GAO, *Management Practices—U.S. Companies Improve Performance through Quality Efforts,* U.S. General Accounting Office, GAO/NSIAD-91-190, May 1991.

Wu, Yuin, and Moore, Willie Hobbs, *Quality Engineering, Product and Process Design Optimization,* American Supplier Institute of Dearborn, Mich., 1985.

2

Statistical Methods

Statistical techniques are an excellent method for measuring quality. This chapter will give the reader an overall understanding of some common statistical problem-solving methods. Less technically oriented readers should skim the equations in this chapter and try to familiarize themselves with the concepts discussed and how statistical techniques can be effectively used. The Central Limit Theorem states, "If a random sample of n observations is selected from a normal population, then, when n is sufficiently large, the sampling distribution of the sample will be approximately normal."

Statistics can be used to infer characteristics of a population by taking a small sample. Several terms need to be defined to understand these characteristics:

Population Mean

Population mean (μ) is the average of a group of data. This is obtained by adding up all of the individual values and dividing the total by the number of individual values:

$$\mu = \frac{\Sigma X_i}{N} \qquad\qquad 2.1$$

where X_i = individual values of each population member
N = population size

Population Standard Deviation

Population standard deviation (σ) is a measure of the dispersion of data from the mean:

$$\sigma = \sqrt{\Sigma(X_i - \mu)^2/N} \qquad\qquad 2.2$$

Sample statistics

Frequently, it is impractical to take measurements from a whole population. Therefore, one uses sampling techniques to estimate these values. When using sampling techniques to infer characteristics about a population, one uses the term *sample statistic*.

Sample average $\overline{X}$

The sample average $(\overline{X})$ can be calculated as follows:

$$\overline{X} = \frac{\Sigma x_i}{n} \qquad\qquad 2.3$$

where x_i = individual value of each sample
      n = sample size

Sample Standard Deviation (S)

When using a sampling technique to estimate the standard deviation, one can calculate the sample standard deviation (S) with the following equation:

$$S = \sqrt{\Sigma(x_i - \overline{X})^2/(n - 1)} \qquad\qquad 2.4$$

$\overline{X}$ and S are used for sample statistics and in most experimental designs. The advantage of using samples is derived from the reduced cost of measuring characteristics from every member in the population.

The normal distribution

To determine if a population conforms to a specification, one can use a measure called capability. A normal or bell-shaped curve is shown in Fig. 2.1. It is symmetric around its center. The figure shows that 2 × 34.13 percent or 68.26 percent of the population falls within ± 1 standard deviation from the mean $\overline{X}$, 95.46 percent falls within 2 standard deviations from the mean, and 99.73 percent falls within ± 3 standard deviations from the mean.

Some population distributions are symmetrical but are not normally distributed. The amount of flatness or peakedness of such a curve is referred to as *kurtosis*. When it has a flatter peak than the normal curve, it is classified as platykurtic. When it has a sharper peak it is classified as leptokurtic (see Fig. 2.2). Fortunately, most symmetrical distributions are approximately normally distributed and the amount of deviation from the normal curve is generally insignificant when utilizing statistical calculations based on the normal curve.

When a distribution is not symmetrical, it is said to be skewed (see Fig. 2.3). When this is the case, statistical calculations based on the normal distributions are invalid. The rest of the statistical calculations in this chapter are based on the assumption of a *normally distributed population*. Therefore, one should verify this assumption before applying them.

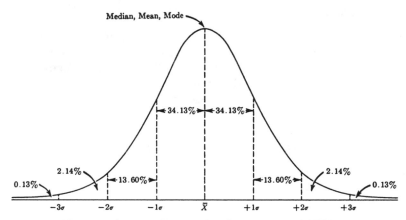

Figure 2.1   The normal curve. (*Reprinted with permission of AT&T.*)

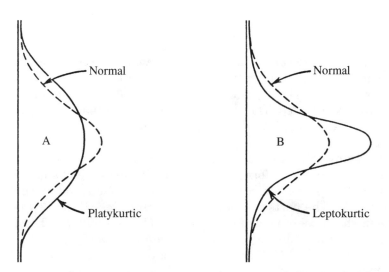

Figure 2.2   Symmetric distributions that are not normal. (*Reprinted with permission of AT&T.*)

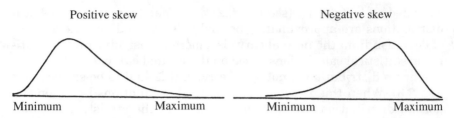

Figure 2.3 Positively and negatively skewed distributions. (*Reprinted with permission of AT&T.*)

Assessing Process (Capability and Process Centering)

To measure the quality of a process, two measurements are used, C_p and C_{pk}. The C_p determines what the process is capable of based on the process standard deviation and the total tolerance specified on the blueprint. It can be calculated as follows:

$$C_p = \frac{\text{tolerance}}{6\sigma} \qquad 2.5$$

The C_{pk} is concerned with the process variance and how well centered it is:

$$C_{pk} = \frac{\overline{X} - NSL}{3\sigma} \qquad 2.6$$

where NSL = nearest specification limit or the minimum of the following two equations:
$\overline{X} - \text{USL}$ (USL = upper specification limit)
$\overline{X} - \text{LSL}$ (LSL = lower specification limit)

Note: when using unilateral specification limits which specify either a minimum value or maximum value, one must use that specification limit to determine C_{pk}. The C_p cannot be properly calculated if only a minimum value is specified. These calculations assume that the populations are normally distributed and the sample size is sufficiently large.

Figures 2.4a through 2.4h illustrate the difference between C_p, C_{pk}, and parts per million nonconforming. Figure 2.4a shows a bell-shaped normal curve. The process is centered so the C_p is the same as the C_{pk}, which is 0.67. The parts per million nonconforming (PPM-NC) is 45,600. When the process is centered and the C_{pk} is 1.00 (Fig. 2.4b), the PPM-NC is 2700. When the process is centered and the C_{pk} is 1.33, there are 63 PPM-NC. Now, the difference between C_p and C_{pk} will be demonstrated. In Figs. 2.4c and 2.4d, the C_p is equal to the C_{pk} because both processes are centered. However, in Fig. 2.4e, the

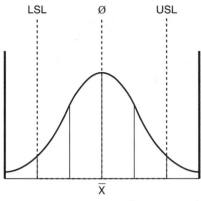

$\overline{X}$

CP = 0.67 (± 2 σ)
CPk = 0.67
Process is centered
Parts per million nonconforming: 45,600

Figure 2.4a–2.4h Comparison between C_p, C_{pk}, and parts per million nonconforming.

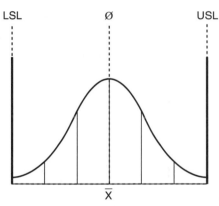

$\overline{X}$

CP = 1.00 (± 3 σ)
CPk = 1.00
Process is centered
Parts per million nonconforming: 2700

Figure 2.4b

process is running toward the upper specification limit. The C_p is 1.67, the same as Fig 2.4d; however, because it is not centered, the C_{pk} is 1.33. The PPM-NC in the centered process with a C_{pk} of 1.67 is 1, but toward the shifted process, with a C_{pk} of 1.33, it is 32. In Fig. 2.4f, 2.4g and 2.4h, this idea is further illustrated. Fig 2.4f shows a centered process. The $C_p = C_{pk} = 2.00$ and PPM-NC = 0. Figure 2.4g also has a $C_p = 2.00$. However, this process is running halfway between the lower specifications limit and the middle of the specification and the C_{pk} is 1.00. The PPM-NC is 1350. This is half of the number in Fig. 2.4b which also has a C_{pk} of 1.00, but PPM-NC is 2700. The

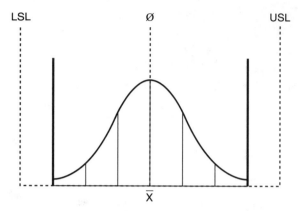

CP = 1.33 (± 4 σ)
CPk = 1.33
Process is centered
Parts per million nonconforming: 63

Figure 2.4c

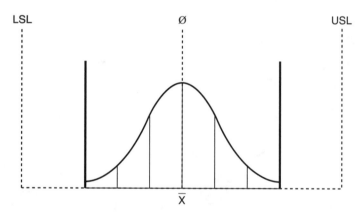

CP = 1.67 (± 5 σ)
CPk = 1.67
Process is centered
Parts per million nonconforming: 1

Figure 2.4d

reason is that the nonconforming percentage is generated solely by the parts below the lower specification limit. The probability of manufacturing a unit beyond the upper specifications limit is extremely low—*much* less than 1 PPM. And finally, Fig. 2.4*h* shows a process that is running toward the upper specification limit. It has a C_p of 2.00, a C_{pk} of 0.67, and is generating 22,800 PPM-NC.

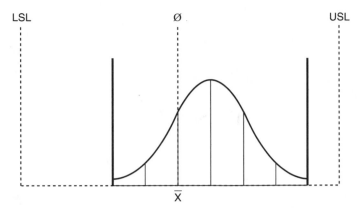

CP = 1.67
CPk = 1.33
Process is running towards the upper specification limit
Parts per million nonconforming: 32

Figure 2.4e

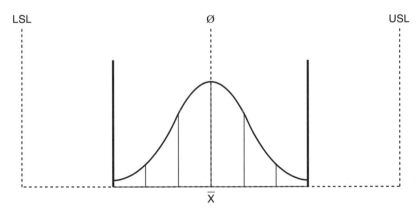

CP = 2.00 (± 6 σ)
CPk = 2.00
Process is centered
Parts per million nonconforming: 0

Figure 2.4f

The Quality Loss Function

The quality loss function shown in Fig. 2.5 demonstrates that the farther away from the nominal specification one is, the greater the loss in the quality of the part. It is assumed to be a parabolic function. This concept is supported by a 1979 finding regarding Sony television sets of identical designs and tolerances. The difference was the manufacturing location: some were built in Tokyo, Japan, and some in San

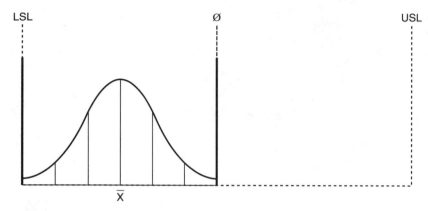

CP = 2.00
CPk = 1.00
Process is running towards the lower specification limit
Parts per million nonconforming: 1350

Figure 2.4g

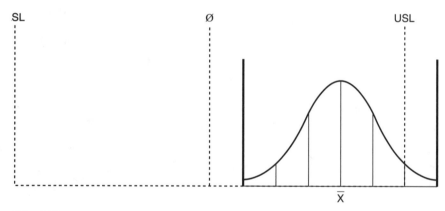

CP = 2.00
CPk = 0.67
Process is running towards the upper specification limit
Parts per million nonconforming: 22,800

Figure 2.4h

Diego, California. The U.S. sets were 100 percent sorted for color density so no sets were shipped that were out of tolerance. Their process had a C_{pk} of 0.58, while the sets manufactured in Tokyo were not sorted, but they had a C_{pk} of 1.00. This allowed approximately three sets per 1000 to leave the plant out of specification. The surprising result was that customers had a preference for the sets built in Japan (see Fig. 2.6).

Interpretation of Loss

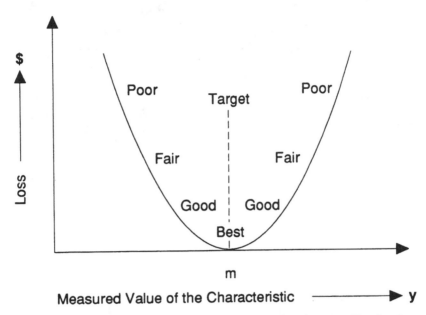

Measured Value of the Characteristic ——————▶ y

Figure 2.5   Taguchi's quadratic representation of the quality loss function. (*Reprinted by permission of American Supplier Institute, Inc., of Dearborn, Mich.*)

Traditional Quality Concept

The traditional approach to quality is illustrated in Fig. 2.7. This diagram shows that traditionally manufacturers perceived that a product was good if it was just slightly inside the specification limit, while it was bad if it was barely outside the specification limit and the two products were very different in their performance characteristics. However, a fallacy exists in this thinking because for all practical purposes, the customer will not be able to detect a difference between these two products in terms of end use or functionality-durability. The reason the Sony sets manufactured in Tokyo were preferred was because, on the average, they were better centered toward the nominal specification. This demonstrates the importance of having quality measuring indexes such as C_p and C_{pk}.

The automotive industry currently has minimum C_{pk} requirements of either 1.33 or 1.67 from their component, equipment and tooling suppliers, depending on the manufacturer. It should be pointed out that to hold a C_{pk} of 1.33 long term, one should have a higher short-term acceptance standard to account for machine wear, raw material

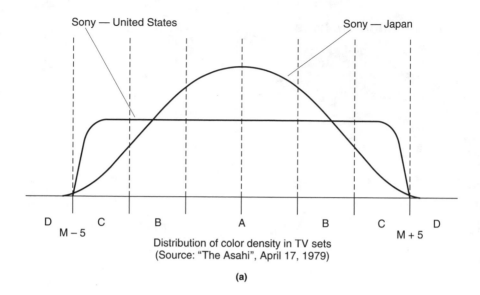

Distribution of color density in TV sets
(Source: "The Asahi", April 17, 1979)

(a)

Types of distribution

Factory location	Approximate type of distribution	Percent defective
San Diego	Uniform	Almost nil
Japan	Normal	0.3%

(b)

Figure 2.6a and b The difference between meeting spec and controlling process—Sony TV. (*Reprinted by permission of American Supplier Institute, Inc., of Dearborn, Mich.*)

Figure 2.7 The traditional approach to evaluating the quality of a product—it assumes that all products within the specification are equally good.

variation, etc., until process improvements can be instituted. The Automotive Industry Action Group Standards dictate that dies, molds, and other wear-related tools should be qualified to account for maximum tool life and suppliers should agree to a quality standard with their customer. The reason for this requirement is because these tools wear to the other end of the specification so they are purposely targeted away from nominal to allow for wear. So, initially, it might have a C_p of 1.67 and a C_{pk} of 1.00, but as the mold wears, the C_{pk} will improve to 1.67 and the C_{pk} will subsequently deteriorate afterward. In order to improve their quality, manufacturing plants have to continually focus their efforts on targeting toward nominal specification and reducing variation.

Statistical Process Control

Statistical analysis through sampling can be used to prevent defects during the manufacturing process. The manufacturing process is monitored and process adjustments are made if a statistically significant change in the process is detected as opposed to waiting until parts are manufactured out of specification.

The technique for doing this is called *statistical process control,* or SPC. SPC generally records measurements of small samples of the characteristic being monitored and plots the data on a control chart. Characteristics can be finished dimensions such as an outside diameter, length, width, etc., or a processing parameter like temperature, pressure, voltage. The data then are analyzed to see if the process has changed. Some of the most common charts are an $\overline{X}$ and R (sample average and range), an individual and moving range, P (proportion nonconforming) and U (nonconformities per unit). The characteristics that are typically charted are critical to the process and can result in problems at the customer or in subsequent manufacturing operations. When determining which characteristics should be charted, the Pareto principle should be utilized so that resources are not wasted. The Pareto approach would prioritize the most important characteristics to be monitored so that resources are effectively used to monitor only significant and critical characteristics.

Selecting Critical Characteristics

To identify the critical characteristics, one can consider the following approach.

From a design standpoint

Critical characteristics can be determined by reviewing the quality problem history and field returns of similar parts and characteristics that cause customer dissatisfaction with regard to safety, reliability, functionality, or appearance if they are not maintained. Characteristics can also be identified by using such techniques as failure mode and effects analysis (FMEAs) and quality function deployment (QFDs).

From a processing standpoint

Some characteristics are critical because of the implications for subsequent processes, assembly operations, etc. If they are not maintained, plant productivity is significantly reduced.

From a quality control standpoint

Based on both design and manufacturing engineering's input, combined with process capability data, the appropriate control methodology can be determined; e.g., some need SPC, others just need to be verified at set-up, and others need initial samples, depending on the process selected. This should be agreed to by an interdisciplinary group which includes representatives from design-development engineering, manufacturing process engineering, quality control, and, when appropriate, the supplier.

$\overline{X}$ and R Charts

An $\overline{X}$ and R chart plots variable data. Two charts are actually used: the $\overline{X}$, which plots the average of a sample, and the R, or range, chart, which plots the range of a sample of measurements (see Fig. 2.8). In Fig. 2.8, the out-of-control point is circled on the $\overline{X}$ chart. There is a comment section on the back of the chart where the operator describes the action taken to get the process under control (not shown). The $\overline{X}$ chart plots each sample of data taken at specified intervals. The sample size and interval of measurements taken must be constant throughout the charting process. To properly estimate control limits and process capability, only points that are "in control" can be used in the calculations. To establish SPC, one needs to perform the following series of calculations to determine control chart limits:

$$\overline{X} = \frac{x_1 + x_2 + \dots + x_k}{n} \qquad 2.7$$

where $\overline{X}$ = average of sample or subgroup
$x_1, x_2, \dots x_k$ = individual measurements
n = sample size, or number of measurements taken, in a subgroup

$$R \qquad = x_{max} - x_{min} \qquad\qquad\qquad 2.8$$
R = range of a sample (or subgroup)
x_{max} = highest value in a sample
x_{min} = lowest value taken from a sample

The dashed lines on the charts in Fig. 2.8 are called *control limits*. They are on the 3 standard deviations of the process variation. They can be calculated as follows. Please refer to Table 2.1 to obtain factors based on the sample subgroup size. To calculate the centerline for the R chart, use the following:

$$\overline{R} = \frac{\text{total of R's}}{\text{no. of samples}} \quad \text{or} \quad \frac{R_1 + R_2 + ... + R_k}{k} \qquad 2.9$$

where $R_1, R_2, ... R_k$ = range of each subgroup
     k = number of subgroups plotted

Control limits for the R chart are calculated by using the following equations:

$$\text{UCL}_R = D_4 \overline{R} \qquad\qquad\qquad 2.10$$

$$\text{LCL}_R = D_3 \overline{R} \qquad\qquad\qquad 2.11$$

where UCL_R = upper control limit for R chart
       LCL = lower control limit for R chart
       D_3, D_4 = constants determined from Table 2.1

To determine the process average for the $\overline{X}$ chart, one performs the following calculation:

$$\overline{\overline{X}} = \frac{\overline{X}_1 + \overline{X}_2 + ... + \overline{X}_k}{k} \qquad\qquad 2.12$$

where $\overline{\overline{X}}$ process average, or centerline of $\overline{X}$ chart
     $\overline{X}_1, \overline{X}_2, ..., \overline{X}_k$ = average value from each subgroup, respectively
     k = total number of subgroups sampled

The control limits for the $\overline{X}$ chart are calculated as follows:

$$\text{UCL}_{\overline{x}} = \overline{\overline{X}} + A_2 \overline{R} \qquad\qquad\qquad 2.13$$

$$\text{LCL}_{\overline{x}} = \overline{\overline{X}} - A_2 \overline{R} \qquad\qquad\qquad 2.14$$

where $\text{UCL}_{\overline{x}}$ = upper control limit for the $\overline{X}$ chart
     $\text{LCL}_{\overline{x}}$ = lower control limit for the $\overline{X}$ chart
     A_2 = constant determined from Table 2.1

VARIABLES CONTROL CHART X&R					
CUSTOMER	PART # 127162	MATERIAL Lexan 500		MACHINE # 8	MOLD # 12741
CHARACTERISTIC DD	SPECIFICATION 20.42/20.62	CAV. # All	GAGE M-1815	SAMPLE SIZE/FREQUENCY 4 per hour	

Date		10/7/92								10/8								10/8								
Time		4:00P	5:00P	6:00	7:00	8:00	9:00	10:00	11:00	12:00A	1:00A	2:00	3:00	4:00	5:00	6:00	7:00	8:00	9:00	10:00	11:00	12:00P	1:00	2:00P	3:00	4:00
Operator		MJ	MJ	MJ	MJ	MJ	MJ	MJ	MJ	CG	CG	CG	CG	CG	CG	CG	CG	KB	KB	KB	KB	KB	KB	KB	KB	KB
Sample Measurements	1	.50	.53	.55	.59	.57	.52	.53	.52	.51	.53	.55	.52	.53	.56	.57	.52	.56	.57	.53	.53	.55	.55	.57	.57	.58
	2	.53	.48	.51	.56	.53	.49	.49	.49	.52	.52	.56	.50	.52	.53	.56	.52	.53	.53	.51	.50	.49	.56	.56	.53	.55
	3	.49	.46	.56	.52	.51	.48	.47	.47	.46	.49	.53	.47	.49	.50	.50	.49	.55	.51	.55	.48	.47	.53	.50	.51	.52
	4	.52	.51	.49	.58	.49	.50	.50	.48	.52	.54	.54	.49	.50	.54	.53	.46	.50	.49	.49	.50	.50	.54	.53	.49	.53
	5																									
Sum		2.04	1.98	2.11	2.25	2.10	1.99	1.99	1.96	2.03	2.08	2.18	1.98	2.04	2.10	2.16	1.99	2.14	2.10	2.08	2.01	1.99	2.18	2.16	2.10	2.18
Average $\overline{X}$		.510	.495	.528	.563	.525	.498	.498	.490	.508	.520	.545	.495	.510	.525	.540	.498	.535	.525	.520	.500	.498	.545	.540	.525	.545
Range R		.04	.07	.06	.07	.08	.04	.06	.05	.04	.05	.03	.05	.04	.06	.07	.06	.06	.08	.06	.05	.04	.03	.07	.08	.06

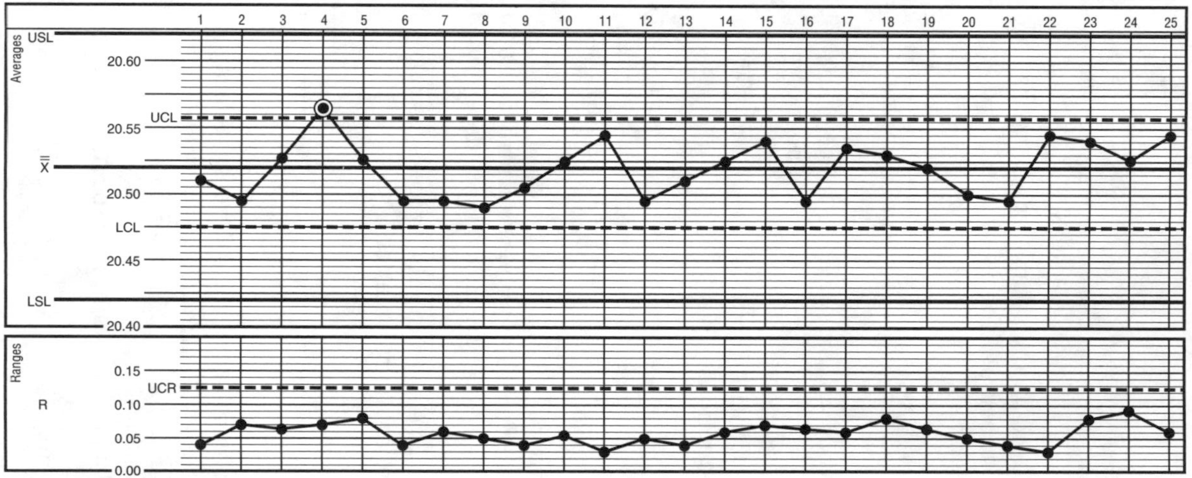

Figure 2.8 An $\overline{X}$ and R chart. Note that the out-of-control point is circled.

TABLE 2.1   Factors Needed to Calculate Control Limits.

n	A_2	D_3	D_4
1	2.66	0.00	3.27
2	1.88	0.00	3.27
3	1.02	0.00	2.57
4	0.73	0.00	2.28
5	0.58	0.00	2.11
6	0.48	0.00	2.00
7	0.42	0.08	1.92
8	0.37	0.14	1.86

SOURCE: Adapted from Western Electric (AT&T), *Statistical Quality Control Handbook,* 1956, p. 12.

The eight most common tests for determining out-of-control conditions are outlined as below. *Note:* These tests apply to both the $\overline{X}$ chart and the R chart:

1. Outliers or freaks—one point beyond either the upper or lower control limits.

2. Trend—seven consecutive points either increasing or decreasing.

3. Run—seven points in a row on the same half of the control chart (between the centerline and one control limit).

4. Stratification—fifteen points in a row in the inner third of the control chart.

5. Mixture—eight points in a row on both sides of the centerline with none in the inner third of the control chart.

6. Run—four out of five points in a row in the outer one-third of the control chart.

7. Run—four out of five points in a row in the outer two-thirds of the control chart.

8. Sawtooth—fourteen points in a row, alternating up and down.

Some companies used tests 1, 2, 3, and 4 only because it is easier for their operators to interpret and they still derive most of the benefits of SPC. Some also find it useful to use modified limits and reaction plans because it is easier for machine operators to interpret them and the other out-of-control conditions rarely manifest themselves or do not significantly impact the finished product. Figure 2.9 is an example of a modified SPC reaction plan used by Technimark, Inc., an injection-molded plastic supplier for women's cosmetic compacts, cosmetic organizers, as well as custom-molded plastic components for the computer, consumer appliance, power tool, and automotive industries. Technimark reacts to a six-point trend. There will be differences between companies depending on their processes and how important it

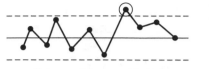

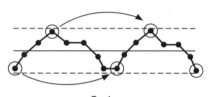

Point outside control limits

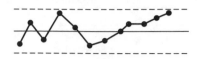

Trend
Six increases or six decreases in a row
Eight of ten increments increasing or decreasing

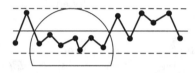

Cycle
Search for repetitive pattern

Run
Seven points in a row above centerline
Seven points in a row below centerline

If an out-of-control condition occurs:
1. Circle the "out-of-control" point
2. Notify your supervisor
3. Further action will be taken from this point by your supervisor in conjunction with quality and production management.

Figure 2.9 Modified SPC reaction plan. (*Courtesy of Technimark, Inc., Randleman, NC.*)

is to react to a trend or run quickly and run the risk of reacting unnecessarily, due to a statistical anomaly, versus waiting longer before correcting the process.

It is important that the process being charted is both stable and is understood well enough that corrective action can be taken to correct out-of-control conditions. If this cannot be done, it will be difficult to implement SPC unless a modified reaction plan is established for out-of-control conditions.

The Individual and Moving Range Chart

The individual and moving range chart can be used to reduce inspection costs; however, it is less sensitive than an $\overline{X}$ and R chart. It is frequently used to monitor

- Material chemistry
- Material properties
- Process control parameters (e.g., pressures, temperatures, voltages)
- Processes which have a high long-term process capability ($C_{pk} \geq$ 2.00) and are not prone to sudden increases in variation

- Accounting figures
- Plant efficiencies

One first charts the individual points X and then plots the moving range MR. The time interval for sampling must remain constant for these calculations. Assuming a normal distribution of the process, the applicable equations are

$$MR = X_{current} - X_{previous} \qquad 2.15$$

where $X_{current}$ = current sample reading (the one just recorded)
       $X_{previous}$ = last individual point plotted

$$\overline{X} = \frac{X_1 + X_2 + \ldots + X_n}{n} \qquad 2.16$$

where $\overline{X}$ = average of all individual measurements
       $X_1, X_2, \ldots, X_n$ = individual readings
       n = number of individual readings taken

$$UCL_X = \overline{X} + 2.66 \times (\overline{MR}) \qquad 2.17$$

$$LCL_X = \overline{X} - 2.66 \times (\overline{MR}) \qquad 2.18$$

where UCL_X = upper control limit of individual chart
       LCL_X = lower control limit of individual chart

The centerline for the moving range chart ($\overline{MR}$) can be determined by using the following equation:

$$\overline{MR} = \frac{MR_1 + MR_2 + \ldots + MR_{n-1}}{n-1} \qquad 2.19$$

Where MR_1, MR_2,...MR_{n-1} are the individual moving range calculations.

The upper control limit is calculated as follows:

$$UCL_{MR} = 3.27\overline{MR} \qquad 2.20$$

The lower control limit for the moving range chart is always zero; that is:

$$LCL_{MR} = 0$$

Where UCL_{MR} and LCL_{MR} are the upper and lower control limits for the moving range chart, respectively.

The same out-of-control criteria on the individual and moving range charts are used as on the $\overline{X}$ and R chart except that when analyzing trends and runs, 8 consecutive points are used instead of 7. In some cases, it may be useful to use an individual and moving range chart for accounting figures, because they have a valid basis for reacting and identifying problem areas rather than having nonscientifically determined standards for identifying significant deviations from budgets. For some individual and moving range applications, a two-standard deviation (2 σ) control limits may be used. They can be determined by multiplying the control limit factor (2.66) by two-thirds standard deviations, or 1.78, and reacting to 5-point runs and trends on the control charts, instead of 8. This increases the chance of reacting to a condition that does not exist; however, overall it reduces the amount of time that a process runs out of control and assures a more rapid response time. Figure 2.10 is an example of an individual and moving range chart used by Brighton Tool and Die to monitor the outside diameter of a thrust washer. They can use this approach because their long-term C_{pk} is above 2.00. Brighton Tool has won several prestigious quality awards from their customers for their performance and QC systems. In Fig. 2.11, Amoco Chemical Co. uses an individual and moving range chart to monitor the calibration status of their melt flow analyzer according to a standard. They also use it to monitor the melt flow rate of their polypropylene product.

Figure 2.12 demonstrates how Amoco's product variation was reduced after applying statistical controls to the pellet count, a critical characteristic. The pellet count is important because it can significantly impact their customer's process when molding plastic products.

P Charts

The P chart (proportion nonconforming) is a method of charting attribute data. It can be used to monitor a product that is

- 100 percent inspected for go/no (a plug gage)
- 100 percent tested (such as a transmission or power tool)
- 100 percent inspected for cosmetic defects (such as a plastic TV housing or a glass picture tube)

The centerline for the P chart, $\overline{P}$, is calculated as follows:

$$\overline{P} = \frac{NC_1 + NC_2 + \dots + NC_k}{n_t} \qquad 2.21$$

BRIGHTON TOOL & DIE

Customer:	Cust. code: BT-1038	Date of Report: 9/17/92
Description: WASHER-DIFF. PIN THR	Characteristic: OUTSIDE DIAMETER	II: GAGE CALIPERS
Part #:	Revision: ENG REL 03JL80	

Special Instructions: CHECK THREE PLACES AND USE HIGHEST   READING

SPECIFICATION	CENTRAL TENDENCY	DISPERSION	DISTRIBUTION	CAPABILITY		PREDICTION
TOL: 0.01180			SD:0.000591	6SD/TOL(Cr): 0.301	ZU: 6.091	% ABOVE USL : 0.00
USL: 1.4134	UCLx :1.411573	UCLr :0.002178	+3SD:1.411573	TOL/6SD(Cp): 3.328	ZL:-13.875	% BELOW LSL : 0.00
TARGET: 1.4075	XDBAR :1.409800	RBAR :0.000667	MEAN:1.409800	SD Type- Cp: 3.328	ZU/3: 2.030	% OUT OF SPEC: 0.00
LSL: 1.4016	LCLx :1.408027	LCLr :0.000000	-3SD:1.408027	R/d2 Cpk: 2.030	ZL/3: -4.625	% IN SPEC :100.00

Calculations based on the previous 25 subgroups.

INDIVIDUALS

MOVING RANGES

SUMMARY

Subgroup	12	13	14	15	16	17	18	19	20	21	22	23	24	25	26	27	28	29	30	31
Samples	1	1	1	1	1	1	1	1	1	1	1	1	1	1	1	1	1	1	1	1
Individual	41000	40900	41000	40900	40900	40900	40900	41000	40950	41000	41100	41000	40900	41000	41100	41000	41100	41000	40950	41000
R	00000	00100	00100	00100	00000	00000	00000	00100	00050	00050	00100	00100	00100	00100	00100	00100	00100	00100	00050	00050
R/d2	00000	00089	00089	00089	00000	00000	00000	00089	00044	00044	00089	00089	00089	00089	00089	00089	00089	00089	00044	00044
Date	06-24	06-24	06-24	06-24	06-24	06-24	06-24	06-24	06-24	06-24	06-24	06-24	08-20	08-20	08-20	08-20	08-20	08-20	08-20	08-20
Time	14:31	14:31	14:31	14:31	14:31	14:31	14:31	14:31	14:32	14:32	14:32	14:32	13:57	13:57	13:58	13:58	13:58	13:58	13:58	13:58

8221   Program written by MAJOR MICRO SYSTEMS, INC. - Copyright 1985

Figure 2.10 An individual and moving range chart used to measure the outside diameter of a thrust washer. (*Courtesy of Brighton Tool & Die, Brighton, Mich.*)

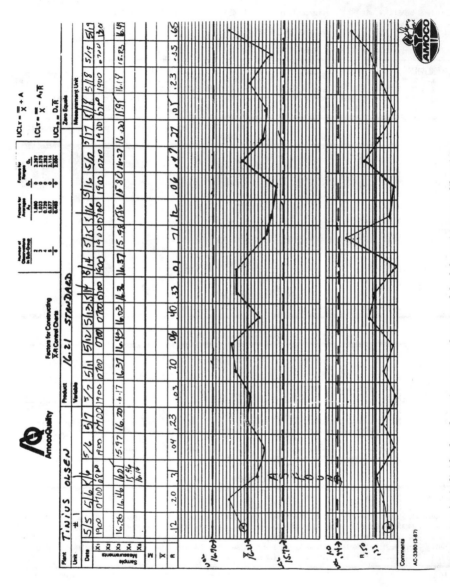

Figure 2.11 An individual and moving range chart used for lab equipment calibration. (*Courtesy of Amoco Chemical Company, Chicago, IL.*)

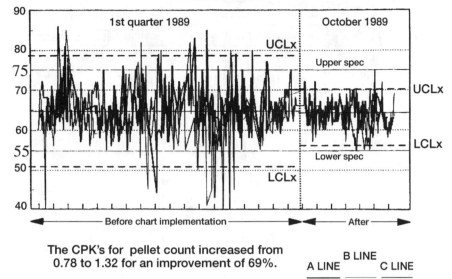

Pellet Count Control Chart
Pellets/Gram

The CPK's for pellet count increased from 0.78 to 1.32 for an improvement of 69%.

A LINE B LINE C LINE

J. J. BARNES 11/16/89

Figure 2.12 SPC reduces the variation of the finished product. (*Courtesy of Amoco Chemical Company, Chicago, Ill.*)

where P = average fraction defective from samples

$NC_1, NC_2,...,NC_k$ = the number of nonconforming units in each sample

n_t = total number of units sampled

The upper and lower control limit is calculated as follows:

$$UCL_p = \overline{P} + 3 \times \sqrt{\overline{P}(1 - \overline{P})/n} \qquad 2.22$$

$$LCL_p = \overline{P} - 3 \times \sqrt{\overline{P}(1 - \overline{P})/n} \qquad 2.23$$

These equations assume an equal subgroup size. The same eight control chart tests to determine whether the process is in control on an $\overline{X}$ and R apply for the P chart. Figure 2.13 is an example of the type of P chart used by Reinz Wisconsin Gasket to monitor visual defects at a cutting operation for their gaskets. The data collection method also has the category of the defect marked so that data can be collected and summarized later for scrap analysis. Reinz manufactures such gaskets as engine cylinder head gaskets, valve cover gaskets, and a

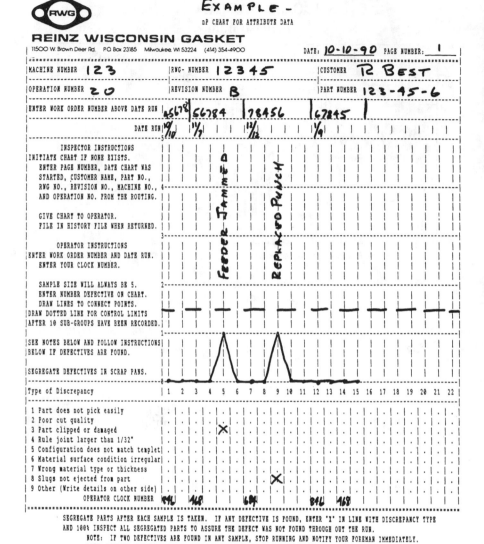

Figure 2.13 A sample *P* visual defects for a die-cut gasket chart. (*Courtesy of Reinz Wisconsin Gasket, Milwaukee, Wis.*)

host of paper and die cut gaskets for customers in the automotive and outdoor products industry. Reinz has won several prestigious awards for quality from their customers and is one of the primary suppliers of gaskets for the Saturn Corporation's engine programs and the Chrysler Corporation's Dodge Viper.

U Charts

The *U* chart is used to measure the number of defects or demerits for a unit. It generally is used for a complex finished product such as an automobile, a washing machine, toaster, recliner, or other finished assemblies. It measures the number of defects per unit based on a specified measurement method.

$$U = \frac{ND}{n} \qquad \qquad 2.24$$

where U = average number of defects per unit
      ND = total number of defects found
      n = number of units evaluated in specified time interval

$$\overline{U} = \frac{ND_1 + ND_2 + \dots + ND_k}{n_1 + n_2 + \dots + n_k} \qquad \qquad 2.25$$

where $ND_1, ND_2, \dots, ND_k$ = number of defects found in each subgroup
      $n_1, n_2, \dots, n_k$ = size of each subgroup, respectively
      k = number of subgroups

The upper and lower control limits for a U chart, UCL_U and LCL_U, are calculated as follows:

$$\mathrm{UCL}_U = \overline{U} + 3 \times \sqrt{\frac{\overline{U}}{\overline{n}}} \qquad \qquad 2.26$$

$$\mathrm{LCL}_U = \overline{U} - 3 \times \sqrt{\frac{\overline{U}}{\overline{n}}} \qquad \qquad 2.27$$

where $\overline{n}$ is the average sample size of each subgroup.

Gaging Issues

There are several types of error or variation associated with a measurement system. They include gage accuracy, linearity, repeatability, reproducibility, and stability. They each relate to different issues as is discussed below.

Gage accuracy   This is the difference between the observed average of measurements and the true average. True average is best established with the most accurate measuring equipment available. Sometimes this is done with a coordinate measuring machine (CMM) which has been calibrated. However, CMMs sometimes do not report true measurements when reporting measurements of flat surfaces and diameters. This is because they use a least-squares algorithm to calculate roundness and flatness.[1]

Gage linearity This is the differences in the accuracy throughout the operating range.

Gage repeatability This is the variation in measurements obtained when one operator uses the same gage for measuring the identical characteristic on the same parts. This is also known as equipment variation.

Gage reproducibility This is the variation in the average of measurements made by different operators using the same gage measuring identical characteristics of the same parts. This is commonly referred to as appraiser variation.

Gage stability This is the difference in the average of at least two sets of measurements obtained with a gage at different times on the same parts.

Gage system error This is the combination of accuracy, linearity, repeatability, reproducibility, and stability.

Note: If a gage has some instability, but is accurate enough for an application, calibration procedures might require the use of an SPC control chart to determine if a calibration adjustment to the gage is needed.

Gage repeatability and reproducibility

Gage reproducibility and repeatability (gage R&R) studies are performed to determine if the gage is acceptable for a prescribed application. This type of gage study measures two kinds of variation as they relate to the amount of variation inherent in the gage hardware and the operator's methodology. All characteristics that are SPC-charted should have gage R&R studies performed on them. The steps to perform a gage R&R study are as follows:

1. Calibrate the gage with a master in the anticipated operating range that is traceable to a recognized standard.
2. Specify the inspection procedure for the operators to follow.
3. Select two or three operators or inspectors who will be using the gage to perform the study.
4. Select 10 parts that are within the specification range for the characteristic being selected.

5. Number the parts from 1 to 10 so that the numbers will not be visible to the persons performing the study.

6. Let the first operator measure the parts in a random order and enter the results in column one. (The number on the part should correspond to the row for that sample number.)

7. Repeat the step and perform the second trial after reordering the sequence of measuring the parts.

8. Perform the same study with the operators again (second trial) and repeat for the third trial if required.

Note: If it is difficult to administer in this sequence, the repeat trials may be done with the same operator at the same time.

9. Perform the calculations with the gage R&R form as specified on the sheet shown in Fig. 2.14.

10. Multiply the $\bar{\bar{R}}$ (the grand range) by D_4 to determine an upper limit for any of the individual readings of the range (R). If any value exceeds this amount, one must identify the cause and correct it. After the cause of the extreme reading has been identified, have the same appraiser repeat the measurements with the same sample(s) that was originally used.

Interpretation of the results

If the gage R&R is

- Under 10 percent error, the gage is acceptable.
- Between 10 and 30 percent, it is acceptable based upon the importance of application, cost of repair, etc.
- Over 30 percent is generally unacceptable. Efforts should focus on improving the gage design.

This form shows that the total gage R&R is calculated. However, this information can be broken down into two contributing sources of variation: reproducibility (appraiser variation) and repeatability (equipment variation). This is useful for troubleshooting analysis. If the predominant error is reproducibility (appraiser variation), one should focus on operator training and measure the same location of the part. If the repeatability error (equipment variation) is large, one should look again at such gage design issues as using precision gears, improving the clamping method, gage rigidity, etc.

There are several commercially available software packages available that perform gage R&R calculations, making the task less tedious.

GAGE REPEATABILITY AND REPRODUCIBILITY DATA SHEET (Long Method)

Operator	A-				B-				C-			
	1	2	3	4	5	6	7	8	9	10	11	12
Sample #	1st Trial	2nd Trial	3rd Trial	Range	1st Trial	2nd Trial	3rd Trial	Range	1st Trial	2nd Trial	3rd Trial	Range
1	.65	.60		.05	.55	.55		0	.50	.55		.05
2	1.00	1.00		0	1.05	.95		.10	2.05	1.00		.05
3	.85	.80		.05	.80	.75		.05	.80	.80		0
4	.85	.95		.10	.80	.75		.05	.80	.80		0
5	.55	.45		.10	.40	.40		0	.45	.50		.05
6	1.00	1.00		0	1.00	1.05		.05	1.00	1.05		.05
7	.95	.95		0	.95	.90		.05	.95	.95		0
8	.85	.80		.05	.75	.70		.05	.80	.80		0
9	1.00	1.00		0	1.00	.95		.05	2.05	1.05		0
10	.60	.70		.10	.55	.50		.05	.85	.80		.05
Totals	8.30	8.30		.45	7.85	7.50		.45	8.25	8.30		.25

$\overline{R}_A$	Sum 8.30	16.55		
$\overline{X}_A$		.83		
$\overline{R}_B$	Sum 7.85	15.35		
$\overline{X}_B$		.77		
$\overline{R}_C$	Sum 8.25	16.55		
$\overline{X}_C$		.83		

$\overline{R}_A$	.05
$\overline{R}_B$	.05
$\overline{R}_C$	.03
Sum	.13
$\overline{\overline{R}}$	.04

# Trials	D_4
2	3.27
3	2.58

$$(\overline{\overline{R}}) \times (D_4) = UCL_R*$$

$$(.04) \times (3.27) = .13$$

Max. $\overline{X}$	.83
Min. $\overline{X}$	.77
$\overline{X}$ Diff.	.06

*Limit of individual R's. Circle those that are beyond this limit. Identify the cause and correct. Repeat these readings using the same appraiser and unit as originally used or discard values and reaverage and recompute R and the limiting value UCL_R from the remaining observations.
Reference: The D_4 constant is obtained from, "Table of Factors for X&R Charts", Figure 9, pg. 12—Western Electric (AT&T) Statistical Quality Control Handbook.

Figure 2.14 A gage R&R study along with calculations for a thickness gage. (*Courtesy of the American Society for Quality Control, Milwaukee, Wis.*)

NOTES: _____

GAGE REPEATABILITY AND REPRODUCIBILITY REPORT

Part No. & Name ___Gasket___   Gage Name ___Thickness Gage___   Data ___9/6/76___

Characteristic ___0.6–1.0 mm___   Gage No. ___X-2034___   Performed By _____

Specification _____   Gage Type ___0.0–10.0 mm___

From Data Sheet: $\overline{\overline{R}} =$ | 0.4 | $\overline{X}_{Diff} =$ | 0.06 |

MEASUREMENT UNIT ANALYSIS

% TOLERANCE ANALYSIS

Repeatability — Equipment Variation (E.V.)

$E.V. = (\overline{\overline{R}}) \times (K_1)$

$= (0.04) \times (4.56)$

$=$ | **0.18** |

TRIALS	2	3
K_1	4.56	3.05

% E.V. $= 100 \ [(E.V.)/(\text{Tolerance})]$

$= 100 \ [(0.18)/(0.40)]$

$=$ | **45.0%** |

Reproducibility — Appraiser Variation (A.V.)

$A.V. = \sqrt{[(\overline{X}_{diff}) \times (K_2)]^2 - [(E.V.)^2/(n \times r)]}$

$= \sqrt{[(0.06) \times (2.70)]^2 - [(0.18)^2/(10 \times 2)]}$

$=$ | **0.16** |

OPERATORS	2	3
K_2	3.65	2.70

n = number of parts

r = number of trials

% A.V. $= 100 \ [(A.V.)/(\text{Tolerance})]$

$= 100 \ [(0.16)/(0.40)]$

$=$ | **40.0%** |

Repeatability and Reproducibility (R&R)

$R\&R = \sqrt{(E.V.)^2 + (A.V.)^2}$

$= \sqrt{(0.18)^2 + (0.16)^2}$

$=$ | **0.24** |

% R&R $= 100 \ [(R\&R)/(\text{Tolerance})]$

$= 100 \ [(0.24)/(0.40)]$

$=$ | **60.0%** |

All calculations in Figure 3-8 are based upon predicting 5.15σ (99.0% of the area under the normal distribution curve).

K_1 is $\dfrac{5.15}{d_2^*}$ where d_2^* is dependent on the number of trials (m) and the number of parts (n), and, the number of operators (g) which is assumed to be greater than 15.

A.V.—if a negative value is calculated under the square root sign, the appraiser variation (A.V.) defaults to zero (0).

K_2 is also $\dfrac{5.15}{d_2^*}$ where d_2^* is dependent on the number of operators (m) and (g) is (1), since there is only one range calculation.

d_2^* is obtained from Table D3, "Quality Control and Industrial Statistics", A. J. Duncan.

K_1 and K_2 values are obtained from "Measurement System Analysis", Chevrolet Motor Division, General Motors Corporation.

Figure 2.14b

Hypothesis Testing—*F* Test

If one wants to know how to determine whether there is a difference in the standard deviation between populations, the test statistic or analysis technique used is called an F test. An example would be to determine whether a characteristic of a product manufactured from new equipment has a higher process capability than that characteristic manufactured from existing equipment such as an inside bearing diameter, or an outside diameter, etc. The F test is calculated as follows:

$$F = \frac{S_1^2}{S_2^2} \qquad\qquad 2.28$$

where S_1 = sample standard deviation of population 1
S_2 = sample standard deviation of population 2
S_1 will be defined as having the larger standard deviation of the two populations, e.g., $S_1 > S_2$.

Assumptions: 1. Both populations are normally distributed.

2. The samples are selected randomly and independently from their respective populations.

The experimental test is determined as follows. The null hypothesis is denoted by H_0. It assumes that there is no difference in the standard deviations of the two populations. The alternate hypothesis, H_a, assumes that the new process (no. 2) has a smaller variance than the old process (no. 1). If the F test is greater than $F_{CL,(\nu_1,\nu_2)}$ where CL is the desired confidence level, ν_1 is the degrees of freedom on population 1 and is equal to $n_1 - 1$ where n_1 = sample size for process 1 and ν_2 is equal to $n_2 - 1$ (n_2 = the sample for process 2), as determined from Table 2.2, then one can conclude that there is a statistically significant difference.

At the onset of the experiment, one must determine a desired confidence interval for making the decision. Frequently, 95 percent is used. A 95 percent confidence level F table is shown in Table 2.2. One calculates $\nu_1 = n_1 - 1$ and goes to that column, and then calculates $\nu_2 = n_2 - 1$ and reads across that row until it intersects the column in ν_1.

This test methodology is illustrated in the following.

Example: Suppose a new screw machine was being purchased to improve the process capability of the outside diameter for a shifter pin. The tolerance on the outside diameter is 0.04 mm. The current screw machine no. 1 has a sample standard deviation of 0.0105 mm and the one that is being considered for purchase, machine 2, has a sample standard deviation of 0.0075. One thousand pieces were manufactured and a 31 piece, randomly selected sample was used

TABLE 2.2   **F Tables for 95% Confidence (Top) and 99% Confidence (Below).**

Critical Values of F (95% Confidence Level)
$F.95\,(\nu_1, \nu_2)$

ν_2 \ ν_1	12	15	20	24	30	40	60	120
12	2.69	2.62	2.54	2.51	2.47	2.43	2.38	2.34
15	2.48	2.40	2.33	2.29	2.25	2.20	2.16	2.11
20	2.28	2.20	2.12	2.08	2.04	1.99	1.95	1.90
24	2.18	2.11	2.03	1.98	1.94	1.89	1.84	1.79
30	2.09	2.01	1.93	1.89	1.84	1.79	1.74	1.68
40	2.00	1.92	1.84	1.79	1.74	1.69	1.64	1.58
60	1.92	1.84	1.75	1.70	1.65	1.59	1.53	1.47
120	1.83	1.75	1.66	1.61	1.55	1.50	1.43	1.35

Critical Values of F (99% Confidence Level)
$F.99\,(\nu_1, \nu_2)$

ν_2 \ ν_1	12	15	20	24	30	40	60	120
12	4.16	4.01	3.86	3.78	3.70	3.62	3.54	3.45
15	3.67	3.52	3.37	3.29	3.21	3.13	3.05	2.96
20	3.23	3.09	2.94	2.86	2.78	2.69	2.61	2.52
25	3.03	2.89	2.74	2.66	2.58	2.49	2.40	2.31
30	2.84	2.70	2.55	2.47	2.39	2.30	2.21	2.11
40	2.66	2.52	2.37	2.29	2.20	2.11	2.02	1.92
60	2.50	2.35	2.20	2.12	2.03	1.94	1.84	1.73
120	2.34	2.19	2.03	1.95	1.86	1.76	1.66	1.53

SOURCE: Adapted from Pearson, E. S., and Hartley, H. O. (eds.), *Biometrika Tables for Statisticians,* vol. 1, 2nd ed., Cambridge University Press, New York, 1958.

to obtain the data for both machines. Does the new machine (no. 2) have a higher process capability than the old machine (no. 1)?

Solution:

Null hypothesis	$H_0: S_1 = S_2$	There is no difference between the two machines.
Alternate hypothesis	$H_a: S_1 > S_2$	The old machine, no. 1, has a larger sample standard deviation for machining the outside diameter than the new machine, no. 2.
Test statistic	$F = \left(\dfrac{S_1}{S_2}\right)^2$	

Verify assumptions

1. Samples were randomly selected and were from separate populations.
2. The histograms generated from the population data (not shown) demonstrated that they probably approximate a normal distribution. This assumption also has been verified previously with this process for similar products.

Decision criteria

$$\text{Reject } H_0 \text{ if } F_{\text{experiment}} > F_{.95,(30,30)}$$

Note: A 95 percent confidence interval is sufficient in this instance, and each sample had 30 of freedom since the number of samples taken from both machines was 31 pieces.

Look up $F_{.95,(30,30)}$ in Table 2.2, it is equal to 1.84.

Calculate

$$F = \frac{0.0105}{0.0075^2} = 1.96$$

Conclusion   Since 1.96 > 1.84, the null hypothesis is rejected. One can conclude with greater than 95 percent confidence that the new machine has less variation and hence has a higher process capability.

   F tests are also commonly used to analyze market research data to see if any conclusions about issues such as customer preferences and demographic and psychographic profiles can be made.

Hypothesis Testing—*t* Test

Suppose one wants to determine if an adjustment they make to a process does a better job of centering it, or suppose someone wants to know if a design change improves a fracture strength. They can use a statistical method of analysis called a *t* test. The following equation is used to determine if there is a statistically significant difference in the mean of two populations. As in the F test, an experiment is established:

Null hypothesis

$$H_0: \mu_1 = \mu_2$$

Alternate hypothesis

$$H_a: \mu_1 > \mu_2$$

Test statistic

$$t = \frac{\overline{X}_1 - \overline{X}_2}{\sqrt{\dfrac{S_1^2}{n_1} + \dfrac{S_2^2}{n_2}}}$$

2.29

Note: Establish the variables so that $\overline{X}_1$ is larger than $\overline{X}_2$ or take the absolute value of the difference between the two variables.

Decision Criteria

$$\text{Reject } H_0\text{: if } t_{\text{experiment}} > t_\alpha$$

Assumptions:

1. Both populations are normally distributed.
2. Random and independent sampling was used.
3. Standard deviations σ_1, σ_2 of the population are estimated by S_1 and S_2, respectively.

where α = confidence limit desired and degrees of freedom are based on smaller of $(n_1 - 1 \text{ and } n_2 - 1)$

n_1, n_2 = sample sizes of their respective populations one and two

The t_α value is easily determined by looking at the row corresponding to the test's degree of freedom and aligning it with the column of the desired confidence interval.

Example: A customer satisfaction survey was performed on a new car. A well-defined satisfaction scale was used to tabulate the total of 10 questions which was used to obtain a score between 0 and 100 (higher numbers indicate higher levels of satisfaction). The data were separated between men and women with the following results tabulated:

	Men	Women
Average satisfaction score	68.5	75.1
Standard deviation	7.1	7.3
Number of respondents	67	62

Is there a difference in satisfaction between the two populations?

Solution:

Null hypothesis $H_0\text{: } \overline{X}_M = \overline{X}_W$

e.g., there are no differences in the average satisfaction ratings between the two population groups of men $(\overline{X}_M)$ and women $(\overline{X}_W)$.

Alternate hypothesis $H_a\text{: } \overline{X}_M < \overline{X}_W$

e.g., there is a difference between the two populations.

Test statistic

$$t = \frac{\overline{X}_W - \overline{X}_M}{\sqrt{S_W^2 / n_W + S_M^2 / n_M}}$$

Verify assumptions

1. The data were plotted (not shown) and both samples approximated a normal distribution.
2. Both populations were randomly selected. Since women and men are population categories that are mutually exclusive, the assumption of independent populations is valid.
3. Since the sample size was larger than 30 for the two populations, the sample standard deviations are good estimates for the standard deviations of the populations.
4. Assume the use of a discrete measuring scale has sufficient resolution to approximate a continuous scale.

Decision criteria   Reject H_0 if

$$t_{.95,61} < t_{calculated}$$

61 degrees of freedom was used, because 62 is the smaller of the two samples and (62 2 − 1) or 61 degrees of freedom. A 95 percent confidence interval is required for this problem.

Look up $t_{.95,61}$ in Table 2.3. Since 61 degrees of freedom is not listed, we will select 60 in the 95 percent confidence interval column. The number is 1.645.

Calculate

$$t = \frac{68.5 - 75.1}{\sqrt{7.1^2/67 + 7.3^2/62}} = -5.20$$

Converting this to a positive number it is 5.20.

Conclusion   Since 5.20 > 1.645, the null hypothesis is rejected and one can conclude that there is a difference in the satisfaction level of that car between men and women. The reason for this difference would require further investigation.

TABLE 2.3   The Student's *t* Table.

	Critical values of t		
Degrees of freedom	$t_{.90}$	$t_{.95}$	$t_{.99}$
10	1.37	1.81	2.76
15	1.34	1.75	2.60
20	1.33	1.73	2.53
25	1.31	1.71	2.49
30	1.31	1.70	2.46
40	1.30	1.68	2.42
60	1.30	1.67	2.39
120	1.29	1.66	2.36

SOURCE: Adapted from Fisher, R. A., and Yates, F., *Statistical Tables,* Oliver & Boyd, London, Table III.

Linear Correlation Studies

The purpose of performing a linear correlation study is to see how one variable changes with another variable. An example of such a situation would be that a casting process engineer wants to determine how pouring temperature relates to the shrinkage in a hole diameter or the hole's true position as it relates to another characteristic. One can determine if these variables relate to each other by calculating the correlation coefficient r. r^2 is the percentage of variation that can be explained by one variable as it relates to the change in the other.

$$r = \frac{1}{n} \frac{\Sigma(X_i - \overline{X})(Y_i - \overline{Y})}{\sigma_x \sigma_y}$$ 2.30

where n   = number of pairs of measurements
  r = correlation coefficient
  x_i, y_i = the respective x and y values for the ith point.

Assumptions

- The correlation must have a rational explanation of the relationship.
- The correlation coefficient r, $-1 \le r \le 1$.
- Both variables are from normally distributed populations.
- The correlation curve varies linearly in the form $Y = A \times X + b$. (A is a coefficient for the variable, and b is where the line crosses the y axis at $X = 0$.)

Degrees of freedom   n $-$ 2 (n is the number of data points obtained in the correlation analysis).

Decision criteria   If the magnitude of the r value is greater than the critical r value specified for in Table 2.4 for the degrees of freedom and the desired confidence level for the experiment, then there is a statistically significant relationship between the two variables. To determine the relative strength of the correlation, Table 2.5 is a useful guide.

Correlation studies are useful for determining significant characteristics that need to be carefully monitored upstream in sequential processes because of their effect on subsequent processes. In the chemical resin industry the plastic resin's melt viscosity is statistically controlled in the finished product because of its impact on their customers' processes. Some manufacturers are starting to statistically

TABLE 2.4   Critical r Values Used to Determine Statistically Significant Relationships between Two Variables.

Critical values of the correlation coefficient r

Degrees of freedom, $n - 2$	95% Confidence	99% Confidence
5	.754	.874
8	.632	.765
10	.576	.708
12	.532	.661
15	.482	.606
20	.423	.537
25	.381	.487
30	.349	.449
50	.273	.354
80	.217	.283
100	.195	.254

SOURCE: Revised from Snedecor, G. W., *Statistical Methods,* 4th ed., Iowa State College Press, Ames, Iowa, 1946, p. 351; and David, F. N., *Tables of the Correlation Coefficient,* London Biometrika Office, 1938.

TABLE 2.5   Relating Correlation Coefficients to a Qualitative Assessment of the Correlation.

Interpretation of r values

r value	Type of correlation
−1.0	Perfect inverse
−0.85	Strong inverse
−0.5	Weak inverse
0.0	No correlation
0.5	Weak positive
0.85	Strong positive
1.0	Perfect positive

control temperatures and pressure in their catalytic processes before the finished product is produced in order to obtain better control of the resin's melt viscosity. Such controls are also possible in injection molding and powdered metal and die casting operations so that the process is statistically controlled in addition to monitoring the finished product. Correlation studies are also performed by economists to discover leading indicators for econometric forecasts.

Reference

1. Sprow, Eugene, "Challenges to CMM Precision," *Tooling and Production*, November 1990, pp. 54–61.

Bibliography

American Society For Quality Control, *Statistical Process Control Manual,* ASQC, Milwaukee, Wis., 1986.

Automotive Industry Action Group, *Fundamental Statistical Process Control* Reference Manual, AIAG, Troy, Mich., 1991.

Automotive Industries Action Group, *Measurement Systems Analysis,* AIAG, Troy, Mich., 1990.

Chrysler Corporation, *TESQA Guide to Quality System Requirements for Tooling and Equipment,* Chrysler Corporation, Highland Park, Mich., 1990.

Chrysler Corporation, *SPC Statistical Process Control Methods,* Chrysler Corporation, Highland Park, Mich., 1989.

David, F. N., *Tables of the Correlation Coefficient,* London, Biometrika Office, 1938.

Fisher, R. A., and Yates, F., *Statistical Tables,* Oliver & Boyd, London, Table III.

McClave, James T., and Benson, P. George, *Statistics for Business and Economics,* Dellen Publishing, San Francisco, Calif., 1985.

Pearson, E. S., and Hartley, H. O. (eds.), *Biometrika Tables for Statisticians,* vol. 1, 2nd ed., Cambridge University Press, New York, 1958.

Snedecor, G. W., *Statistical Methods,* 4th ed., Iowa State College Press, Ames, Iowa, 1946, p. 341.

Western Electric Co., *Statistical Quality Control Handbook,* Delmar Printing Co., Charlotte, NC, 1985.

3

Reducing Product Development Time

Speed in developing products or services allows companies to obtain a differential advantage over their competitors with the result of achieving improved profit margins and higher volumes. Therefore, to maximize a company's profitability, it is necessary to get a quality product to market in as little time as possible. Several methods can be used to reduce product development time. Having a shorter lead time has several benefits including:

- The product's life will be increased, because it will be in the market ahead of its competition. Assuming that all products and/or features become antiquated at the same time, the firm who introduced the product or feature first will have had the longest life.

- The product will be more profitable because it enters a market with less competition and fewer product substitutes so a higher price can be charged which, of course, increases the profit margin. This is especially true for innovative products. However, innovation costs may be higher because that company has to spend more on research and development working out an innovation's problem areas. If a product is easy to imitate in a short period of time, the profit advantage can be minimal.

- Product development costs per unit are reduced because less administration, labor, and engineering time was used to develop the product.

- Interest expenditures are reduced to finance corporate projects since the product development time and hence the finance period have been shortened.

- Errors in market forecast and projections are reduced because the time difference between market research projections and product introductions is less. Also the time to allow for possible technology changes introduced into the marketplace is reduced.

Tradeoff Considerations

When reducing the product development time, one must evaluate the tradeoffs between up-front investment to reduce the schedule and the resulting increase in profits. Factors that must be evaluated in the tradeoff evaluation process include

1. *The incremental profit available over the life of the product vs. the incremental investment required to reduce product introduction time.*   Higher initial investment may result from a compressed schedule due to crunch time, additional engineering and support personnel, overtime wages, etc. A simple ratio should be calculated:

$$\frac{\text{Increase in present value profits over the product's life by shortening introduction time}}{\text{Present value cost increase required to compress the schedule}}$$

Overhead cost overruns should be understood as they relate to the profitability of the product so that management can determine whether it is profitable to apply additional resources to complete a project in a more timely fashion. Ratios greater than 1.0 indicate that it may be desirable to compress the schedule.

2. *The impact on product unit cost relating to overhead costs for a development cost overrun.*   This requires an estimate of product volumes for the life of the product. The cost can be easily calculated in terms of the following:

$$\frac{\text{Development cost overrun}}{\text{Anticipated volume over the product's life}}$$

This cost is important because a manager can appreciate the reduction in unit profits for an overrun of the development budget.

3.   The ratio of

$$\frac{\text{Manufacturing cost per unit}}{\text{Percent change in sales volume}}$$

is important, because this fraction shows the economies of scale achievable for manufacturing costs as they relate to production volume. Manufacturing overhead and set-up costs per unit, as well as volume discounts for purchased material, are generally major factors in product cost as it relates to volume.

4. *The interest expense to finance the project during the time of its development overrun.*

Reducing Development Time

There are many approaches and considerations that can be used to reduce product development time including using project teams, improving up-front planning, writing clear product specifications, freezing the product specifications at a specified date, and process mapping.

Utilize project teams

Utilizing interdisciplinary project teams whose participants are involved at the onset of a project can greatly reduce development time and improve the probability of a project's success. Chrysler Corporation changed to this management method and was able to reduce the time it took to develop a car from 60 months to 40. They introduced three vehicles that were well received by the press and the marketplace: the Dodge Viper, the Grand Cherokee, and the LH platform (Concorde, Intrepid, and Vision). They were also able to do this with fewer engineers, reducing the number from over 1000 to about 850 for the LH. However, some of the productivity improvement was accomplished by delegating some portion of the design work to outside suppliers and by reducing staff. On the LH platform, Chrysler's marketing, engineering, manufacturing, purchasing, and finance all were involved up front before decisions were made and those areas all worked together to resolve issues when they arose.[1]

Team members should work in the same office or near each other, when possible, to enhance communication and the exchange of ideas. Also, where appropriate, all of the team members should be dedicated full time to this project and not have other project responsibilities because this will detract from a timely implementation of the project schedule. There are, however, some situations in which certain task requirements are minimal and the team cannot justify full-time participation by one employee. The top priority for those individuals must be to support team efforts and to avoid slowing down the project schedule due to lower priority assignments. If conflicts exist, they must be brought to the attention of the project leader, so that these issues can be resolved by the management that oversees several projects and that has the ultimate responsibility for all projects and resources. Resolution of such conflicts requires reinforcing their annual goals and should be included in their performance review by a panel of representatives with different project groups.

This approach enables sufficient resources to be allocated up front, which assures that a better job is done in the planning phases of a project. When adequate resources are allocated initially, a project will have fewer problems associated with poor planning, which in turn will result in lower development costs and a more timely product introduction. The costs to correct problems later in a development cycle are greater the closer they are to the product introduction. It is important to have all disciplines involved up front for several reasons. First, all parties are allowed to have their input in the project so that all of the different viewpoints are considered. Second, it generates a stronger commitment and vision to make the project successful than it would if these players had to implement someone else's ideas. Therefore, it is *not* recommended to hand off parts of the project to other people who perform the same tasks during the development process. One exception would be if development facilities were in different locations for different aspects of a project and it was not economical to have the same people follow through the whole project. Third, interdisciplinary involvement reduces traditional department conflicts such as those between manufacturing and design or marketing and engineering because these people are working toward a common goal and are in more frequent contact; hence they will be in a better position to appreciate the other disciplines' perspective on an issue.

The Team Leader

All project team members should report directly to a team or group leader who ultimately reports to a general manager or project team leader. The team leaders should behave as coaches to their subordinates and manage by walking around. They should encourage the free flow of ideas and all ideas should be given fair consideration. The project team leader should be an avid supporter of the project, one who is a "product champion." Such a person will not be discouraged by setbacks because of his or her strong belief in the project and will be committed to making it work. The management should encourage some risk taking in developing the project and allow for mistakes without censuring efforts that fail; otherwise communication barriers will exist with the management and team members, and design efforts will be compromised. The critical suppliers who perform design work or manufacture critical components should also be involved early in the design process and considered as part of the team. The team members should have some autonomy in approving capital expenditures so that unnecessary delays are not incurred waiting for the procurement of prototypes, equipment, market research information, etc. Finally, as added incentive, successful project teams should be rewarded in some manner for their efforts. It is also important for the team members to have the authority to make decisions and have the resources to carry them out; otherwise, unnecessary delays or poor development work will ensue.

In some instances it will be necessary to utilize a person who specializes in a specific task. In such a situation, their time should be scheduled in with their management's commitment to support the development schedule as a priority.

Maximizing resource utilization

When using a project team management approach it is important to take advantage of economies of scale with other products and teams within the company. Efforts should be made to utilize common components wherever possible. By using components off of the shelf, advantages are achieved in

1. Utilizing engineering resources by reducing redundant efforts for similar components.
2. Taking advantage of reduced tooling costs on a piece price basis because higher volumes increase the chance that a tooling's useful life will be expired.
3. Reducing setup costs on a per unit basis because each manufacturing run will be longer to accommodate the increased volume.
4. Reducing administrative expenses by having fewer part numbers in the system for both the manufacturing plants and service, as well as for computer files and blueprint storage and maintenance.

In practice many engineering compromises will have to be accepted for this approach to work. However, by reviewing the situation from the customer's eyes this situation will be less difficult. Frequently, an engineer will want a special part designed for an application rather than use a shelf design because performance will be improved somewhat. Suppose this improvement can be achieved, but the product will cost the customer 10 percent more (this includes the mark-ups in the distribution and retail change). Most consumers would barely notice this difference, and from their perspective, it is not worth the extra money. This thinking process has to be used by all engineers when evaluating such tradeoffs. They should be involved with regular customer contacts and in developing and interpreting market research information so that their perspective is not polarized from a technical specialist's view of the product. Therefore, the use of common and standard components should always receive extensive consideration before designing a new part for the same application.

Coordination between project teams

A system should be established in which project teams share technological breakthroughs, discoveries, and solutions to problems that are encountered. This coordination mechanism should involve efforts to commonize designs and use standard components in order to maximize the efficiency of resource utilization which reduces administrative and engineering resource requirements, as well as manufacturing costs. Similar systems and discussions should exist between marketing, finance, purchasing, and manufacturing groups as they relate to issues in their specific disciplines. Technological breakthroughs in areas relating to a company's *core technologies* must be shared between groups. Core technologies are those product areas where a company has a strength or a need to have a competitive advantage; these product areas are generally engineered and manufactured in house or their designs and processes are kept proprietary. For example, a power tool manufacturer might consider motors, switches, gears, and housings as core technologies, while bearings, fasteners, wire chords, and batteries would be purchased technologies. An auto company might regard its engines, transmissions, frame-unit body, and suspension as proprietary, while seats, shock absorbers, and cassette stereos might be purchasing components.

Developing standard part manuals

Standard part reference manuals should be developed for commonly used components to utilize the cost advantages of such. Examples of such components would be fasteners, washers, spring clips, springs, connectors, wire, bearings, motors, gears, capacitors, resistors, computer chips, etc. The components that are included in a standard parts manual depend on what types of components are frequently used in a particular industry. Emphasis should be placed on using such components unless it is in the customer's best interest to pay the higher total cost for a specially designed component. Additionally, specialized components that apply to a particular industry such as flexible pressure hoses, pivot arms, switch toggles, etc., should be used in as many applications as possible to achieve economies of scale, provided that it is beneficial from the customer's perspective. Black & Decker used this thinking and achieved great cost savings by substantially reducing the number of motor sizes used in both their power tools and household consumer appliance products. Achieving economies of scale should not prevent product improvements such as trying new design approaches, material applications, and new technologies. In fact, one new product can include a new component design. If it proves to be successful, it can be used with other product lines. This approach also reduces a company's risk exposure with new technologies.

New product selection

New product ideas can be determined from a variety of sources. All sources of input should be given fair consideration and any "not invented here" tendencies should be censured and avoided. Sources may include customers, marketing personnel, engineers, manufacturing personnel, etc. New products will generally address:

- New product and service ideas/concepts
- Existing product problems/performance issues
- Existing market problems or customer needs
- New technology breakthroughs
- New manufacturing technology or materials
- New uses for an existing product

While reviewing these concepts the team should analyze potential competition and product substitutes to determine if it should be given further consideration. Once a concept is agreed to be worth pursuing by the team, a feasibility study should be performed if any new technologies are involved.

Product development objectives

The objectives of a product development effort should be clearly understood by all team members. They should include a focus on meeting all key performance and quality objectives, minimizing product and development costs, and effectively completing tasks in the least time possible or ahead of schedule. The team members should continuously focus their efforts and decisions toward achieving customer satisfaction by meeting or exceeding objectives with regard to product *performance, quality, cost, and schedule,* all of which improve profitability.

Timely reviews after each development phase

When a phased product development cycle is used, the management should review the program at the date specified on the product development schedule. The project should be stopped only when the management specifically authorizes a project to be terminated. If the management does not respond, the team will continue according to the schedule and assume that it is a "Go" project. This approach does not cause unnecessary product development delays since getting the product to market quickly is so critical. Many concept origination and feasibility projects will be canceled. However, this is time that is well spent and will enable the management to have an opportunity to choose from the projects that will most probably have the highest profitability. This phased approach reduces each project's risk because unprofitable projects or ones that have a lower probability of success can be canceled before excessive development costs are incurred and valuable resources wasted.

Scheduling

Once the feasibility phase has been completed, team members should develop a project timing chart for completing the next phase of the project. The reason that schedules can be established only after the feasibility and research has been performed is because the successful completion of research is not predictable because there are too many unknowns. However, if desired, a schedule of research tasks and experiments can be established on a monthly or quarterly basis. All team members should mutually agree to a product development schedule. They should use their experience with past projects to determine these schedules. To maximize the accuracy of their estimates, they should break down the tasks into all of the steps to be taken and project the time for the minitasks. It should be laid out on project management software, which is usually in the form of a network diagram, program evaluation, and review technique (PERT) or critical path method (CPM) chart.

Teams should meet regularly, perhaps weekly, to communicate project status and issues to the team leader. The leader should record the minutes and update the project status on the project management timing chart software. This information should be summarized and shared with all team members on a timely basis and should help to instill a sense of urgency in the project participants. When a project is broken down into phases, it makes it easier to track milestones' progress as each task is achieved.

Each task that is completed should have the quality assurance principal of "independent verification" applied to it. Therefore, all designs, manufacturing processes, financial analysis, market research, etc., should be reviewed and formally approved by another qualified individual to assure that nothing significant was overlooked. In addition to "management by walking around" and other less formal project reviews, there should be only a few formal design and project status reviews to see if the project should go onto the next level of commitment. These reviews should be scheduled in advance with upper management so that the project is not delayed either waiting for approval to go onto the next phase, or important management concerns requiring attention are not delayed.

Improved up-front planning

A key to avoiding delays is to properly research and analyze the market and technology early in the development project. The project engineers and marketing personnel should visit customers together to identify customer needs, applications, product features, and uses. It will also give them clues as to what educational efforts will be needed to introduce the product and how to make it user-friendly. A review of warranty items and reasons for losing any previous customers should be identified so that a new product design can address these issues. Then, an estimate of the market size and sales forecast should be established and the target market defined. International markets should be researched for products that are being considered for export. The team must realistically acknowledge what design tradeoffs exist and that the market is changing. However, the team must establish a specification which they agree not to change after a certain date. Changes not permissible would include items such as performance criteria or feature selections. This is called a *specification freeze*. The specification should not be frozen until several prototypes have been field tested and the best and most reliable variations have been accepted. Product improvements can be established for later introductions. Any specification change after the freeze point must be approved by management because it can jeopardize the product's introduction date and hurt profitability. Therefore, strong consideration must be given before making any changes to the specification after it has been frozen.

By having a fast feedback information system such as a hotline or customer satisfaction survey after product introduction, additional product improvements can be defined for the next iteration of the product. By utilizing a planning technique known as quality function deployment, which will be discussed later in this book, the team can improve the speed at executing product launches because it assures effective planning and customer focus.

Reducing Product Engineering Time

There are many approaches that can be used to reduce the time to engineer a product. Six methods for achieving this objective will be discussed:

1. The time to engineer a product can be reduced by breaking down a product into *design modules.* For example, a shaded table lamp would have several modules including the wiring, electric wall plug, housing, light socket, and lamp shades. The light socket can be broken down further to include wiring connections, a switch, and a light-bulb holder. The socket interfaces with the lightbulb and the wiring through soldered leads. Another example of modules in a car would be the instrument panel, the stereo, the glovebox, etc. The instrument panel can be broken down into several modules including the fuel gage, tachometer, speedometer, oil pressure gage, voltage gage, etc. The speedometer can be broken down further into several modules such as a speed sensor, speedometer cable, analog gage, etc. Each module will try to use a reliable, proven technology or a standard component that is already being manufactured. The advantage of this approach is that the product should not have many development problems; hence it can be designed and developed quickly and it will be reliable. The disadvantage is that it can raise the product cost because breaking a product into modules can be more expensive (unless one takes advantage of using economies of scale by using components that are used on other products). Also by using modules and standard components, the performance standards may be compromised by not using the newest technology. Engineering optimization may be compromised by using standard parts instead.

2. Determine the amount of excess performance in the design so that it can be adapted for changing market requirements without requiring substantial capital investment. Generally, a price is paid for excess performance, but it can substantially save money for the whole product line if it can be used in other applications that were not originally planned. An example would be to design a common computer housing for both a low-cost personal computer (PC) and a higher performing, higher option PC. The housing will have to be larger than needed for the low-line PC and require larger tooling and a higher material cost. However, an economy of scale is achieved by allowing for common tooling for the two units (obviously there are other factors to consider in such a situation such as whether the low-line PC customers prefer a smaller housing, etc.).

3. The product should be designed with robustness in mind to allow for product adaptations and modifications if market requirements change. For example, some cars have the capability to have features added and are marketed with different options and interiors as different products. The basic family car model Plymouth Acclaim is essentially the same as the sporty Dodge Spirit ES except that the ES has a performance suspension, air dam, more powerful engine, and some other option package differences.

4. The kind of interface must be defined between modules.

5. Each module should undergo a *risk analysis*. If a module has a high risk because it is a new technology that was proven in a feasibility study with a small sample of handmade parts and limited field testing, or is being used in a new application, it should have a contingency plan or backup system which uses a proven technology even if either the performance will be compromised or the cost higher as long as these penalties still allow the product to be marketed profitably. These contingency plans are critical to assure a timely new product introduction and prevent marginal products from being sold to customers because a reliably performing alternative was not established. Modules should also be selected for systems whose technologies are anticipated to change rapidly. A module can be grouped into three risk categories: low, medium, and high risk. A brief explanation should be included next to the risk category for each module included in a project risk assessment report.

6. It is better to implement incremental changes to a product in mature industries rather than radical changes because of the risk of quality problems. This risk can be reduced by effective product testing and field trials of new technologies with low-volume products, applications, or small sample production lots in order to reduce customer exposure. A power tool manufacturer sends some prototypes and pilot builds to carpenters and building construction sites many months before their products are introduced to the general public where they can learn about opportunities for product improvements and identify quality problems. A personal computer manufacturer may have a number of prototypes tested with office customers. Before releasing a product on a mass scale, software manufacturers can test approved software with customers to determine if any bugs exist which were not discovered in development.

Tracking Prototypes

Some suppliers do not give the same priority to prototype compo-nents that they give to production orders because late shipments have a perceived less deleterious effect. This can cause expensive delays in the development process, especially if a prototype build is on the critical path. A formal system should be established with the purchasing organization as well as the receiving area or mail room to assure that prototype orders arrive in a timely fashion. Prototype orders should be tracked for scheduled arrival dates versus actual delivery. All late and overdue shipments should be periodically reported for management review. The purchasing agent should be responsible for communicating to suppliers the importance of meeting prototype delivery dates when components do not arrive on time. When feasible, penalty clauses should be included in the purchase order agreement for late prototype deliveries.

A crucial consideration when determining sources (both internal and external) should be their ability to manufacture prototypes and production tools in short periods of time relative to their competitors. This is critical so that either more iterations of prototypes can be manufactured before releasing the final design or product development time is reduced. This allows the product designers and engineers more opportunities to improve the products than they would have if prototype components took longer to procure.

Specification Writing

Writing a clear product specification is critical to the project's success. A product spec summary should be as brief as possible, perhaps one page, because it will be easier for the development team and management to focus on the project objectives if it is summarized. However, depending on the product complexity, the specification itself can be substantially longer. It should also be developed by utilizing interdisciplinary involvement with team representatives from engineering, manufacturing, marketing, purchasing, quality assurance, customer service, etc. Product specifications should be written quantitatively to avoid misunderstandings and misinterpretations. It should occur after a review of business trends in that industry and market, identifying emerging technologies and product substitutes, anticipating potential competition, and completing customer visits.

The specs should acknowledge design and cost tradeoffs and be designed for a family or complete line of products to accommodate add-on features. The specification should include the following information:

- User needs that are satisfied and the product purpose
- Target users and their abilities
- Product features and functions broken down into two categories: needs and wants
- Performance requirements from the customer's standpoint
- Reliability goal
- Physical operating environment the product will be used in
- Maximum quality and warranty goals
- Safety, liability, government, or regulatory requirements
- Patent issues

- Potential for design modifications or adaptations for other applications
- Required documentation for service, training, and maintenance manuals
- Warranty policy
- Technical support policy
- Selling price to distribution channels
- Maximum manufacturing cost
- Distribution channels
- Development budget
- Capital expenditure budget
- Product Launch or Introduction Date
- Lead time to fill customer orders

Process Mapping

Another approach that can be used to reduce product development time is called *process mapping*. It is a technique which reviews the current development process. The objective of each step in the process is clearly defined and the completion time is assessed. This approach begins with an interview of key personnel of previous projects and a discussion ensues of previous delays and bottlenecks in operations. Then the total development process is established on a flowchart and the completion time for each task is listed. The management then reviews each task with special focus on the critical path items and looks for ways to reduce the completion time of each task and to improve the process. Then the results are monitored and tracked to determine if any improvements were implemented. Using this process, even one cycle of improvement can take years to complete, but can yield many long-term benefits for the corporation in terms of reducing development costs and time. It would be valuable to involve suppliers to participate in such a task, because they are frequently asked to compensate for a company's errors and the management is not made aware of the implications of such efforts. Additionally, it will offer opportunities to improve the communication loop with suppliers.

Conjoint Analysis

Conjoint analysis can be a form of market research in which customers prioritize the features and options for a product, as well as the price that they are willing to pay for each feature. After collecting this information, it is entered into a computer and analyzed. This can help identify important features, pricing issues, and market segments. This is especially helpful if demographic information is collected when performing the research. After gathering the data, it is useful to classify product feature information into two categories: *needs* and *wants*. A need is a feature that is expected of the product and is critical to its market success, while a want is a desirable feature, which will enhance a customer's "delight" for that product. This will help the product development team focus efforts to assure a timely new product launch, should financial constraints, product development problems, or time delays occur.

Helpful Hints

Early in the project, creativity should be encouraged and supported by the management. Many prototypes should be made to identify key features and customer perceptions about the product. Prototype tooling should be as representative of production tooling as possible to avoid process changes which can affect product performance. Sometimes parts of the prototype tool, die, or mold can be used in the final production tool.

Early in development, it can sometimes be beneficial to make rough forms of dies before the final detail work is fully completed. This approach is used by Honda when manufacturing body stampings and greatly reduces their product development time. Occasionally the die requirements change, and they have to pay a cost penalty to manufacture the stamping on an accelerated schedule; however, this is an infrequent occurrence.[2]

Castings should have excess machine stock to allow for subsequent design changes. Machining lines and progressive dies should have blank or dummy stations to allow for later engineering changes and process improvements. Although these approaches involve some risk and cost more money at first, they generally save money by a large margin over the life of the product.

The product specification should be frozen at an agreed upon date by the project team. No modifications to it can be allowed unless market changes occur and the schedule is adjusted accordingly. This approach will assure a timely product introduction and avoids product quality problems. If the project is running behind schedule, the management must devote additional resources to assure the project is completed as scheduled. They can add more labor to project assignments, approve overtime, pay for compressed time, reprioritize issues at bottleneck tasks, compress time for some of the remaining tasks, and perform assignments concurrently or in parallel. When the management realizes that a project is no longer profitable and is considering canceling it, they should base their cost analysis on the costs associated with completing the project and ignore all costs that have already been put into it. The reason is that those costs are sunk and should not affect future investment decisions. For example, if the tooling and development costs are $2 million and are 75 percent complete, and an additional $500,000 would need to be spent to complete it, the decision to proceed further with the project should be based on the remaining $500,000. If it turns out that the project will have acceptable profitability with a $500,000 investment, but not the $2 million, the project should be a go because the $1.5 million already invested is already lost money. This approach will help a company to "cut its losses." The only reason to cancel the project at that point would be if other projects were identified which would generate substantially greater income for the organization, by utilizing those resources.

The project team should focus its priorities on meeting the minimum critical specifications before devoting efforts to exceeding them and working on the less critical features. This will allow for the project to be completed on time and neglect the less critical specifications which will not have as substantial an impact on sales (providing that the product is still acceptable). Unless time permits, such less important features can be added as a product improvement at a later date. It is important to have the team maintain administrative documentation of the product, drawings, meetings, etc. Additionally, the documentation for feasibility studies that could not be successfully proven, should be saved because if a new technology emerges, the previous research performed will prove worthwhile.

It is important to assign full-time manufacturing personnel to the project. Their salaries should be paid as part of the new product development budget. It is also wise to rotate team members into other areas for temporary assignments so that they can develop an appreciation for the other functional areas of the company's operations. They should be assigned the less complex assignments and be given adequate supervision.

After the project has been completed, a project review should occur to determine what can be learned from the process and what improvements can be made for future projects.

A product development procedures manual should be developed and accompany a training class for all team participants so that they all understand the process. It should be revised as information is learned from the postlaunch program reviews and again after warranty reports have been received.

All follow-up work (warranty feedback), service manual improvements, etc., can be handled by other staff members or by requiring the project team to devote full time to these activities for a period of time after the project's completion. However, this responsibility may detract from the success of other new product development efforts. The team can also work on adaptations to new product lines and features.

Incentives

The project teams who successfully complete their assigned task should be given some kind of reward. The reward can be based on some kind of merit system which measures the product's performance with respect to the goals set for profitability, program completion date, warranty, customer satisfaction measures, and performance standards. The reward can be in many forms such as recognition, monetary, a party, dinner, etc.

References

1. Daniel, Charles Ross, "Eagle Vision TSI • Dodge Intrepid ES • Chrysler Concorde • Beyond the Horizon in Chrysler's Salvation Sedans," *Motor Trend*, June 1992, pp. 78–83.
2. Womack, James P., Jones, Daniel T., and Roos, Daniel, *The Machine that Changed the World,* Rawson Associates, New York, 1990, pp. 116, 117.

Bibliography

Clark, Kim B., Fujimoto, Takahiro, and Chew, Bruce, "Product Development in the World Auto Industry," Brooking Papers on Economic Activity, No. 3, 1987.

Fujimoto, Takahiro, "Organizations for Effective Product Development: The Case of the Global Motor Industry," PH.D. Theses, Harvard Business School, 1989 Tables 7.1, 7.4, and 7.8.

Peters, Thomas J., and Waterman, Robert H., Jr., *In Search of Excellence,* Warner Books, New York, 1983.

Rosenau, Milton D., Jr, *Faster New Product Development—Getting the Right Product to Market Quickly,* AMACOM, New York, 1990.

Smith, Preston G., and Reinertsen, Donald G., *Developing Products in Half the Time,* Van Nostrand Reinhold, New York, 1991.

4

Performing Market Research

Market research is concerned with obtaining information to better understand customer preferences, wants, and needs. It is used to assist the decision-making process for determining marketing and other business strategies. This research helps reduce the uncertainty associated with making such decisions but does not totally eliminate it. When used effectively, market research will clarify how to understand the customer's decision-making process as well as understand the reasons for liking or disliking aspects and features of products. This information will help the development engineer translate customer preferences, desires, and needs into product features. In many instances, the potential benefits of performing market research are not explored to their full potential because it is frequently used to determine only whether customers like or dislike a particular product.

Types of Market Research

There are four classifications of the type of market research performed: primary or secondary, qualitative or quantitative, exploratory or conclusive, and strategic or tactical. *Primary research* is concerned with obtaining data to provide new information. An example would be to hire a research firm to understand which features an industrial vacuum cleaner manufacturer should incorporate into a new vacuum cleaner by surveying potential industrial customers. *Secondary research* is concerned with reviewing existing records and studies to obtain information. It is generally a lot less expensive to utilize than primary research; however, it may not address specific issues as well as primary research would. Secondary research can be obtained by reviewing studies published in trade journals, reviewing previous studies, and reviewing industry and demographic trends.

Qualitative research involves obtaining information which will give the researcher a "feel" for the topic to be explored but does not utilize any quantitative studies. It generally uses anecdotes to give the researcher such an overview of the topic. It is used for determining quantitative research strategies. Common techniques include focus groups and in-depth interviews. Qualitative research can be performed by doing phone interviews with a company's top five customers to understand what can be done to be a better supplier to them. On the other hand, *quantitative research* is performed in order to acquire knowledge regarding empirical evaluations of attitudes, behavior, or performance. This type of research is what managers should use to develop marketing plans. Quantitative research would involve performing either phone interviews, store-mall intercepts, or mailings with a specific set of questions and responses. It will use a random sampling technique and statistically analyze the results.

Exploratory research involves gathering information to obtain insights which can be used to generate a hypothesis for later testing but is not recommended for generating conclusions. Performing a focus group with customers is an example of exploratory research. *Conclusive research* tests a hypothesis and generates statistically valid conclusions from which management can greatly reduce risk and take action on. An example of conclusive research would be performing a statistically valid random sample of a company's customers (both large and small) to determine how the company can better satisfy their needs. That research might measure differences in preferences between large and small customers as well as regional differences.

Strategic research is concerned with identifying a marketing approach to be used in marketing a company's products to the general population. It might be used to identify a theme that could create the best image for the company in the customer's eyes, while *tactical research* is used to identify methods to be used in marketing products and services to specific *market segments* and *target markets*. Market segmenting is used to develop several products by identifying differences in customer preferences and placing them in different product categories. Segmenting can be established by differences in product application, customer type, customer business size, geographic region, customer usage rate, product use classification, etc. A target market is a classification of a type of customer who would share common interests in their purchasing of a particular product. An example would be to identify the customer preferences of eye shadow with females over the age of 40 whose family income exceeds $50,000.

The Research Process

To properly perform market research, one must first determine the objectives of the research. This is crucial and can result in many costly errors if the issues are not well defined. Next, research strategies will be developed. If not enough is known about the topic, an exploratory approach, such as a focus group, should be used. Selecting a capable vendor to perform this task is of paramount importance, because an inexperienced, low-cost source may not provide the depth of information that might be revealed if a talented researcher is selected. After the exploratory research is completed, a more quantitative type of research method should be selected. The questionnaire design should be based on the information generated from the focus group in order to determine the importance and magnitude of the issues. The conclusive research can be conducted in several ways including mail surveys, mall intercepts, store intercepts, personal interviews, and telephone surveys. The market research firm should first design the survey, then pretest it, and then request that the customer review the questionnaire before commencing with the study. Then, they must select a method which assures that a representative sample is used. The sample should be unbiased and statistically significant. After collecting the data, the information is coded and entered into a computer program which analyzes the data and determines any statistically significant issues. The researcher confirms that these items are properly addressed to assure that the research is both valid and reliable. A research report is issued which summarizes the findings. Once completed, they can develop a marketing plan or strategy for a particular product line.

Research Methods

Some of the types of research and their associated processes and methodologies are discussed including focus groups, mail surveys, telephone surveys, personal interviews, field trials, market trend analysis, and customer satisfaction surveys.

Focus groups

Focus groups are group interviews conducted with typically 6 to 10 people who are led by a moderator. The moderator leads a group discussion about a specified topic in order to uncover the participants' views regarding that subject. The sessions usually last between 1 and 2 hours. Generally, three to six separate group sessions are held with different participants before completing the research; however, the total number of groups can range from 2 to 20.

The focus group can reveal information concerning

1. Customer attitudes

2. Customer motives—why people behave the way they do

3. Consumer needs and wants

4. Customer values and lifestyles

5. New product possibilities

6. How new product concepts are received.

This information can be used to identify product refinements and improvements for greater customer appeal.

This approach is exploratory; it cannot reveal quantitative information that has statistical validity regarding consumer preferences, market potential, etc., and should not be used for such purposes. Thus, the focus group reveals attitudes, while the large sample survey can measure their importance.

An important part of developing the discussion guide is planning. Defining the problem and the objectives of the research will identify the type of people to interview so that the respondents who participate properly represent the market segment to be studied. This will also help to establish the discussion topics. A moderator guide should be developed to help the moderator keep to an agenda. The guide usually will include an introduction for the group, an explanation of the ground rules, an introduction of the participants, and finally lead into the discussion topics. Sometimes the group members are first asked to write down their thoughts pertaining to a particular issue before commencing the discussion.

These sessions should be conducted in a relaxed, informal atmosphere because this helps respondents admit feelings that they would be more reluctant to disclose in a more formal environment. The moderator needs to be trained to be proficient in both interviewing and interrogation techniques. Sometimes they will have to use both humor and hostility to help reveal customer feelings. Moderators sometimes use a technique to test out a product concept by explaining what it is and telling them the reasons "that they should use it." This approach is used to test their reactions to such statements and better understand the customer's perspective. Focus groups are usually recorded on film or are observed with a one-way mirror.

Focus groups are frequently used to test advertising concepts. Such sessions are begun with a brief introduction and discussion of the ground rules; then a few questions are asked to break the ice pertaining to the respondents' background and their use of the product that will be advertised. The respondents are then shown the advertisements and given a questionnaire to record their responses. Then a discussion ensues about their reactions, the reasons for their feelings about a particular ad, and their anticipation about the effectiveness of the advertisement.

When preparing questions for a focus group, the researcher must remember that they are trying to understand the customer's process of making decisions, not their conclusions. This can be done by identifying what was sought or wanted. The information that is learned can be classified into three categories: direct experience, social influences, and the media. This breakdown allows for a further analysis.

After conducting the group, it is recommended to send a questionnaire of an exploratory nature to the participants in order to obtain further thoughts and recommendations about a product. This can reduce a participant's bias and fears from peer pressure. It also allows the participant time to think about the product and develop new ideas and suggestions.

The advantage of the focus group is that the information can be obtained in a short time frame at a relatively low cost and can reveal new product ideas. However, it is of an exploratory nature and should not be treated as a substitute for further quantitative research because of the small samples that were not randomly selected.

Sources of new product ideas

Lawton and Parasuraman's research revealed that 60 percent of industrial new product ideas came from research staffs, engineers, salespeople, marketing personnel, and other employees and executives of the firm. This same group generated 46 percent of new product ideas for consumer applications. Another 26 percent of industrial new product ideas came from users and 30 percent came from users of consumer products.[1] The management can review focus group films and reports to help further identify these opportunities.

Mail surveys

Mail surveys are used because they are a relatively inexpensive way to collect quantitative data. Response rates vary but are usually between 5 and 10 percent.[2] Higher response rates occur when the participants have a special interest in participating in the research. For example, one can assume that a higher response rate will be achieved when a researcher surveys chairpersons of Fortune 500 companies to identify how far along they are at developing a total quality program because this is a topic of interest in many of those companies. Most surveys are designed to require less than 5 or 10 minutes of the participant's time in order to maximize responses. Mail surveys are frequently not classified as conclusive research because of the potential bias in the survey result. The bias results from the low response rates. It is possible that the respondents represent a certain personality type more than another. For example, busy people who are always on the go may respond less than people who have more free time. These two categories of people may utilize a different criterion for making decisions, and might institute an inherit bias in the survey results.

Telephone surveys

Telephone surveys are perhaps the most frequently used method for performing market research. The telephone interview can allow the interviewer the flexibility to ask open-ended questions as well as answer multiple choice questions. The response rates are usually substantially higher than mail interviews. The length of time varies depending on the nature of the customer-manufacturer relationship. Business-to-business interviews typically last approximately 20 minutes but are substantially shorter with random phone calls from a phone list. These interviews require some training on the part of the interviewer. In addition to having the survey pretested, the interviewer's method of reading the survey should be pretested before interviewing on a full-time basis to uncover any biases or errors in their method. Once their technique is satisfactory, they should always read the questionnaire verbatim when performing the interview to maximize the consistency of the research and minimize any interviewer bias. To assure an unbiased sample when addressing the general public, the phone calls are made at specified intervals, for example, calling every 100th name in the phone book, after randomly selecting a first name to call. The first name can also be selected from a predetermined market research list. The results generally are considered reliable enough to draw conclusions about the whole population.

Some of the key issues to consider when selecting telephone interviewers include that they should have

1. A euphonic, relaxed voice and conversational qualities in their speaking patterns.
2. Diplomacy and patience when talking with customers.
3. Promptness; that is, they should phone their customers at arranged times, when applicable.

Additionally, the interviewer should not have other job responsibilities which can detract from their effectiveness on this assignment. They should also be trained on the proper interviewing technique and to interview for the specific item assigned.

Personal interviews

Personal interviews can provide more in-depth analysis of a topic than mail interviews and phone interviews. The cost to perform them is higher than other interviews. Although the information to be obtained can be both qualitative and quantitative in nature, the cost is higher and is not justified in many cases. The time it takes to collect the data is longer than mailings and phone calls. Interviews frequently can last more than an hour. The advantage is that personal interviews can be used to evaluate new product ideas. It is therefore prudent to encourage respondents to talk as much as they desire, because a lot of valuable knowledge can be elicited from remarks they made during the interview.

To assure that a representative sample is selected, researchers may be given instructions to select every 10th person walking into a mall or store who fits a specified demographic profile such as females between the ages of 20 and 45. This approach will eliminate affinity bias in which researchers select people similar to themselves. Sometimes quotas for several specified categories are required to be interviewed until the research is completed. This allows them to identify different market segments. Also a representative demographic region must be selected by choosing stores, malls, and shopping centers from cities, suburbs, and rural areas spread around the regions identified for study. In business interviews a similar approach can be used with the business customers.

Field trials

Field trials offer the advantage of having a product studied to see how consumers would actually use the product and then determine its strengths and weaknesses. This information offers the advantage of having extended usage and reduces the respondents' ability to anticipate responses by actually observing their responses to a product. Some companies perform field trials in stores to see if customers will try a new product over their competition.

Customer database analysis

It is important to analyze the company's market position in the various target markets and geographic areas. The analysis should include revenues and profit margins by product in each area as well as the customer. This analysis should answer the following questions:

1. How long does the average customer maintain a business relationship?

2. How many customers are there? What is the percentage of business done with each customer for each product line/product mix? What is the profit margin with each?

3. How many customers have been lost last year? and in the previous 5 years?

4. How are sales distributed by geographic location and industry segment?

5. Which products are in growing markets and which are in declining markets? Does this vary by geographic area?

After obtaining the information which answers these questions, one can determine a strategy for researching the market segments in order to better satisfy their market needs.

Market trends analysis

Market trends analysis is done to identify markets that are growing, shrinking, and remaining steady. It uses demographic data and industry trends from sources such as trade journals to identify changes in market segments and geographic regions. It is very useful to identify products that should be developed to take advantage of such trends. It can also point out upcoming problem areas for the company.

Customer satisfaction surveys

Customer satisfaction surveys are conducted to

1. Prevent the loss of existing customers by identifying problem areas so that they can be addressed before the business relationship deteriorates.

2. Identify new market opportunities by identifying customer wants that are currently unsatisfied.

3. Improve market positioning and strategies by identifying new segments or how customers used the wrong product in a given application.

4. It can identify the strengths and weaknesses of both the company and its competitors. This will help a company to know what strengths should be promoted and what weaknesses need to be improved.

5. This survey can also help customers become aware of other products and services that a company offers.

6. Who or what factors within a customer's organization will determine how purchase selections are made. This is crucial because it

can help realign priorities and resources to better address those issues so that the customer will be more likely to select their products for future applications.

Questionnaire Design

Designing questionnaires is an iterative process. It frequently takes half a dozen iterations before the survey is acceptable to be submitted to a customer for review. After it is reviewed, it is given a pretest to see if the questions require further clarification. When presenting the questions to respondents, it is important to assure them that honest answers are more helpful and that anonymity will be assured so that they will not be judged by their responses. There are many types of questions that can be used. The most common are discussed below.

Likert scale

A Likert scale is a measurement of intervals of a characteristic. It is used to test the amount of agreement or disagreement with a certain opinion. Most commonly it has between five and seven intervals ranging from "strongly disagree" to "strongly agree." The statements should represent the scope of thoughts regarding a product and its features. An example would be

Strongly disagree	Disagree	Neither agree nor disagree	Agree	Strongly agree
1	2	3	4	5

Questions asked may include something like: Please answer the question below using a 1 to 5 scale, as shown above, in which 1 means that you strongly disagree while 5 means that you strongly agree.

1. The XYZ Company's computer processes information fast. _____

2. The software is difficult to utilize. _____

The purpose of using an odd-numbered scale is to show indifference, that is, neither agree nor disagree, and the reason for using a five- or seven-point scale is to provide several categories to discern magnitudes of responses. The researcher should pick half of the questions to have what is known as a positive bias toward the product and half to have a negative bias toward the product. This is to eliminate a phenomenon in respondents known as "nay sayer bias" and "yeah sayer bias." In the example given, question 1 has a positive bias and question 2 a negative one.

Semantic-differential scale

The semantic-differential scale is used to identify customers' perceptions regarding important customer attributes of a particular product. It uses two adjectives which are bipolar opposites to test the extreme views of a topic. Half of the questions should list a positive attribute (e.g., durable) first and half should list a negative (e.g., unattractive) attribute first. It would be introduced to the respondent as follows:

Please place a check mark in the space to indicate your opinion regarding this product.

	1	2	3	4	5	6	7	
Durable	_____	_____	_____	_____	_____	_____	_____	Fragile
Unattractive	_____	_____	_____	_____	_____	_____	_____	Attractive
Light weight	_____	_____	_____	_____	_____	_____	_____	Heavy

Stapel scale

The Stapel scale is used to determine how well various adjectives describe a topic. It is easier to establish than a semantic differential scale, because a researcher does not have to identify bipolar opposites of a given topic. A questionnaire may be established as follows:

For each of the adjectives listed below, indicate how well it describes the product. Use the following numeric choices: $-5, -4, -3, -2, -1, +1, +2, +3, +4, +5$. A -5 indicates that it is an extremely poor description, and a $+5$ means that it is an extremely accurate description.

_____ Easy to use

_____ Unreliable

_____ Convenient

_____ Expensive

Half of the questions should describe positive attributes (such as convenient) and half negative attributes (such as expensive) to minimize bias. In the example given above, zero was omitted from the scale to force the respondents to take a position that is not neutral.

Adjective checklist

The adjective checklist is a simple way of determining how respondents view a particular product. It might be written as follows:

Please place a check mark near the item that describes this product.

_____ Easy to use

_____ Unreliable

_____ Convenient

_____ Expensive

The advantage of this method is its simplicity in determining general attitudes; however, it does not quantify the magnitude of those attitudes. Half should describe positive attributes and half negative.

Rank order comparisons

Rank order comparisons are used to identify preferences between products. However, they do not identify the magnitude of the differences. The question will typically be structured as follows:

Please rank the following by placing a 1 next to the stereo speakers that is best overall, a 2 next to the speakers that are second best, and so forth.

_____ EPI

_____ JBL

_____ Bose

_____ Pioneer

_____ Kenwood

_____ Technics

This approach is good to use for field trials. In such a case, the questionnaire could be redone and brand names eliminated from the products and questionnaire to avoid a perceptual bias.

Paired comparison

The paired comparison is an alternate of the forced comparison; however, it is a more direct A-B comparison between products. Again, it is a relative scale and does not measure the magnitude of differences or preferences. It might be structured as follows:

In each of the following pairs, please select the speaker which has a better sound:

_____ EPI   or _____ JBL

_____ JBL   or _____ Bose

_____ Bose   or _____ Pioneer

_____ Pioneer   or _____ Kenwood

_____ Kenwood   or _____ Technics

This approach could also have some additional comparisons to determine if the results have consistency by converting the data to a rank-order scale based on product comparisons.

Comparative scale

Sometimes comparative scales are used which also demonstrate the magnitude of differences between products. However, it does not provide the researcher with quantitative data, only with relative magnitudes of product preferences. It might be described as follows:

For the following questions, place a number in the box which best describes your assessment between the two speakers. Please use the following rating criteria:

Much better	better	About the same	Worse	Much worse
5	4	3	2	1

The JBL speaker has a sound that is _____ than the Bose speaker.
The Bose speaker has a sound that is _____ than the Pioneer speaker.

Constant sum scale

The constant sum scale is used when it is necessary to learn the relative proportions of a particular issue. An example would be as follows:

Allocate a total of 100 points among the following speakers depending on how much you like the sound quality. The more you prefer the sound, the more points should be allotted to that particular speaker (please check to make sure that the allocated points add up to 100).

_____ EPI

_____ JBL

_____ Bose

_____ Pioneer

_____ Kenwood

_____ Technics

Total = 100 Points

The number of products that should be compared for a given attribute should be kept below 10 to avoid excessive complexity for the respondent. Once the data are tabulated, they can be broken down into percentages easily.

Multiple choice questions

The multiple choice question has the advantage of being versatile and can offer the researcher a lot of information to determine issues and preferences. The primary things to remember are to assure that all categories are mutually exclusive, that the choices are fewer than 10, and that the respondents understand the meaning of the choices. The multiple choices should encompass about 90 percent of the answers; however, an all-encompassing topic should be included such as "other (describe)_____."

Issues to Remember When Developing Questionnaires

When designing questionnaires, there are several items to review to assure that the question will not be unnecessarily biased and that the question is clearly asking what is intended. The following principles should be considered when editing questionnaires.

Avoid asking double-barreled questions. A double-barreled question has two parts but is asked as one question. An example of such a question is as follows:

1. Do you like listening to loud Rock and Roll music? Yes_____ No_____

This question will cause some respondents to be confused and generate erroneous answers. Suppose several respondents like Rock and Roll music but not loud; some would respond yes to the question because they like Rock and Roll music (even though not loud), while others with the same preferences and tastes would respond no because they do not like it loud. The best approach would be to make it two questions, such as

1-a. Do you like Rock and Roll music? Yes_____ No_____ (If no, please go to question 2.)

   If yes, do you like listening to it loud? Yes_____ No_____

Avoid asking leading questions. Leading questions are also known as loaded questions. They have a tendency to direct a respondent to a certain answer. An example of this is illustrated as follows:

How much do you like Crest toothpaste?

This type of questioning leads the respondent to assume a favorable bias for the product. A better way of asking this question would be

How much do you either like or dislike Crest toothpaste?

This kind of question should not be avoided in some questionnaire designs such as a Likert scale in which the respondent indicates that they either strongly agree or strongly disagree with a statement (provided the questionnaire is balanced by asking as many positive questions as negative questions). Another more blatant example is as follows: Do you clean your bathroom with a disinfectant on a weekly basis as is recommended by the board of health to prevent the spread of disease to your loved ones? This question is biased because it implies that someone is being negligent of their family members by not cleaning their bathroom weekly. The question should be more objectively asked as follows: Do you clean your bathroom on a weekly basis? If the sponsor wants to educate the respondent as to the importance of using their brand of disinfectant, it should be addressed after the respondent completes the questionnaire.

Avoid one-sided questions. One-sided questions emphasize only one aspect of an issue. Consider the following example:

1. Do you feel that brand Z is worth a higher price as compared with brand X?

A more neutral way of asking this question would be

1. Do you believe that brand Z is worth paying a higher, lower, or the same price for than brand X?

One-sided bias can also be implied by the choice selection; e.g., when you purchase a new copy machine, how important is the sort feature?

a. Of paramount importance

b. Extremely important

c. Important

d. Slightly important

e. Not important

This question incorporates a one-sided bias because four out of five choices are used to imply that it is important. A more neutral alternative would be to provide the following choices:

a. Very important

b. Important

c. Neither important nor unimportant

d. Unimportant

e. Very unimportant

Avoid implicit assumptions. Implicit assumptions take for granted a person's habits or understanding regarding a particular topic. An example is in the following question: Do you drink coffee when you get to work? This question assumes both that a person drinks coffee and that they go to a workplace. It is also a double-barreled question. It can be rewritten into screening questions such as

1. Do you drink coffee? Yes_____ No_____
   (If no, go to question 5; otherwise continue on to question 2.)
2. Do you work at a job other than at home? Yes_____ No_____
   (If no, go to question 4; otherwise continue on to question 3.)
3. Do you drink coffee when you arrive at work? Yes_____ No_____

The use of "if no, go to question 5" is known as *branching*. Care should be taken so that the branching used is not excessively difficult to follow. Another example of implicit assumptions is to assume that different respondents have the same quantitative definition for "a lot" or "a little"; for example,

4. How much coffee do you drink in a day?
   a. A lot
   b. Some
   c. A little

Question 4 might be reworded as follows to eliminate the respondents' differences in perspective:

4. On the average, how many cups of coffee do you drink in a day?
   a. 1 cup
   b. 2 cups
   c. 3 cups
   d. 4 cups
   e. More than 4 cups

Avoid sponsor bias.   Sponsor bias results when the sponsor asks a disproportionate number of questions involving its products as compared with its competitors. This can be avoided by asking an equal number of questions regarding the sponsor's product and the competition's products.

Avoid response overlap.   Response overlap occurs when questionnaire categories are not mutually exclusive. For example, when asking a demographic question, the following example will illustrate:

1. What is your annual family income?
   a. $0–$10,000
   b. $10,000–$25,000
   c. $25,000–$40,000

d. $40,000–$60,000
e. $60,000–$100,000

This set of choices has two problems with it. First, each response category is not mutually exclusive because if a family earns exactly $25,000, they could answer correctly by recording either b or c. Also if a family earns more than $100,000, there is no choice for them. A solution to these problems is shown in the response choices below:

a. $0–$10,000
b. $10,001–$25,000
c. $25,001–$40,000
d. $40,001–$60,000
e. More than $60,000

Other Issues to Consider When Developing Questionnaires

Other issues to consider when reviewing survey questions are to assure that the questions are easy to understand so that they are concise and utilize vocabulary that is understood by the respondents being interviewed. They should be designed so that the least sophisticated respondent will be able to understand and follow the survey format. All surveys should be pretested so that final revisions can be made before the survey commences.

Designing the format

There are several methods for designing the format. Sometimes sections are grouped by the main theme or content of a particular section. An example would be to have three sections: demographic, consumer lifestyles, and consumer preferences. The demographic questions are included in almost all surveys because they identify information about the respondent's age, sex, geographic area, income, etc. Other formats are designed according to the scaling method used; for example, one might have three sections: Likert scale (strongly agree/disagree), paired comparison, and multiple choice. They also are sometimes formatted by topic. An example for a stereo manufacturer would be to group questions in the following categories: speakers, cassette decks, turntables, compact disks, and receivers. The designer should try to assure that there is a smooth flow between topics.

The questions should ask the potentially least threatening questions first in order to break the ice to put respondents at ease and not scare them. This helps to set the stage for the rest of the questionnaires. Euphemisms should be used whenever possible. Demographic questions such as annual income and age can be perceived as being threatening; therefore, they should be included at the end of the survey.

Sometimes a technique known as *skirting* should be used to obtain information that may be sensitive to the respondent. The following example is for a manufacturer of a drug called "Brand D" which is used to treat diarrhea:

1. Have you ever heard of a product named Brand D?
2. Have you ever seen it at a friend's house?
3. Has a bottle of it ever been in the house that you have lived in?
   (If no, go to question 6.)
4. Did a family member use the product?
   (If no, go to question 6.)
5. What did they think of the product's effectiveness?
6. Have you ever used the product?
   (If no, go to question 8.)
7. What did you think of the product's effectiveness?

This questioning technique will make it easier for the respondent to answer that question honestly.

The directions must inform the participant that honest responses are needed so that they can be the most helpful. The instructions must be both clear and concise. They should be included in any section of the questionnaire where confusion may arise. Finally, each page on the survey should be numbered in case the questionnaire sheets become shuffled.

A *survey introduction letter* or *speech* must be prepared for respondents to help them understand the purpose and scope of the survey as well as to put them at ease. It should be limited to one page, whenever possible. This introduction should address the following items:

1. Explain what the survey topic covers.
2. Explain the sponsor of the survey or at least a description of the industry they are in.
3. Describe the potential benefits and importance of the information and what it will be used for.
4. Indicate why the respondent was selected.
5. Explain the level of difficulty anticipated in completing the questionnaire (generally, it should be relatively easy).
6. Describe the time required to complete the questionnaire (it is recommended to be short in most instances).

7. Assure that confidentiality will be maintained.

8. Explain the date that the questionnaire must be returned by (if it is a mailing).

9. State that a self-addressed stamped envelope is included (if it is a mailing).

10. Thank the respondent for his or her cooperation.

Determining sample sizes

Determining the proper sample size cannot always be done by using a scientific approach because frequently population variances are unknown. The equations that are used to determine sample size selection utilize the population variance in the calculation as a variable. When it is known, the task is fairly straightforward. However, it is possible that the variance for a customer's perception of a product can change from the time that research was previously performed to the time the current survey is being issued. This could be a result of changes in customer sentiment and preferences due to product substitutes and changes in the marketplace. Experience and judgment frequently play a large role in the decision-making process. The objective is to establish a cost-effective sample that is representative of the population being studied.

The sample size should be such that it will be large enough to validate the smallest demographic classification of the data. For example, if one wants to know taste preferences of women over 50 as well as the whole population included in a survey, the sample size must be large enough to assure that a statistically valid number of respondents are included who are women over 50 years old.

There are some general rules of thumb that can be used:[2]

1. If the sample size is less than 30, it is usually too small to draw conclusions from.

2. Rarely is more than 10 percent of a population required for a sample, provided that the population is *greater* than 500.

3. For populations greater than 10,000 units, the sample size would be between 200 and 1000.

4. For populations of 5000 units, the sample would be between 100 and 500.

Other factors that should be considered in determining the sample size are discussed as follows:

1. If the cost to the company of erroneous conclusions is large compared to the cost of increasing the sample; it is cost-effective to have high confidence in the data and utilize a larger sample size.

2. If the respondents have large similarities, smaller sample sizes can be used.

3. The question requiring the tightest confidence interval will determine the sample size (this assumes the respondents have a relatively consistent response variation from the other questions being surveyed).

4. If a lot of subsample categories will be analyzed to determine market segments, the sample size selection will need to be increased.

An equation that can be used to determine the required sample size is as follows:

$$n = \left(\frac{Z_{\alpha/2}\sigma}{E} \right)^2 \qquad 4.1$$

where   n   = required minimum sample size

$Z_{\alpha/2}$ = constant based on desired confidence level with data. (Use Table 4.1 to determine factors.)

σ = population's standard deviation

E = total margin of error divided by 2 or amount of error that results should be, within plus or minus this amount

After the samples are taken, one can calculate the error margin for each question by rearranging Eq. 4.1 and solving for E, the error term, as is done in Eq. 4.2:

$$E = \frac{Z_{\alpha/2}\sigma}{\sqrt{n}} \qquad 4.2$$

One can calculate E by using S as an estimate for σ, assuming that the sample was sufficiently large (perhaps larger than 32).

TABLE 4.1   **Factors for a Given Confidence Level.**

Confidence Level	$Z_{\alpha/2}$
.90	1.65
.95	1.96
.98	2.33
.99	2.57

SOURCE: Revised from Table I of Hald, A., *Statistical Tables and Formulas,* John Wiley and Sons, New York, 1952.

Auditing the survey

While the data are being collected, one should arrange to have some people who are on the interviewer's phone list or interview list audit the interview method for objectivity and accuracy. There should be some method of tracing the responses to see that they were accurately recorded. Obviously, the interviewer should not know which one of the calls will be an auditor; however, if they know that they will be audited, their methodology will more likely be objective and the data recorded with higher accuracy. If the auditor is not a proper sample representative, their data should be identified and discarded before analyzing the data.

Data analysis

When designing a questionnaire, one should plan a coding scheme for each question. When the results are in, they should be coded and entered into a database. Each survey input should be numbered so that the data can be verified. Once all of the data have been correctly loaded onto a database, the analysis can be performed by the computer.

The data are then analyzed for relationships. The company may look at the percentage of respondents. The researcher should be able to calculate the margin of error for the data. The results may be reported as follows for the question regarding speakers:

1. Please rank the following by placing a 1 next to the stereo speaker that is best overall, a 2 next to the speaker that is second best, and so forth. (*Author's note:* these results are strictly hypothetical and model numbers were not included.)

Model	Average
EPI	2.5
JBL	1.9
Bose	2.9
Pioneer	4.0
Kenwood	4.7
Technics	5.0

Note: An alternate approach would be to label the speakers A through F to eliminate brand perceptual bias. This would identify sound preferences better by eliminating brand name bias.

The data for Likert scales (strongly agree/strongly disagree) are usually printed out in percentages for each example.

Scale category	Total %	Over 40 years, %	Under 40 years, %	t	F
Strongly agree	25	15	35	*	
Agree	35	23	47	*	
Neither agree/disagree	20	30	10	*	
Disagree	15	24	6	*	
Strongly disagree	5	8	2		

*The data show significance at the 95% confidence level.

In the example shown, the data were broken out into demographic categories to determine differences between age groups. The data showed that the variances between age groups did not change (according to F-test results); however, the means did (as shown by the t-test results in 4 of the 5 choice categories) at a 95% confidence level. The research data are frequently compared with different demographic categories to see if any statistically significant differences exist.

Research Process

It is important for the researcher to be intimately familiar with the objectives of the research in order to properly design the research strategy. It is therefore necessary for the researcher to obtain or be provided with the following information before developing a market research plan:

1. A background of the problems, issues, and uncertainties of the topic to be explored.
2. The information that is desired to be obtained once the research is completed; that is, what questions should the research results be able to answer.
3. The time allocated for completing the research.
4. The budget constraints (if known).
5. A commitment from the survey sponsor to support the researcher if any additional background information is needed.

The research process should be planned using the following 10 steps:

1. Specify what information is needed; this usually takes several meetings between the researcher and the sponsor.
2. Estimate the value of each piece of information requested; this helps the researcher to prioritize efforts and to provide the most cost-effective research. It is frequently classified into three cate-

gories: high, medium, and low priority. High priority is essential to the research, while low priority provides background information; medium is somewhere between the two.

3. Determine what research has been done regarding this topic in the past. It is invaluable to save time and effectiveness in developing a research methodology.

4. Choose the data collection method such as focus group, mailings, phone, or personal interviews.

5. Select the data processing method or the type of software that will generate the best results.

6. Given the budget constraints, determine if it is better to survey a large sample briefly or a smaller sample in more detail with more extensive questioning.

7. Determine the sample size required and the experiment design (questionnaire format and type).

8. Specify the methodology (printings, mailings, interviewers' phone calls, etc.) and cost.

9. Describe the report format.

10. Summarize the costs of the research process and the time it will take to generate the final report.

Then the implementation phase of the market research begins. The 10 primary steps are

1. The survey is designed.

2. It is pretested with about 5 to 10 respondents to identify questions that need clarification and improvement.

3. It is reviewed with the sponsor.

4. The survey is fielded.

5. The data are prepared; they are summarized or coded, and then entered and verified for accuracy of the entry into the computer.

6. The preliminary data analysis occurs.

7. A meeting is held with the sponsor to discuss findings and any additional analysis that is required.

8. The data are analyzed and summarized to identify significant findings.

9. The report is prepared and presented to the customer.

10. The sponsor develops a marketing strategy based on the findings and other information available.

Once the research has been performed, the research report should

1. Provide an executive summary which typically is 1 to 5 pages.
2. Indicate the actions to be taken based on the results; it should include the value and the risks and consequences.
3. Identify the limitations of the survey. All surveys have some inherent limitations and could have been designed better. The researcher and sponsor must both have an appreciation for this so that open communication can be freely shared.

One of the goals in marketing and advertising is to educate the consumer on how new products can benefit them by first creating an awareness and then changing the customer's perception about a product so that they can create a want. These research techniques can be used to evaluate customer awareness and perceptions of a product. Once the data have been analyzed, either advertising strategies can address the issues effectively or product changes can be made to better accommodate customer preferences.

The principles in research questionnaire design can also be used to understand other aspects of business. One application would be to survey internal department customers to understand how the hosting department could better address their internal customers' needs.

Researching the Market Correctly

In 1985 the Coca-Cola company embarked on a marketing strategy which introduced a reformulation of their Coke product. This radical change was made in order to address concerns about perceived taste preference changes with the younger customers. Pepsi-Cola had a different formulation which was sweeter and was increasing sales at a faster rate than Coke was during this period. Pepsi had also surpassed the sale of Coca-Cola in the grocery store segment of the market. The Coca-Cola Company had market research conducted which was designed to determine if a sweeter formulation of Coke was preferred to the original formulation. The research performed was a brief, one-sip comparison which generally did not divulge the brand names. Typically, when such research is performed, consumers are told to separately sip different sodas—in this case several formulations of new Coke, Coca-Cola original formula, and Pepsi. These would be identified with numbers such as 697 and 483 (because no. 1 and no. 2 or product A vs. B can induce perceptual distortions from consumers). The consumer's palate is cleaned to eliminate residual taste effects from the previous test before sipping a new soda. The consumers' preferences were then recorded. The research was conducted with over 200,000 people over a 4-year period and showed a preference for Coke's new formulation. The results generally revealed a preference for the new Coke formulation 61 percent of the time (the results, however, did vary in certain geographic regions).[3] Coke concluded from the market tests that the new formulation would be more popular and changed the formula in their Coca-Cola brand products that were marketed. Loyal consumers complained vehemently about the change, and the company eventually went back and remarketed the original formulation as Coca-Cola Classic to reestablish brand identity. The reasons for this apparent discrepancy between the market research and the market results were due to flaws in the research design. The question that Coke really wanted the research to answer was, "What product will be the most popular in the marketplace?" However, the market test was designed to answer was, "What formulation has a better flavor in a brief taste test?" The research methodology did not simulate the users' actual usage and consumption patterns. A one-sip taste test may show a preference for a sweeter formulation. However, a more extended consumption may yield different results. To some consumers the sweeter product may seem "too sweet" or "less thirst quenching" after drinking a whole can. Therefore, the testing should have been performed over a few weeks with consumers practicing normal consumption patterns and quantities including at meals, in movies, while participating in sporting events, etc. This approach would have had "ecological validity" because it would have had representative test information regarding actual consumption patterns. The research methodology had further flaws because it also neglected to account for consumer psychological responses to a Coke which had a strong history in the American culture and had been the same throughout the 20th century. Hence, a change to such a "stable product" was not well received and threatened the consumers' emotional ties to the product. The market research did not account for this type of effect. Good market research should have included the whole gamut of market issues including

1. Taste testing

2. Packaging design

3. Distribution and sales chain

4. Product advertising

5. Product name

The marketing effort may also have overlooked the *mass market fallacy,* which essentially states that companies have a tendency to target their products after the biggest market to have the largest sales. However, this type of thinking often neglects to consider that the mass market will usually have the most competitors and, as a result, will have lower profits. Instead, it is frequently more prudent to market a product targeted at a market niche which does not have any competition, and higher profit margins can be realized. Because of this phenomenon, Coke was probably better off marketing their product to their market niche than trying to compete more heavily in a market niche which was already dominated by Pepsi.

References

1. Lawton, Leigh, and Parasuraman, A., "So You Want Your New Product Planning to Be Productive," *Business Horizons*, December 23, 1980, p. 31.
2. Alreck, Pamela L., and Settle, Robert B., *The Survey Research Handbook,* 1985, Richard D. Irwin, Inc., Homewood, Ill. 60430.
3. Bernstein, Charles, "A classic lesson: 'Gut feel' vs. research," *Nations Restaurant News*, August 5, 1985, p. 9.

Bibliography

Alreck, Pamela L., and Settle, Robert B., *The Survey Research Handbook,* Richard D. Irwin, Homewood, Ill., 1985.

Hald, A., *Statistical Tables and Formulas,* John Wiley and Sons, New York, 1952.

Alsop, Ronald, "Coke's Flip-Flop Underscores Risks of Consumer Taste Tests," *Wall Street Journal*, July 18, 1985, p. 27.

Johnson, Richard M., and Olberts, Kathleen A., "Using Conjoint Analysis in Pricing Studies: Is One Variable Enough?" 1992.

Kilman, Scott, "Coca-Cola Co. to Bring Back Its Old Coke," *Wall Street Journal*, July 18, 1985, p. 2

Market Research Intelligence, Sales and Marketing: The Role of Market Research, Market Research Intelligence, Catharpin, VA, 1991.

Monroe, Kent B., *Pricing Making Profitable Decisions,* McGraw-Hill, New York, 1990, pp. 111–118.

Rosenau, Milton D., Jr., *Faster New Product Development—Getting the Right Products to Market Quickly,* AMACOM, New York, 1990.

5

Quality Function Deployment

"Luck is a residue of design."

(paraphrase) BRANCH RICKEY

Quality function deployment (QFD) is a technique which can be used to assure that a product is designed and manufactured to exceed customer expectations. Reportedly, it was first used at the Mitsubishi Kobe Shipyard in Japan.[1] QFD utilizes market research of customer requirements, engineering's technical description of that information, and competitive analysis from both customer and technical viewpoints. The information is presented to show how engineering design standards, descriptions, and tests relate to customer requirements for both existing and competitive products. Therefore, QFD is a process which integrates product requirements with product development. The information is also presented to show any interrelationships between engineering requirements and market tests. This helps identify the important and difficult customer issues and design requirements that the development team should focus on. Finally, it shows any design tradeoffs that may be present. All of the information listed is summarized in a matrix called a *house of quality*. Finally because QFD is a team-oriented management approach, it is ideal to incorporate with a product development team's matrix organization.

Benefits

The benefits of QFD have been reported to be:

1. *Reduces the number of engineering changes required.* This results from a better understanding of customer requirements, earlier

manufacturing involvement, and a more preventative focus early in the design process. Engineering changes have been reduced by 30–50 percent.[1]

2. *Reduces product development time.*   Estimates indicate that the time to introduce new products can be reduced by one-third to one-half as much time when using this approach.[2] Such improvements require dedicated team members and concurrent engineering techniques.

3. *Lower start-up costs.*   Toyota reported that their start-up costs were reduced by 61 percent between 1977 and 1984 by using this method.[2] This is demonstrated in Fig. 5.1. The cost savings are a result of a combination of reduced engineering and tooling changes, fewer repairs, less scrap, and fewer administrative resources required to resolve problems.

4. *Reduced warranty.*   This comes about from improved designs and manufacturing controls. The QFD method includes a review of existing as well as potential warranty problems and competitive product designs to generate improved approaches. Reported warranty claims have been reduced between 20 and 50 percent from QFD.[1]

5. *Greater customer satisfaction.*   QFD seeks to understand and address customer requirements. It also offers opportunities to identify unexpected customer wishes and "delight" them so that

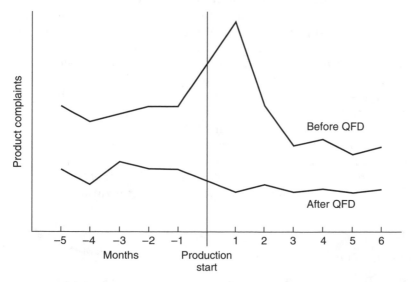

Figure 5.1   A comparison of production start-up problems at Toyota before and after the utilization of QFD. (*Reprinted by permission of American Supplier Institute, Inc., of Dearborn, Mich.*)

product innovations are created and hence customer expectations are exceeded.

6. *Increased cooperation and teamwork between departments.*   Since all functional areas are represented and working together, they develop a better appreciation for other departments' work and are better able to work out solutions between conflicting objectives in order to please their customers.

7. *A well-documented project history and information base.*   It can be used for future reference for other related projects.

The House of Quality

The format for performing a QFD varies. However, a basic method will be described. It is constructed in a matrix called the *house of quality.* The house has several sections or rooms as is shown in Fig. 5.2.

1. The left portion of the matrix, called the "what" room, specifies the voice of the customer. It answers the question, "What requirements should be satisfied, or are there any special features which the customer would be delighted to discover?" These requirements are sometimes grouped in primary, secondary, and tertiary categories. A primary requirement might be general categories such as good reliable operation. A secondary requirement describes a general category such as "is durable, easy to operate, looks good, and does not leak." The tertiary requirement is a more specific classification of the secondary requirements. For example, if the secondary requirement is "looks good," then the tertiary requirement would be "is shiny," "no blemishes," and "appealing shape." Each of these tertiary requirements is then given a numerical importance rating, on a scale of 1 to 10, in which higher is more important. This rating should be determined from market research when possible.

2. Beneath the roof of the correlation matrix is the "how" room, which answers the question, "How can these customer requirements be met in terms of design requirements?" This information is broken down into primary, secondary, and tertiary requirements top to bottom, respectively, as is shown in Fig. 5.3. The tertiary requirements are the actual design verification methods. The tertiary design requirements are then identified numerically for reference later. The classifying process can be performed by a process known as *grouping.* It helps to combine and classify ideas into respective categories. This technique will be discussed later in the book. Above the primary requirements is a row that defines whether the design requirement will specify a minimum, a maximum, or a target value. This is shown just beneath the roof of the house or correlation matrix in Fig. 5.2.

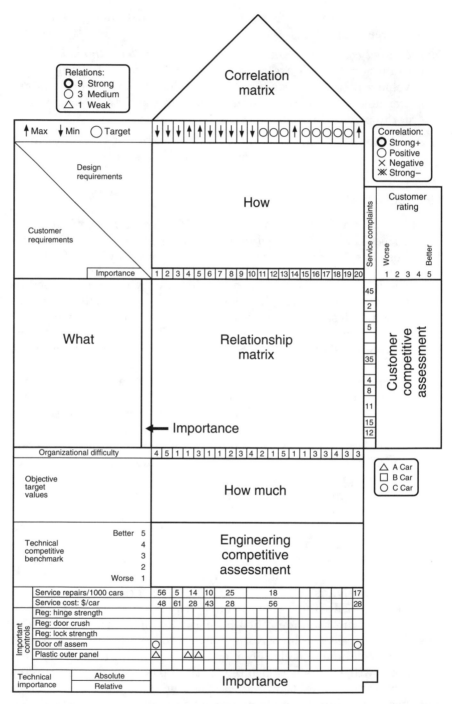

Figure 5.2 The house of quality matrix. (*Reprinted by permission of American Supplier Institute, Inc., of Dearborn, Mich.*)

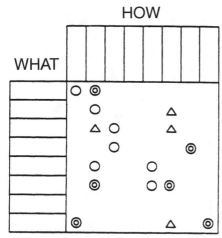

△ WEAK RELATION

○ MEDIUM RELATION

◎ STRONG RELATION

Figure 5.3 How and what room relationship matrix and the associated strength of the relationship. (*Reprinted by permission of American Supplier Institute, Inc., of Dearborn, Mich.*)

3. The room that joins the "how" room and the "what" room is the *relationship matrix*. It links the kind of relationship between the engineering design requirements and the voice of the customer. A circle within a circle signifies a strong correlation between the two, while a single circle shows a moderate correlation and a triangle a weak correlation. Beneath the relationship matrix is a row that estimates the anticipated level of difficulty that the company will encounter in order to achieve the design goals. Again, a 1 to 10 or a 1 to 5 rating scale is generally used.

4. The box beneath the relationship matrix is called the "how much" room and can be clearly seen in Fig. 5.4. It lists the engineering specification which will satisfy customers' requirements. This quantifies the design objectives and provides reference values, should it be determined that customer requirements are not met and the specifications need to be changed.

5. At the top of the rooms is the roof, called the *correlation matrix* (Fig. 5.5). The purpose of this is to identify design tradeoffs from the "how" room that are likely to occur. Design tradeoffs are inevitable, and it is important that they be identified so that the project's goals are realistic. The symbols used in the roof are

A double circle, indicating a strong positive correlation
A circle, indicating a positive correlation
An X, indicating a negative correlation
A double X, indicating a strong negative correlation

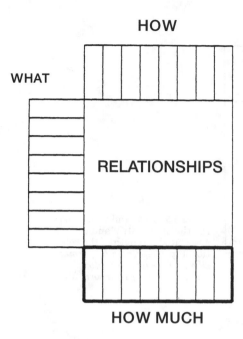

Figure 5.4 The relationship matrix and the "how much" room. (*Reprinted by permission of American Supplier Institute, Inc., of Dearborn, Mich.*)

Negative correlations can be addressed in two manners. The first is to redesign the product to eliminate the tradeoff. However, one must be careful to identify any new tradeoffs incurred as a result of the design change. The second method is to determine an optimization target in which the design tradeoffs are factored with their relative importance to the customer considered.

Two separate competitive assessments are performed in two separate boxes or rooms (Fig. 5.6). A technical assessment is usually performed by engineering, and the other, which is a customer rating, is generally performed by marketing. Typically, marketing will first identify market opportunities, and engineering follows up with a technical feasibility assessment of the product and features. However, marketing and engineering are frequently involved in aspects of each of these tasks to assure full team involvement and a greater understanding of the issues between customer preferences and wants and technical tradeoffs.

6. The *engineering competitive assessment* collects the data in engineering terms and records it on the chart. Each item is scaled separately as it relates to its relative merit for each test from good to bad. Engineering's competitive assessment is recorded below the "how much" room and corresponds to the "how" room column. An importance rating is then assigned to each test on an appropriate scale, possibly 1 to 10 (Fig. 5.7).

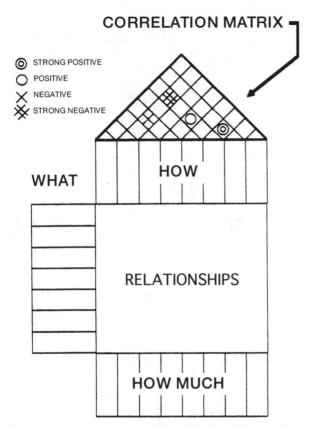

Figure 5.5 The correlation matrix. (*Reprinted by permission of American Supplier Institute, Inc., of Dearborn, Mich.*)

7. *Marketing's competitive assessment* corresponds to the "what" room. This is called the *customer competitive assessment room*. The service complaint column lists items in which current warranty items are significant using a weighted scale of 1 to 10. It is located between the relationship matrix and the customer competitive assessment room. This *competitive benchmarking* helps identify current best-in-class designs as well as identifying the strengths and weaknesses of each design. It can be used to identify areas to focus engineering's efforts to obtain a competitive advantage. It is also useful to generate selling points by demonstrating a new product's superior features.

Benchmarking is a useful tool only when products with the best-in-class features are used for comparison purposes. Best-in-class refers to the best product in a similar price classification and market segment. This is important to consider because it may be unrealistic for a product to achieve the same level of performance for a fraction of the cost

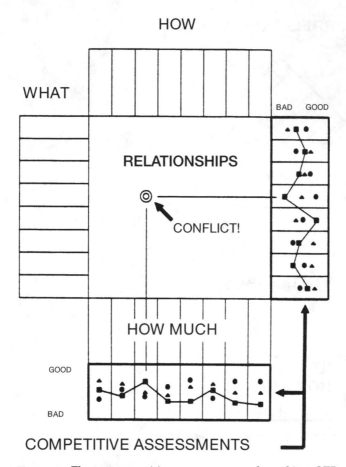

Figure 5.6 The two competitive assessments performed in a QFD: Marketing and engineering. (*Reprinted by permission of American Supplier Institute, Inc., of Dearborn, Mich.*)

of the *best* competitive model. It may be useful to perform competitive analysis with a product that is considered the best because it may lead to creative, cost-effective innovations in product design.

If a discrepancy exists between an engineering technical assessment and marketing's customer competitive assessment, it is a sign that the current engineering design requirements need to be revised to reflect true customer requirements.

Preliminary Research Required to Perform QFD

In order to perform QFD effectively and in a proficient manner, the company should have systems which are formally in place and can rapidly obtain some of the following information relating to the product being researched:

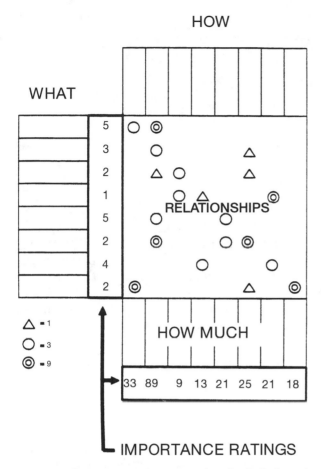

Figure 5.7 Importance ratings are assigned to both the technical and customer requirements. (*Reprinted by permission of American Supplier Institute, Inc., of Dearborn, Mich.*)

- Warranty data and field return information
- Process capability studies
- Plant Problems such as scrap, rework, and returns
- Customer surveys
- Market surveys
- Focus groups
- Competitive analysis from both an engineering and customer perspective
- Government agency and consumer advocate group complaints and concerns

- Lawsuits
- Trade industry leaders determining technology trends
- Salespeople
- Trade show information
- Trade journal information
- Suppliers
- Customer feedback

Project Planning Recommendations

The process works because of its interdisciplinary involvement focusing on team building skills which results in successful conflict resolution in which team players respect opposing views and perspectives. It is recommended that a company select an existing product in which improvements are desired and use it as a QFD pilot project. An interdisciplinary team should be assigned to the project. The team should consist of six to eight people with representatives from the following areas, as appropriate:

Marketing	Market research	Competitive analysis
Quality assurance	Manufacturing	Engineering
Supplies	Facilitator	

1. The manager of these employees must communicate the importance of the project to the employees and assure that they can devote the appropriate amount of time to the project. The employees should receive long-term support from their manager, who must understand that this process will appear to have slow progress initially. The significance of management's support is paramount and cannot be understated. Management should also support the technique because it develops team building and an appreciation for the issues facing other functional areas.

2. The facilitator or leader cannot dominate the discussion because of his or her status or personality. QFD requires everyone's support in order to be successful. The decision making requires group consensus and support.

3. The process can generally take about 20 hours if the research has been properly developed and prepared before each meeting. Therefore, it is advisable to reduce the meeting time to 2 to 3 hours and have 7 to 10 meetings.

4. The initial project will be a lot slower than subsequent projects because of the learning curve, and it may take time to establish systems to collect pertinent data.

5. Periodically evaluate the QFD process and determine if there are opportunities to improve it. There are many variations that have been used depending upon the application.

6. Documentation of the process successes and opportunities for improvement during the project is the key to modifying it to the business culture. A well-trained facilitator, along with management support, are the critical elements of a successful output.

The Completed QFD Matrix—Examples

In Fig. 5.8, a completed QFD matrix is shown for a car door. The customer survey identified that it is most important for the door to open easily, the window crank to be easy to reach and operate, the lock to be easy to operate and not freeze, and for the door to not allow water leaks. QFD is not a document that can be reviewed in a few minutes; it takes some time for one to become familiar with all of the issues involved. So we will just review one characteristic. The customer characteristic "key oper easy" refers to the customer desire to have a locking system that makes it easy to lock and unlock the door with a key. B car and A car have comparable levels of customer satisfaction; however, they are both rated slightly higher than C car. The engineering translation of this is to define the key unlock effort. The specification is a 5 in-lb maximum. Currently, it is a warranty problem in 25 out of 1000 cars. This specification correlates strongly with the customer requirement "key oper easy" and weakly with key insertion effort. Other specifications which weakly correlate with this customer characteristic are the freeze test and a key insertion effort test. In the correlation matrix there is a weak correlation between the key unlock effort and the key insertion effort. Cars A, B, and C were all relatively close in this regard. The relative importance of the engineering specification of it on a 1 to 10 scale was 7.

The QFD technique can also be applied to a new product which does not currently have any competition. A mini QFD was performed on a spring-loaded secondary retaining clip by an automotive supplier. The existing design was made of spring steel. The supplier visited with its customer's engineering group to understand all of the functional requirements of the clip. They went back to their offices and listed the customer requirements and assigned importance ratings to each. The top issues were for it to pass the sealing test after it was

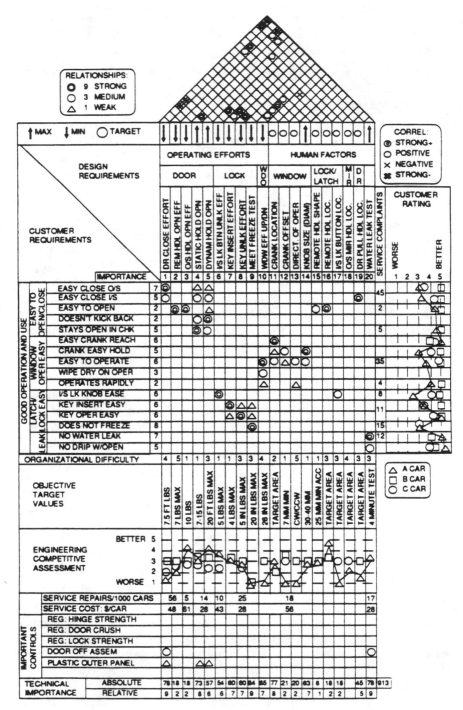

Figure 5.8 A completed QFD matrix for a car door. (*Reprinted by permission of American Supplier Institute, Inc., of Dearborn, Mich.*)

Type of correlation
◉ Strong positive
○ Moderate positive
△ Weak

Technical requirement	Go-No Go Seal check (10)	Perform redundancy ret. (9)	Ease of assembly (8)	No rattle (6)	Fit 1/2" diameter (3)	Durability: vibration, heat (6)	Removable for service (4)	Cheaper than metal (7)	Absolute	Relative
Use box-type structure to encapsulate fitting	○	◉	○	○	◉	○		△	261	4
Sufficient wall thickness to provide integrity	○	◉	○	△	△	○		○	245	6
Material with properties of yield/heat/impact requirements		◉	◉	○		◉	○	○	288	2
Living hinge — snap fit		◉	◉		△	◉	○	○	261	4
Lead in — tapered ends	○	△	○	◉	○				163	10
Two distinct pieces that fit together		◉	○	△			○	○	◉	244	7
Smooth sliding surface	○		◉	△	○		○		154	12
Snap fits	△	○	◉	○	○	○	○	○	213	8
Tight fit to tube	◉	◉	○	◉	◉	○	△		321	1
Multipiece design		◉	○	△	◉	○	○	◉	271	3
Quick release feature	△	○				○	◉		121	13
Tool access	△	○				○	◉		121	13
Multiple cavity tools								◉	72	17
Simple tool design without cams				○	○			◉	117	15
Colorized material		○						◉	117	15
Rib for structural integrity		◉					◉	◉	207	9
Use ribbing to act as a flexible plastic washer	◉		◉					△	161	11

Figure 5.9 A mini QFD matrix for a plastic retaining clip. *(Reprinted by permission of Warren Division of Black & Decker, Mt. Clemens, Mich.)*

assembled onto the unit, to perform the redundancy retainer function, and, finally, to determine if it was easy to assemble at the customer's assembly facility. These customer wants were translated into design requirements. A design was developed with a plastic clip, and they were able to convince the customer to test it out. The clip resulted in a cost savings to their customer of more than 40 percent. Figure 5.9 shows the analysis technique.

QFD identifies both customer requirements and delights. Then, it evaluates the tradeoffs required to meet those objectives. It also tries to use the value-added concept to determine if the cost of some features outweigh the benefits and vice versa. When used properly, QFD determines the best method to manufacture good-quality products in a cost-effective manner. Whenever a tradeoff is being evaluated, the project members must always base their decision on "what the customer would want." The designers should use design flexibility in designing the product, which allows for later adaptations and versions of the product for other markets. For example, the Ford Motor Company is designing a modular engine which has three versions: a V-8, a V-6, and they plan on introducing an in-line 4-cylinder, which is tentatively scheduled to be manufactured in 1998. This approach was taken to allow for common tooling and components which have enough flexibility to manufacture all versions of the engine yet reduce tooling and component costs for engines which can be used in different applications.

References

1. Vasilash, Gary S., "Hearing the Voice of the Customer," *Production*, February 1989, pp. 66–68.
2. American Supplier Institute, *Quality Function Deployment: Implementation Manual for a Three Day QFD Workshop,* 1989 American Supplier Institute, Dearborn, Mich., 1989.

Bibliography

Bossert, James L., *Quality Function Deployment: A Practitioner's Approach,* ASQC Quality Press, Milwaukee, Wis., 1991.

6

Failure Mode and Effects Analysis

Failure mode and effects analysis (FMEA) is a preventative approach used to design products and processes which assure that both design and manufacturing quality objectives consistently meet customer requirements. To perform an FMEA on both a component's design and manufacturing process, one must utilize a team approach to help identify the potential failure modes to customers. The word "customers" is all-inclusive, including end users, manufacturing and assembly plants, and service and other departments. The format used can help identify the higher risk aspects of a design and manufacturing process. This information can be utilized to prioritize efforts for performing design modifications and process improvements which can reduce that risk.

The design FMEA tries to identify and prevent potential design problems by reviewing failure histories and anticipated customer uses and abuses, as well as current design practices with similar parts. It assumes that the part will be manufactured correctly.

The process FMEA assumes that the designs are correct; therefore, a process must be selected which will have sufficient capability and controls to assure that subsequent customer(s) and end user(s) will not have any problems with the product. It reviews previous problem histories and current manufacturing practices in order to select appropriate processing and control methods.

Although performing a design and process FMEA requires separate disciplines and people, there must be an interaction between the two functions. The design engineer should select designs that have realistic specifications for a given manufacturing process. This is known as "process-driven designs" and should be a major design consideration.

If a design characteristic is extremely critical and/or process-sensitive, prudent design practice would dictate that the component should be redesigned. This approach reduces the risk of having either manufacturing or customer problems.

A manufacturing process engineer must also talk with design engineers to inform them of any process sensitivities and difficult tolerances to maintain. This will assist design engineers with setting priorities for redesigning the product. Process engineers must also talk with design engineers to identify critical dimensions so that they rank their priorities according to performing process improvements.

The early communication between manufacturing and design can be called simultaneous engineering and can reduce development time as well as both product and tooling costs.

Design FMEA

The design FMEA is a preventative method of systematically documenting the design issues involved and taking corrective action so that the failures do not occur with customers. The information helps designers prioritize the risky aspects of a design so that it can be modified to improve the product.

The FMEA should be performed and/or reviewed by an interdisciplinary team in order to better anticipate possible failure modes. It should be used in conjunction with design reviews.

Design Reviews

A design review should include an interdisciplinary team of experienced engineers and manufacturing and marketing personnel (where appropriate) who can review the design for reliability, cost, and customer satisfaction, according to a checklist, similar to the one shown in Fig. 1.6. It is especially beneficial to have technically astute members who are independent from the project review the design. They should not have any vested interest in showing a good or bad review to the management—their goal is to perform an objective, professional, and constructive review. They should have some advanced notice of the product objectives and the design approach taken before issuing any comments. This advanced notice allows the review team to effectively evaluate the design. The review should discuss all of the items on a checklist. All items do not have to be addressed with a given design; however, the team should have a general consensus that the compromises and tradeoffs with the design were appropriate and improvements are not feasible or appropriate under the current circumstances design goals and timing objectives. When improvements are identified, all suggestions should be reviewed. The suggestions should be discussed in a constructive manner so that items discussed are phrased in terms of improvement opportunities rather than in terms of harsh criticism. Negative criticism is counterproductive and builds in-house fighting which will have a deleterious effect on teamwork. Those suggestions that the review team agrees have the most merit should be documented by the review coordinator and evaluated for follow-up at a later meeting. Possible methods for making the changes should also be listed on this report. A second review meeting should be scheduled, after the changes can be implemented.

The team should begin by reviewing histories of test failures and warranty problems encountered with manufacturing or assembling similar components. It should also review what is different between this part and similar components to help identify potential problems.

A design FMEA is a living document and should be revised for all engineering changes, and as new failure modes are observed or anticipated.

How to Perform a Design FMEA

Each item on the design FMEA has been numbered in Fig. 6.1. After describing the part or component name and number, the subcomponent for a section being analyzed, and all of the other information requested in the heading of the form, the guidelines for completing each section should be followed and are discussed below.

1–11. Fill out the heading and other information as requested.

12. *Part function* Briefly describe the important functional aspect(s) of the part. If the component has several functions, they should be listed separately in the column.

13. *Failure mode* List the ways that the component can fail to perform its intended design function. This can include failures in other components in a system as well as its design function. Every failure mode that the part or component could conceivably have should be listed.

The failure mode should anticipate failures that could occur under extreme usages. For example, a personal computer used by a customer on a manufacturing floor may be exposed to an oily environment that can cause problems with electrical connections rendering the unit inoperative. Environmental conditions such as dust, moisture, salt, ammonia cleaner, heat, cold, etc., should be anticipated. In addition, normal operating errors and customer abuses such as

CHRYSLER MOTORS

DESIGN
FAILURE MODE AND EFFECTS ANALYSIS

Page _1_ of _3_

Subsystem/Name _____ /Rear Axle Housing Shaft

Model Year/Vehicle(s) _____ 1985/E-Body

Primary Design Responsibility _Dept. 5000, Chassis Systems_

Other Depts. Involved _Warranty, Manufacturing_

Plant(s) and/or Supplier(s) Involved _Plant A & Supplier XYZ_

① P = Probability (Chance) of Occurrence
② S = Seriousness of Failure to the Vehicle
③ D = Likelihood that the Defect will Reach the Customer
④ R = Risk Priority Measure (P×S×D)

⑥ Final Design Deadline _____ 1/2/84

⑦ Prepared by _John B. Dole_   Print / Signature

⑧ Reviewed by _E. D. Smith_   Print / Signature

⑨ FMEA Date (Orig.) _1/2/82_ (Rev.) _10/12/83_

1=very low or none   2=low or minor   3=moderate or significant   4=high   5=very high or catastrophic

⑩ NO.	⑪ PART NAME PT. NUMBER	⑫ FUNCTION	⑬ FAILURE MODE	⑭ MECHANISMS & CAUSE(S) OF FAILURE	⑮ EFFECT(S) OF FAILURE	⑯ CURRENT CONTROLS	⑰ P.R.A. ⑱ P	⑲ S	⑳ D	㉑ R	㉒ RECOMMENDED CORRECTIVE ACTION(S)	㉓ ACTION(S) TAKEN	㉔ P.R.A. P	S	D	R	㉕ RESPONSIBLE DEPARTMENT (INDIVIDUAL)
1.	Tube - Rear Axle Housing - 2568-xx	Support to rear axle assy.	• Fracture	• Inadequate wall thickness	• Loss of rear brakes/ loss of vehicle control	None	2	5	5	50	Run general and rough road durability at minimum thickness	Product change to increase wall thickness Approval 4/83	1	5	3	15	EQ & R (J.J. Smith) SQA (J.L. Smith)
				• Inadequate material		None	1	5	5	25	Material's engineering approval required before drawing release	Approved 6/83	1	5	2	10	Engg. (J.J. Smith)
			• Loose press fit to center section	• Tolerance stack-up		Spec. 2562	3	5	5	75	Revalidated at minimum thickness	Product change to increase tube O.D. by .062" approved 6/83	1	5	2	10	SQA (J.L. Smith) EQ & R (J.J. Smith)
			• Yield	• Improper mat'l.	• Accel brg. wear	None	1	3	5	15	Material's engineering approval required before drawing release	Same as earlier	1	3	2	6	Engg. (J.J. Smith)
				• Inadequate wall thickness	• Improper vehicle attitude	None	2	3	5	30	Same durability test as listed earlier	Same as earlier	1	3	3	9	EQ & R (J.J. Smith) SQA (J.L. Smith)

Figure 6.1   A design FMEA. (*Courtesy of Chrysler Corporation.*)

knocking a lamp off of a table, dropping a power tool from a ladder, or dropping a heavy coffee cup onto a computer keyboard should also be identified. Some typical failure modes include:

Cracked	Sticking	Short-circuited
Deformed	Worn	Open-circuited
Corroded	Oxidized	Vibrating
Leaking	Fractured	Scratched
Component interference	Rubbing	Burned
Melted	Separates	

The failure mode should be described in physical or technical terms, such as open-circuited, not as a symptom noticeable by the customer, such as inoperative.

Failure modes can be identified by reviewing warranty data, quality problem reports, and test reports with similar components. Also an interdisciplinary brainstorming session can reveal other possible failure modes.

14. *Mechanism and cause(s) of failure*   Document every conceivable cause of failure assigned to each failure mode. The failure mode assumes that everything will be manufactured to the engineering specifications and the potential failure is due to an unsuccessful design effort. Some causes of design failures include

Incorrect tolerances specified
Inappropriate material specified
Inadequate assembling instructions
Insufficient lubrication capability
Inadequate design life assumption
Inadequate stress-bearing capabilities
Inadequate end-user application assumption
Inadequate circuitry rectifiers
Inadequate warning manual
Incorrect profile specified
Incorrect clearance specified
Insufficient sound deadener
Insufficient heating or cooling capacity
Imbalance
Resonance
Overloaded current supplied
Incorrect thickness specified
Incorrect electronic component specified
Incorrect edge radius specified
Material incompatibility

Poor environmental protection

Inadequate maintenance instructions

15. *Effect(s) of failure* Document the effects of the failure in terms of what the customer might experience. List all of the effects on the finished product on which this component will be used.

If the failure is one that will not comply with a regulatory agency test, state this (e.g., noncompliance with UL test #XX). (Note: This also applies to CSA, BSI, EPA, NRC, etc.) Some possible effects of the failure might include

Poor appearance

Intermittent operation

Noisy

Oily

Rough

Excessive effort required

Inoperative

Partially operative (operates with reduced capability)

Safety hazard—electrical shock

Safety hazard—physical injury

Unpleasant odor

Will not assemble

Jams machinery and/or shuts down manufacturing assembly line

16. *Current controls (method of design verification)* Document all current methods of design verification that are intended to demonstrate the design's adequacy. They can include

Durability and reliability testing	Finite elements analysis
Environmental testing	Weibull analysis
Regulatory agency testing	Assembly process verification
(e.g., UL, EPA, FMVSS, etc.)	Tolerance stack-up analysis
Computer simulations	Customer observation
Thermal shock testing	Creep relaxation tests

17. P.R.A. This stands for priority risk assessment; these columns are used to calculate the risk priority measures (RPM) to prioritize engineering improvement opportunities.

18. *P (Prob)* Probability of failures during the design life. Enter the numerical value (1 through 5) that reports the number of failures anticipated during the life of the part based on the design life assumptions. The design life assumptions should be documented and filed along with the FMEA. Use the following guidelines (the numbers vary for different failure rates in different industries; for example, in the electronics industry, divide the following failure rates by 100):

	Probability of Failure Guidelines	
Factor	Qualitative probability of failure	Anticipated design life failure rate
1	Very low	<2 per 10,000
2	Low	2 to 10 per 10,000
3	Moderate	11 to 25 per 10,000
4	High	26 to 50 per 10,000
5	Very high	>50 per 10,000

Note: Some companies use a 1 to 10 scale because they feel it is more discriminating and has more resolution. Proponents of a 1 to 5 scale will argue that assessing these probabilities is somewhat subjective, so there is no need for further accuracy.

Figure 6.2 is an example of a design FMEA for an engine oil filter performed by Champion Laboratories. It uses a 10-point rating scale. Their FMEA was 22 pages long for this product.

19. *S (Sev)* Severity of the failure to the customer or manufacturing process; enter the numerical value (1 through 5) based on the following guidelines:

	Severity Assessment Guidelines	
Factor	Summary	Description
1	None	Not noticeable by customer
2	Minor	Slight customer annoyance
3	Significant	Noticeable dissatisfaction
4	High	Inoperable feature or product; no build condition
5	Catastrophic	Customer injury, fails regulatory requirement

20. *D (Det)* Probability that a design problem will be detected by the chosen design verification program (DVP). Enter the numerical value (1 through 5) based on the following guidelines:

	Chance of Detection by Design Verification Program	
Factor	Summary	Description
1	Very high	DVP will detect a design problem.
2	High	DVP should detect a design problem.
3	Moderate	DVP may detect a design problem.
4	Low	It's unlikely the DVP will detect a design problem.
5	Very low	DVP does not exist to detect a design problem.

21. *R (RPM)* Risk priority measure. This can be calculated by multiplying the values in the previous three columns by the following equation:

$$\text{RPM} = \text{Prob} \times \text{Sev} \times \text{Det} \qquad \text{(1 through 125)}$$

If the risk priority measure (RPM) is larger than a predetermined value (perhaps 17), the engineering group should undertake efforts to reduce the calculated risk through corrective actions. Regardless of the risk priority measure, additional evaluations should be given to the causes of failures for items that have a severity of 4 or 5 to assure zero failures. However, if the design verification program demonstrates a failure or inadequacy, corrective action is required, regardless of the RPM.

Potential Failure and Effects Analysis
(Design FMEA)

COMPONENT Engine oil filter | OUTSIDE SUPPLIERS AFFECTED ______ | PREPARED BY: ______
PRIMARY DESIGN RESPONSIBILITY Product design | MODEL YEAR/VEHICLE(s) 1990 models and prior years
OTHER AREAS INVOLVED ______ | ENGINEERING RELEASE ______ | FMEA DATE: ORIG. (6-09-82) REV. (1-10-90)

Part name/ Part number	Part function	Potential failure mode	Potential effect(s) of failure	SEV. (1-10)	Potential cause(s) of failure	OCC. (1-10)	Design verification	DET. (1-10)	Risk priority number	Recommended action(s)	Responsible activity	Resulting: Action(s) taken	Resulting: SEV. (1-10)	Resulting: OCC. (1-10)	Resulting: DET. (1-10)	Resulting: Risk priority number
Oil filter assembly	Integrate all individual component functions in a disposable unit for filtering engine oil.	Leakage @ roll seam	Loss of engine oil with severe engine damage possible	8	Improper flange design Improper forming roller design Inadequate material thickness Engine oil system malfunction	2	Durability testing: Impulse fatigue Hydrostatic burst Vibration Road test Cold hydro-static burst Torque to tighten test	1	16	None required						
		Leakage @ gasket	Loss of engine oil with severe engine damage possible	8	Incorrect torque specified	1	Durability testing: Impulse fatigue Hydrostatic burst Vibration Road test Cold hydro-static burst	1	8	None required						

Figure 6.2 A design FMEA for an engine oil filter assembly with a 10-point rating scale. (*Courtesy of Champion Laboratories.*)

The RPM value should be used to prioritize the redesign and product improvement efforts.

22. *Recommended corrective action(s)*   A brief description of the recommended corrective action should be entered in this column. If corrective action is not needed, then write NR (not required) in that column. Corrective action should be recommended for all designs with a risk priority measure greater than the predetermined value (17). The risk priority measure can be reduced by

- Revising the verification program
- Redesigning the component
- Selecting different materials

Corrective action should be focusing on identifying design improvements. They can be obtained by performing analysis such as

- Tolerance, stack-up studies
- Geometric dimensioning
- Finite element analysis
- Additional testing requirements
- Designed experimentation

23. *Action(s) taken*   Describe the action that was actually taken and the implementation dates.

24. *Revised RPM*   After the action has been implemented, evaluate the corresponding RPM, using the same analysis procedure in steps 18 to 21.

25. *Responsible person / due date*   Document the person responsible for implementing the recommended corrective action along with a target completion date.

Process FMEA

The process FMEA is a systematic method of documenting possible product failures that can result from the selected processing methods. This information is used to prioritize corrective action and processing improvements.

The product failure can be either a failure for the end-use customer, a subsequent manufacturing operation, or a service center.

The process FMEA assumes that the engineering specifications are correct and that the current design will meet the design's intended function.

The process FMEA can be performed by an interdisciplinary team including design manufacturing and quality engineers to improve the identification of product failures due to processing problems. The team should review the process flowchart, subsequent manufacturing operations, the design FMEA, anticipated processing problems, and both process capability studies and quality problem histories with similar parts *before* identifying failure modes. A design engineer can help the team understand the failure modes as well as improve his or her knowledge of the processing issues associated with a component. A process FMEA can be performed in conjunction with a manufacturing process review (see Fig. 1.7) in a manner similar to the design review format. Review team members should include representatives from manufacturing, quality, engineering, and marketing.

A process FMEA, like a design FMEA, is a living document and should be updated for all process changes and improvements or failures experienced.

How to perform a process FMEA

A process FMEA has been performed for a portion of an automobile axle housing in Fig. 6.3. After describing the part or component name and number, any subcomponent for a section being analyzed, and the rest of the information requested on the form's heading, the guidelines for completing each section should be followed and are discussed below listed in order of the respective columns:

1. *No. (operation number)*   List the operation number defined in the flowchart or process routing sheets. If several processes are performed at one station, break down the station. For example, if operation 10 has a drill ream and tapping operation, then number them 10a, 10b, and 10c, respectively.

2. *Part name, part no., and process description*   List the affected part(s) name and number(s). Then write a brief description of the process or operation being utilized. Examples would be rough grinding, pouring, machining, turning, molding, assembly, plating, etc. It is desirable to separately list the processes or operations performed by one piece of machinery or station in order to break down the elements. For example, a screw machine can have form turn, shave, cut-off, feed indexing, etc., at different indexing stations. A molding operation has mold closing, injection stroke, cooling time, and mold opening stroke, as well as raw material feed and three zone heating before this.

To assure that all aspects of the processing are analyzed, it is recommended that the process description should follow all of the steps in the process.

3. *Function part and process (process purpose)*   Concisely describe the function that this process performs or the purpose of using this process.

PROCESS FAILURE MODE AND EFFECTS ANALYSIS

CHRYSLER MOTORS

Subsystem/Name __Axle Housing__

Model Year/Vehicle(s) __1990__

Primary Design Responsibility __Power Train__

Other Depts. Involved __SQA, Manufacturing, Process & Reliability__

Plant(s) and/or Supplier(s) Involved __Chrysler and Tubing Supplier__

Final Design Deadline __December 1986__

Prepared by __A. B. Jones__ (Signature)

Reviewed by __A. R. Smith__ (Print) (Signature)

FMEA Date (Orig.) __3-15-86__ (Rev.) __5-15-86__

P = Probability (Chance) of Occurrence
S = Seriousness of Failure to the Vehicle
D = Likelihood that the Defect will Reach the Customer
R = Risk Priority Measure (P×S×D)

1 = very low or none   2 = low or minor   3 = moderate or significant   4 = high   5 = very high or catastrophic

NO.	PART NAME PART NO. & PROCESS	FUNCTION PART & PROCESS	FAILURE MODE	MECHANISM(S) & CAUSE(S) OF FAILURE	EFFECT(S) OF FAILURE	CURRENT CONTROLS	P.R.A.			RECOMMENDED CORRECTIVE ACTION(S)	ACTION(S) TAKEN	P.R.A.			RESPONSIBLE DEPARTMENT (INDIVIDUAL)
							P	S	D	R			P	S	D	R	
13	– Axle tube – TJ234 – Grinding operation – Centerless grinder no. 2	– Press fit tube for integrity of housing assembly – Grind the O.D. & the corner radius	Oversize diameter	• Measurement error – Master out of calibration – Measuring equipment malfunction – Improper use of gauge	– No build condition – Improper fit – Requires excessive force in assy – Possible flange cracks – High scrap – Low production – Could reach in the field & fail	– 2 pcs. checked per hour – Gauge calibration every two weeks – Inadequate operator training or instructions	3	5	3	45	– Implement X̄ - R chart after proving process potential of Cp ≥ 1.33 – Check gauge to a master every shift & record the results – Conduct gauge R&R to see if gauge is capable – Train operation in proper use of gauge & variable chart	– Capability study conducted 6/86 – Operator trained in gauge check & calibration 5/86 – Gauge R&R done. Gauge improvement order released 6/86	1	5	2	10	– SPC co-ordinator – Plant quality engineer
				• New operator – Limited set up knowledge – Limited machine knowledge – Overadjustment based on one piece sample – Limited SPC charting knowledge	Same as above.	– Foreman approves the setup – Foreman changes the settings on the machine	3	5	3	45	– OJT with formal SPC training as a prerequisite for job – Display set up instructions on the equipment – Do's & don'ts list	– Operator scheduled for formal SPC 8/86 – Set up instructions posted 7/86 – Do's & don'ts list posted & reviewed with all operators 7/86	2	5	2	20	– SPC training co-ordinator – Manufacturing & process engineering

Figure 6.3 A process FMEA. (*Courtesy of Chrysler Corporation.*)

4. *Potential failure mode*   Discuss the way a part or assembly could fail to meet engineering specifications. A failure could be a failure to meet the internal process specifications which are necessary in order for subsequent operations to meet the final engineering specifications. The assumption is made that internal process specifications have been correctly derived from studies. Also it assumes that all previous operations and purchased material had effective controls and were manufactured to the appropriate specifications. Those operations should have been analyzed to validate this assumption. If this analysis was not performed, it should be done before proceeding further. The process engineer also analyzes the component so that in-process specifications can be quantified. In-process specifications are different from formal product specs because in-process characteristics are needed either to control other finished product specifications or subsequent operations; otherwise these dimensions may be out of spec. Suppose, for example, a certain tolerance must be held on a finished product diameter. This dimension can only be held by performing four operations: rough machining, finish machining, rough grinding, and finish grinding. The print specifies the final tolerance, but the manufacturing engineer needs to specify the "in-process tolerance" *for the first three operations* in order to be able to manufacture to the blueprint specification. Also, all items critical to subsequent operations or end users that are not specified by design engineering must be identified. For example, the blueprint may not specify that a part must be clean; however, it is unacceptable to a customer if the product is received dirty. Examples of failure modes include

Bent	Nicked	Short-circuited	Warped
Flash	Burrs	Over- or undersized	Soft or hard
Misaligned	Brittle	Discolored	Open-circuited

Note: Any out-of-specification situation or unacceptable condition would be considered a failure mode.

5. *Mechanism and cause(s) of failure*   Briefly list all possible causes of each assigned failure. The cause should be designated such that remedial efforts can be taken to correct the situation. Some examples would be

Improper furnace controls	Inadequate clamping
Handling damage	Inadequate gating
Worn tool	Improper machine setup
Incorrect speeds, feeds	Inadequate machine maintenance
Inadequate process monitors	Inadequate gaging
Noncapable process	

6. *Effect(s) of the failure*   Describe the effects of the failure in terms of what subsequent operations or end users might experience. Some examples include

Leaks	Shakes
Inoperative unit	Cosmetic dissatisfaction
Noisy	Imbalance
Difficult to, or will not, assemble	Intermittent operation
Cracks or fractures	

Note: If the effect of the failure involves potential noncompliance with regulatory agency requirements, document this (e.g., may not comply with UL #XX, FMVSS #XXX, etc.).

7. *Current controls*   Describe the controls that either prevent the failure mode from occurring or will detect the defect. They can include items such as SPC, preventative maintenance, 100 percent test, locating fixture, set up verification, etc.

8. *P (Prob)*   Probability of manufacturing this defect. Use the following table to determine how frequently this defect will be manufactured *based on the minimum long-term process capability*. The probability for each cause of a defect should be separately analyzed (1 through 5). The numbers vary for different failure rates with different applications and industries.

Factor	Qualitative probability of the cause of failure	Anticipated process failure
1	Very low	≤63 per million ($\pm$ 4σ)
2	Low	64 to 465 per million ($\pm$ 3.5σ)
3	Moderate	466 to 2700 per million ($\pm$ 3σ)
4	High	2701 to 5000 per million
5	Very high	>5000 per million

9. *S (Sev)*   Severity of the defect. Use the following table to determine the seriousness of the defect to either subsequent operations or the end user (1 through 5).

Factor	Summary	Description
1	None	Not noticed by customer
2	Minor	Slight customer annoyance
3	Significant	Causes significant customer dissatisfaction or requires major rework or repairs
4	High	Unit fails to perform intended function or shuts down assembly line
5	Catastrophic	Can cause a safety hazard for end user or fails regulatory agency requirements

10. *D (Det)*   Probability that the defect will reach the customer. Use the following table to determine the factor (1 through 5).

Factor	Summary	Description
1	Very low	Controls will catch/prevent the defects
2	Low	Controls should catch/prevent the defect
3	Moderate	Controls sometimes catch/prevent the defect
4	High	Controls occasionally catch/prevent the defect
5	Very high	Controls will not catch/prevent the defect

11. *R (RPM)*   Risk priority measure. Calculate as follows:

$$\text{RPM} = \text{Prob} \times \text{Sev.} \times \text{Det.} \quad (1 \text{ through } 125)$$

If RPM is greater than 17, the process and quality engineers should perform corrective action to reduce this risk. If the severity has a rating of 4 or 5, additional evaluations should be performed to assure an adequate zero defect process and control method.

12. *Recommended corrective action(s)*   Briefly describe the recommended corrective action. If none is required, write NR (not required) in that row. Recommended action can include designed experiments, on-line controls, SPC, 100 percent testing, preventative maintenance, improved set-up methods, ordering additional equipment, and gaging. The emphasis should be on preventing defects.

13. *Action(s) taken*   Briefly describe the actions taken and the implementation date.

14. *R (revised RPM)*   After the action has been implemented, evaluate the corresponding RPM using the same analysis procedure in steps 8 through 11.

15. *Responsible person/due date*   Document the person responsible for implementing the recommended corrective action along with a target completion date.

Figure 6.4 is a process FMEA for an oil filter performed by Champion Laboratories. Figures 6.5 and 6.6 are tables that summarize the probabilities for assessing the factors for both design and process FMEAs.

Potential Failure Mode and Effects Analysis
(FMEA)

COMPONENT: Assemble oil filter
PRIMARY DESIGN RESPONSIBILITY: Oil Filter Assembly
OTHER AREAS INVOLVED: Mfg. Services, Maintenance
OUTSIDE SUPPLIERS AFFECTED: No
MODEL YEAR/VEHICLE(S): 1990 inclusive
ENGINEERING RELEASE: 9-09-83
PROCESS PREPARED BY: Cary Moudy
FMEA DATE: (ORIG) 6-09-82   REV. 1-15-90

Part name/ Part number	Process function	Potential failure mode	Potential effect(s) of failure	SEV. (1-10)	Potential cause(s) of failure	OCC. (1-10)	Current controls	DET. (1-10)	Risk priority number	Recommended action(s)	Responsible activity	Action(s) taken	Resulting OCC. (1-10)	SEV. (1-10)	DET. (1-10)	Risk priority number
Oil filter assembly 16-00000	To combine shell, element assembly and lid assembly into an unpainted finished filter via a roll seaming operation joining shell and lid assembly	Misalignment of element within filter assembly	Engine oil not filtered	8	Operator error	1	Inspection S Article 604-3.8.1, 3.8.3, 3.9, 3.10	1	8	None						
		Inadequate seam resulting in possible filter leakage	Loss of oil	8	Wrong 1st roller set-up	5	Numbered	4	160	100% Test	Operator	Jan. 1990	4	8	5	160
			Starvation of engine	8	Wrong 2nd roller set-up	5	Numbered	4	160	Saw hook 3 pieces	Set-up	Jan. 1990	3	8	3	72
			Engine failure	8	Wrong chuck set-up	6	Numbered	4	192	Lab evaluation	Auditor	Jan. 1990	2	8	2	32
			Loss of customer	8	Sealer set-up	8	PM system	2	128	x Bar and R	Supervisor	Jan. 1990	1	8	2	16
					Wrong material shell	3	Incoming receiving	5	120							
					Wrong material cover	3	Incoming receiving	5	120							

Figure 6.4 A process FMEA for an engine oil filter assembly with a 10-point rating scale. (*Courtesy of Champion Laboratories.*)

Design FMEA Risk Priority Rating Criteria

Factor	PROB (PROBABILITY OF HAVING A FAILURE DURING THE DESIGN LIFE)*	SEV (SEVERITY OF OCCURRENCE)	DET (PROBABILITY OF DETECTION IN DVP)
1	Very low (<2 per 10,000)	None (not noticeable)	Very high (DVP will detect a design problem)
2	Low (2 to 10 per 10,000)	Minor (slight annoyance)	High (DVP should detect a design problem)
3	Moderate (11 to 25 per 10,000)	Significant (noticeable annoyance performance degraded)	Moderate (DVP may detect a design problem)
4	High (26 to 50 per 10,000)	High (inoperable feature/product— no build condition)	Low (DVP should not detect a design problem)
5	Very high (>50 per 10,000)	Catastrophic (customer injury or fails regulatory requirement)	Very low (DVP will not detect a design problem)

If Prob × Sev × Det > 17, corrective action is required. If the design verification plan demonstrates a flaw or failure, corrective action is required.

If Severity is 4 or 5, additional consideration of the adequacy of the design and design verification program should be given.

*Note: The above table applies to the electromechanical industry. However, these guidelines may be changed to suit specific applications or industries. For example, the electronics industry should reduce these incidents by a factor of 100 (e.g., divide the factors for the probability of having a failure during the design life by 100).

Figure 6.5 Table used to select factors for a design FMEA.

Process FMEA Risk Priority Rating Criteria

Factor	PROB (PROBABILITY OF OCCURRENCE)*	SEV (SEVERITY OF OCCURRENCE)	DET (LIKELIHOOD THE DEFECT WILL REACH THE CUSTOMER)
1	Very low $\leq$63 per million $>(\pm 4\sigma$ minimum long-term process capability)	None (not noticeable)	Very low (controls will catch or prevent the defect)
2	Low 64 to 465 per million ($\pm 3.5\sigma$ minimum long-term process capability)	Minor (slight annoyance)	Low (controls should catch or prevent the defect)
3	Moderate 466 to 2700 per million ($\pm 3\sigma$ minimum long-term process capability)	Significant (causes significant customer dissatisfaction, or requires rework or reduces plant efficiency)	Moderate (controls sometimes catch or prevent the defect)
4	High 2701 to 5000 per million	High (unit fails to perform intended function or line will be shut down)	High (controls occasionally catch or prevent the defect)
5	Very high >5000 per million	Catastrophic (can cause a safety hazard for end user or machine operator or fails regulatory agency requirement)	Very high (controls will not catch or prevent the defect)

If Prob $\times$ Sev. $\times$ Det >17, Corrective action is required.

If severity is 4 or 5, additional consideration of the adequacy of the design and design verification program should be given.

Note: The above guidelines may be changed to suit specific applications or industries.

Figure 6.6 Table used to select factors for a process FMEA.

Bibliography

Bechtel Power Corporation, *Reliability Engineering Methods, No. 2.1; Failure Mode and Effect Analysis,* Bechtel Power Corporation, Ann Arbor Power Division, Ann Arbor, Mich., 1978.

Chrysler Corporation, *Failure Mode and Effects Analysis Manual,* Chrysler Corporation, Highland Park, Mich., September 1986.

Ford Motor Company, *Potential Failure Mode and Effects Analysis,* Ford Motor Company, Dearborn, Mich., September 1988.

Hollenback, J.J., Jr., *Failure Mode and Effects Analysis.* Society of Automotive Engineers, Inc., Warrendale, Pa., 1977.

IEEE Std. 352-1975, *IEEE Guide for General Principles of Reliability Analysis of Nuclear Power Generating Station Protection Systems,*

Ireson, W. G., *Reliability Handbook,* McGraw-Hill, New York, 1966.

Juran, J. M., *Quality Control Handbook,* 4th ed., McGraw-Hill, New York, 1988.

7

Reliability Testing and Design Verification

Engineers are supposed to translate customer requirements and needs into product performance specifications as well as component and part specifications. The design FMEA helps to determine the required tests for a given product or component. QFD helps to determine how well the test program assures that the design meets customer needs. This chapter will discuss some approaches to formalizing testing and verification methods in order to maximize organizational efficiency. It will also discuss a method to verify product reliability by using a technique known as Weibull analysis.

Documenting Test Procedures

It is important to document the test and/or verification method as well as the test methodology for several reasons:

1. It standardizes the test approach between products, and it can expand the database to determine any correlation between the real world and customer problems.

2. It results in more organizational efficiency so that engineers do not have to "reinvent the wheel" by developing their own test for similar products.

3. It assures consistency between tests and people. It therefore allows for comparison between products (competitive and internal) and can assist problem-solving analysis.

4. The knowledge of an experienced engineer is shared with others and that knowledge is not lost should that individual leave the department due to a change of employment, fatality, retirement, etc.

5. It also makes it easier to train a new engineer, allowing for easier transitions during job rotations. This enables an organization to develop more well-rounded engineers with cross-functional experiences.

An example of a documented test procedure for an impulse test (a durability test) is shown in Fig. 7.1. Champion Laboratories uses a quality test and Metrology manual which documents their test procedures and inspection methods. Champion makes high-quality oil filters and has won quality awards from all of their O.E.M. (original equipment manufacturer) customers who participate in such programs. They have an extremely well documented quality assurance system.

Design Handbooks and Guides

There are also advantages to be derived from documenting basic design approaches and information in a *design handbook* when products or components have similarities. The benefit is that an organization can obtain the best approaches as agreed to by several experienced engineers. They also can have tables of information that were derived at the company's test facilities and can be used by future designers. Design handbooks can serve as a vehicle to train new engineers so that their productivity is higher. Additionally, the company does not lose the knowledge that an experienced engineer had, should that person leave the company. However, the author of such a document may intentionally leave important information out of the report if they are concerned about their security. Therefore, a reward system must be in place to offer this individual other positions in the company in terms of a job rotation and also assure job security in the event of hard economic times.

Another useful document to develop is a *design guide*. It can give the engineer realistic design parameters to design products from a product durability, customer satisfaction, and manufacturing process capability standpoint. For example, this booklet might tell an engineer typical clearances that are used in one section of a moving component so that noise problems do not arise. It may also recommend wall thicknesses for structural members of a given component for a given output level to assure that it meets the durability criteria. It also lists typical tolerances that can be achieved for a given manufacturing process. For products made in a casting, stamping, or injection molding process, design guides have been written to inform design engineers of approaches to be taken to assure that the component is easy to cast, stamp, or mold so that tool life is maximized and scrap is minimized.

Sometimes, the information included in design handbooks and design guides is combined in one design manual. Periodically,

CHAPTER 9

MECHANICAL TESTS

These test methods describe laboratory testing of filters to prove their mechanical integrity. Filters are tested to determine vibration fatigue life, pressure impulse fatigue life, and hydrostatic burst pressure strength of the housing material and construction. These tests simulate conditions of engine vibration, engine lubrication system cyclic pressure pulsation, and maximum pressure surge. The test condition values should correspond with those actually measured on the intended engine applicable when such information is available.

The test methods and equipment have been developed primarily for use on filters of the spin-on type, but can be adapted for evaluation of replaceable element type filters no greater than Class 3 size as defined in Federal Specification F-F-351-c. Any mounting plates, brackets, bases, external lines, or other components peculiar to the actual engine filter mounting arrangement should be duplicated as closely as possible.

NOTE: The described methods and/or equipment may be modified to accommodate other sizes and types of filters for specific applications.

1. Pressure Impulse Fatigue Test

1.1 Scope--This test simulates conditions of lubrication system cyclic pressures encountered by the filter during engine operation.

1.2 Test Materials--Test Oil: SAE J1260, Standard Oil Filter Test Oil (RM 99) or as specified.

1.3 Test Apparatus--See Fig. 16.

1.3.1 Brown and Sharpe No. 1S Rotary Gear Pump or equivalent.

1.3.2 1 hp, 1725 rpm motor.

1.3.3 2 gal (7.6 L) capacity sump with heater capable of maintaining 212°F (100°C).

1.3.4 Eagle Signal Corp. Flexopulse Timer (model 4A71, type CA100A60202) or equivalent.

1.3.5 General Controls Type K-108 solenoid (Catalog No. K10CA137T and K-10AA137T) or equivalent.

1.3.6 Durant Corp., Electric Counter, Model No. 6-Y-1 MF or equivalent.

1.3.7 Ashcroft Dura-switch Model No. 4077 pressure shut-off switch or equivalent, wired to shut test stand down in event of over-pressure.

1.3.8 Direct acting pressure relief valve adjustable to 0--200 psi (0--1380 kPa).

1.3.9 Tubing, valves, and gages.

1.3.10 Float type low fluid level shut-off switch.

1.3.11 Test filter mounting fixture (Fig. 3) or base required.

1.3.12 Test apparatus connected in accordance with Fig. 16 and wiring diagram (Fig. 17).

1.3.13 Tektronix type 564 oscilloscope with memory feature or equivalent.

1.3.14 Shield.

1.4 Test Preparation

1.4.1 Fill sump with test fluid and circulate through the bypass circuit allowing the temperature to stabilize to 160 ± 5°F (70 ± 3°C).

1.4.2 Install test filter and circulate test fluid through it to purge all air from the filter.

1.4.3 Set timer to provide the required cycle frequency and set system relief valve to test pressure required.

1.4.3.1 The timer and relief valve adjustments must be made to produce the test wave form as required. See Fig. 18 for a test wave form of the pressure impulse showing the pressure-time cycle. The shaded area shows the percent variation of pressure and time permissible from the required wave form. Note that the slopes of

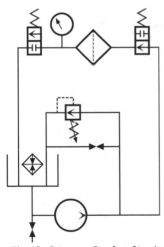

Fig.16 - Pressure Impulse Stand

33

Figure 7.1   A page from an engineering manual. Shown is a test procedure for impulse fatigue test (a durability test) for an oil filter (*Courtesy of Champion Laboratories.*)

test procedures, design handbooks, and design guides need to be reviewed and updated as better methods and changes in technology dictate.

Design Verification

There are many methods that are used to verify if the design of a component meets or exceeds its requirements; however, there is usually a preferred approach for a given application. Frequently, there are many aspects of a design that must be verified. Test programs and other verification means are used to simulate any type of failure that may be experienced. The most significant types of customer uses and abuses must be anticipated. Sometimes, customer uses are not discovered until after a complaint has been issued. It is therefore important to have a feedback system which analyzes that usage pattern so that it can be incorporated into future testing programs.

A simple example of a customer misuse has occurred with wooden dresser drawers. The wooden handles have to be designed either to withstand a 250-lb person standing on them, or to make it impossible to do so. The reason for this is that customers have used these handles like a stepladder and they have broken. Despite the product misuse, customers have been unhappy with those dressers, so the manufacturers improved the design to avoid the negative exposure. However, while moving, if a customer placed corrosive chemicals inside a wood dresser drawer, causing the wood to be damaged, it might be prudent for the manufacturer *not* to make any design changes to address this situation. The inside of the drawer was designed to store clothes, not corrosive chemicals, and wood cannot withstand that kind of product misuse. Also, it is unlikely that there will be a significant number of such instances of that kind of product misuse from their customers.

Usually test programs are designed to be more severe and to accelerate the failure in order to reduce product development time. Some of the most common methods for design verification are discussed below.

Tolerance stack-ups are used to determine component interference, fit or gaps between components, and the amount of variation in a finished characteristic based on dimensions that contribute to that variation. Sometimes a customer may complain because a product's mating parts either do not fit, have excessively large gaps, or do not align well, yet all components meet specification. This is because a tolerance stack-up was not properly performed.

Environmental testing is used to simulate the environment that the component (or finished product) will be operating under. For example, plastic components are tested in an ultraviolet (UV) light chamber with various prescribed intensities and cycles to simulate the effect of the sun's UV rays. A diver's watch may undergo water-immersion cycle tests in a pressurized tank to simulate field conditions. A wood-working power tool may be cycle tested in a chamber surrounded with sawdust to determine if the bearings and motor components are adequately protected in such an environment.

Another form of environmental simulation is chemical resistance testing. To simulate the effect of possible chemicals that a unit may be exposed to, appropriate testing is performed. A car may be exposed to a variety of solvents to determine if it can perform adequately and demonstrate adequate part protection when exposed to chemicals that the auto might be exposed to. A similar test can be performed with a household consumer appliance. Also a review of chemical compatibility between mating components in addition to the environmental uses should be performed. For example, some plastics such as styrene and ABS degrade substantially when exposed to certain oils. Therefore, such plastics should not be used in applications in which they could possibly be exposed to those oils. Additionally, when processing steel components that mate with such plastics, one has to assure that the steel component is free of those oils. A motor manufacturer once changed the cutting oils used to process their electric motor's armature shafts. This caused a significant warranty problem for their customer who assembled an ABS plastic rotating component onto the shaft. The component subsequently degraded, causing failures of the finished product.

Computer simulations are used to identify component interference problems. They can also be used to predict how a product will perform. For example, when designing an engine for a given vehicle, the auto manufacturers use computer programs which can predict the vehicle's acceleration and fuel economy depending on the projected engine's size, bore, stroke, cylinder head design, car weight, coefficient of drag, type of transmission, gear ratio, etc. This saves a substantial amount of development work up front and ultimately assures proper vehicle performance and economy. Computer simulation is also used to design parts for manufacturability. Plastic component designs are downloaded onto a program which analyzes how well the component will process. It determines the molding parameters, optimal gate locations, and time required to process the part. It also shows part cooling to identify warpage problems. This saves a lot of money and time by discovering problems early in the development process and preventing program delays and expensive tooling and equipment modifications downstream.

Regulatory agency testing must be performed to meet all requirements specified by the regulatory body. It is important to coordinate this with the agency so that the program is not delayed unnecessarily.

Customer and engineering specifications must also be included in the test program and documented according to appropriate requirements.

Finite element analysis is a computer technique which can be used to calculate the anticipated stresses, heat transfer rates, fluid flow characteristics, or magnetic flux densities for a product. This requires knowledge of material and physical properties. This is usually done before durability and stress tests. However, the results should be verified with actual stress and strain measurements (where possible) as well as durability tests.

Creep relaxation and cure curve analysis are methods that can be used to infer characteristics about a design or material by extrapolating data from a relatively small amount of test time. Cure curves use accelerated test methods to plot curing characteristics of rubber. Creep measures the deformation of a material, under a constant stress and sometimes elevated temperatures, over time.

Customer observation, focus groups, and field trials are a means to uncover any remaining product problems before the product is released. Sample production units are obtained and are given to customers to use. Either they are asked to assess the product's performance from a durability and features standpoint, or the customer's behavior is observed without his or her knowledge.

Field trials are typically performed by obtaining customers who represent a very severe usage of the products. Sometimes, problems are experienced with units that were not discovered in the test programs. The information is invaluable to prevent faulty products from being released to customers. An industrial power tool manufacturer places prototype tools with a construction company to identify any difficulties encountered. An automobile manufacturer tests new transmissions with a cab fleet in San Francisco where the steep hills cause the transmissions to experience severe usage. The cabs accumulate a lot of miles in a relatively short period of time, so product problems can be addressed early, limiting the manufacturer's exposure.

Assembly trials are a means of verifying that the components fit together and are easy to manufacture. Sometimes minor design changes can greatly improve processability and reduce assembly labor and the assembly line's cycle time. It can also demonstrate characteristics that need to be specified to assure that the machines can process a part. For example, a stamped part had a small burr in it that would jam automated assembly equipment at the customer's facility. The burr was acceptable by industry standards. The solution was to not allow burrs on one edge of the part. The component supplier then added a tumbling operation to the process for a minor change and the problem was eliminated.

Durability and reliability testing is very important to determine how well a unit will fare in actual usage. These tests are designed to accelerate the incidence of failures to determine a design's adequacy for a given application. Frequently similar products have different durability tests depending on the end-user application. For example, a consumer drill may only have to pass a 150-hour cycle test, while an industrial drill may require a 600-hour test. To design the consumer unit to meet the industrial test requirements would add unnecessary expense to the product and the consumer would not benefit from it because it would never get used enough to justify the higher price. There are many different types of tests that a product must meet. Each one tries to evaluate the design for different possible failure modes. These failures can range from maximum stress to cycle testing, current surges, thermal shock, etc. The better the test, the more quickly it can uncover the design flaw being sought. However, it should not be unrealistically severe in that it will require an unnecessary increase in product cost. If the test requirements do not reflect the customer use for the expected useful life of the product, there should be a continual effort to develop more severe tests with shorter test time requirements, which still simulate the failures that would occur in actual customer usage. Automobile manufacturers and defense contractors use a combination of laboratory tests and outdoor field trials. When a test program is reduced, it greatly reduces product development time as well as the amount of support services (engineering test budget) while freeing up test resources for other applications. It is important to assure that all components tested in development are as representative of the final production components as possible. Therefore, efforts should be made to utilize the actual manufacturing processes that will be used in the final production. The prototype molds and dies should be similar to the final tools in molding and gating patterns. The components should be manufactured using the production press tonnage, speeds, and feed rates. Occasionally, prototype pieces work well and pass all tests, while there are problems with units made from the final production processes. One engine head gasket manufacturer made sample prototypes for their customer which passed all durability tests.

However, when they made the final production parts, they used a different press tonnage. This resulted in quality problems for their customer and delayed the new product introduction date. They also incurred an expensive repair bill. Because of these differences, it is also a good idea to have the manufacturer of the prototypes document the process used, measure all dimensions, and perform the appropriate physical tests to assure that the components meet requirements. It is not uncommon to have a lot of product development and test time lost troubleshooting a problem attributable to a quality defect that should have been prevented. Reliability testing can be evaluated by using Weibull analysis, which is a method that can be used to quantify the expected reliability of the production population of a component or assembled unit.

Weibull Analysis

Weibull analysis either tests components to failure or to a multiple of the specification limit and uses this data to determine characteristics about a product's population design reliability. It can be used to determine conformance to a given test criterion or specification. It might be used to determine the life of a motor, bearing, switch, connecting rod, shaft, etc., on a cycle test. Weibull analysis is also used to determine material strength in a fracture test.

Weibull analysis is a very effective method that can be used to infer durability or strength characteristics about a population or design from a relatively small sample. The Weibull curve is not normally distributed. This is desirable since many characteristics that are tested to failure are not normally distributed but fit the Weibull curve. The two-parameter Weibull reliability equation is as follows:

$$R(x, \theta, \beta) = \exp - \left(\frac{x}{\theta}\right)^{\beta} \qquad 7.1a$$

where $R(x, \theta, \beta)$ = reliability or proportion of sample which will pass test requirements as it relates to x, θ, and β.

β = Weibull slope or the shape parameter which determines the shape of the distribution.

θ = characteristic life (determined by projecting the 63.2% reliability point, from the y axis, onto the Weibull line and reading the corresponding value on the failure axis, the x axis; this will become clearer after reading the chapter).

x = variable or characteristic being tested to failure, e.g., time, number of cycles, tensile stress, fracture force, stress, burst pressure, etc.

exp $= e$, base of the natural logarithm, a constant approximately equal to 2.71828.

To determine the reliability for a given sample size, Weibull slope, confidence level, and useful life ratio, assuming that no test failures occurred, one can use the following equation:

$$R\,(C,\,\text{ULR},\,\beta,\,n) = (1 - C)^{\left[\frac{(\text{ULR}^{-\beta})}{(n+1)}\right]}$$ 7.1b

Where ULR = useful life ratio.
    C = required confidence level of data [typically either C90 (90% confidence) or C95 (95% confidence) is used].
    n   = sample size.

The useful life ratio is a comparison of how severe the test procedure is to the real-world performance at a specified reliability level. It is the level of severity of the engineering test program compared to the severity of customer field usage at a specified length of use at a required reliability level.

Equation 7.1b is also used to determine sample sizes requirements for a given reliability goal (by rearranging the variables and solving for n) once both the Weibull slope and a useful life have been determined and a confidence level has been specified.

The Weibull curve has different characteristics depending on the value of the Weibull slope, β.

$\beta < 1$ This usually signifies infantile failures that can be attributed to manufacturing defects, if a proven design was tested and the proper tolerance analysis and testing has already been performed.

$1 < \beta < 3.5$ The curve is skewed left toward the lower failure point. The data will have more scatter than those with lower Weibull Slopes.

$\beta > 3.5$ The curve is skewed to the right toward the higher failure points. The data will be more consistent with less scatter.

$3.0 < \beta < 4.0$ This means the curve is approximately normally distributed.

Typically, complex systems consisting of several components, such as an engine, would exhibit a low Weibull slope on their failure plots due to large data scatter. This is because on engine dynamometer durability tests several different types of failures may occur. One engine failure may be due to a crankshaft, another could be due to an exhaust valve, and another a timing chain. However, an individual component, such as an exhaust valve, would have a higher Weibull slope on a bench test. This is because the failure mode would probably be more consistent. For example, the valve failures might all occur at a filet on a neck of the valve stem and would result in more consistent number of cycles to failure during bench testing.

Procedure to perform a Weibull analysis

1. Determine the desired conformance level (e.g., 95 percent, 98 percent, 99 percent) of the population (or test sample).

2. Determine if the testing will be to failure or if attribute testing will be used.

3. Determine the sample size requirements from Table 7.1a or 7.1b if the information is known. Table 7.1a is a general guideline. Table 7.1b is a more precise method for determining sample sizes for attribute testing to a test standard, e.g., suspend the test if it passes the test standard and testing to failure is not required. However, Table 7.1b does require knowledge of the Weibull slope ß and knowledge of how the testing method correlates to real-world performance. If customer duty cycles are known and the test method simulates those cycles and has correlated with real-world failures, then one can estimate the useful life ratio. If a test is 2.5 times more severe than customer usage for its expected useful life of the product at R95 (a 95 percent reliability level), then the useful life ratio would be 2.5. The higher this ratio, the smaller the sample size required for performing suspended attribute tests. Table 7.1b assumes that the required reliability is proven if no test failures are demonstrated. If the useful life ratio is unknown, one should assume that this ratio is 1.0 to be conservative. However, efforts to correlate test data with the real world should commence to validate this assumption.

4. Test the component or unit according to the documented procedure.

   a. *If testing to failure,* one should record the failure point. The failure point can be in terms of cycles, hours, stress, force, etc.

TABLE 7.1a   Sample Size Selection for Weibull Analysis at Various Confidence Levels.

Failure variable testing		Suspended attribute testing	
Conformance level	Sample size	Conformance level	Sample size
0.95	6	0.95	13
0.98	12	0.98	34
0.99	20	0.99	68

NOTE: These are general guidelines. Attribute testing based on a 50% confidence level.
SOURCE: Revised from American Society for Quality Control, Automotive Division, Statistical Process Control Manual.

TABLE 7.1*b* **Sample Size Selection Table for Suspended Attribute Testing to an Engineering Specification at 90% Confidence Level***

Useful life ratio	Weibull slope, β											
	1.0		1.5		2.0		2.5		3.0		3.5	
	R90	R95	R90	R95	R90	R95	R90	R95	R90	R95	R90	R95
1.0	21	44	21	44	21	44	21	44	21	44	21	44
1.5	14	29	11	23	9	20	7	16	6	13	5	11
2.0	10	22	7	15	5	11	3	7	2	5	1	3
2.5	8	17	5	11	3	7	2	4	1	2	1	2
3.0	7	14	4	8	2	4	1	2	1	1	1	1
3.5	6	12	3	6	1	3	1	3	1	1	1	1

*For required reliabilities of 90% (R90) and 95% (R95), at various useful life ratios and Weibull slopes.
NOTE: This table assumes that no failures will occur.

However, when performing variable data analysis, once the Weibull slope has been determined, suspended attribute testing can be used and testing can be terminated before failure. The failure level should be determined by cost and availability of components and test facilities. However, the test sample size must meet the guidelines specified in Table 7.1*b* for validity.

b. *If attribute data are being used,* test all of the components to the specification. If all components in the sample meet the requirement, then one assumes that the design meets the requirement according to the specified confidence level. If a failure occurs, corrective action must be performed. It is recommended to test at least three components to failure so that information relating to the Weibull slope can be obtained and more information regarding proper sample size selection can be assumed.

The test sample sizes can be reduced if testing time is increased because increasing test time correspondingly increases the useful life ratio. Test time and sample sizes can be varied to either reduce development costs or accommodate parts and test time availability. This approach can also be used to minimize related development expenses or reduce product development time (whichever is most desirable under the circumstances).

NOTE: Steps 5 to 11 (below) apply only when testing to failure with variable data.

5. When testing to failure with variable data, organize the data in rank order from lowest to highest. For example, if six components were tested and the results were as is shown in Fig. 7.2*a,* the failure data should be ranked in order as is shown in Fig. 7.2*b. Note:* The example discussed is a hypothetical example and does not reflect actual test data or performance parameters for a motor.

6. Use the median rank table (Table 7.2a) to determine the corresponding median rank value for each failure point. List the rank ordered data for the corresponding median rank value. This is shown in Fig. 7.3.

The median rank value was used because the curves can be highly skewed; therefore, the median value is a more representative measure of central tendency than the mean for this analysis. That is why the tables were selected based on median rank values. Equation 7.2 can be used to calculate a reasonable approximation of the median rank values:

$$\text{Median rank order percentage} = \frac{(j - 0.3)}{(n + 0.4)} \qquad 7.2$$

Where j = rank order number
   n = sample size or number of items tested to failure

7. Use Weibull paper to plot the data. The x axis will be hours, number of cycles, failure strength, stress, etc. The y axis will be the median rank percentage.

8. Draw a straight line of *best fit* through the plotted points. Half of the points should be on one side of the line and half on the other. This is illustrated in Fig. 7.4. In some instances, a few curved lines will make a best fit of the data. Such failure plots have separate portions with different slopes. When this occurs, each section has to be separately analyzed with a straight line connecting each section.

Component no.	Failure value, hours
1	850
2	175
3	512
4	266
5	314
6	731

Figure 7.2 a Raw data for six components tested to failure.

Rank order, hours
175 (lowest)
266
314
512
731
850 (highest)

Figure 7.2 b The data after it has been reorganized in rank order.

TABLE 7.2*a*   Median Rank Table Used for Weibull Analysis

Median Ranks

j	Sample size n									
	1	2	3	4	5	6	7	8	9	10
1	50.0	29.3	20.6	15.9	12.9	10.9	9.4	8.3	7.4	6.7
2		70.7	50.0	38.6	31.4	26.4	22.8	20.1	18.0	16.2
3			79.4	61.4	50.0	42.1	36.4	32.1	28.6	25.9
4				84.1	68.6	57.9	50.0	44.0	39.3	35.5
5					87.1	73.6	63.6	56.0	50.0	45.2
6						89.1	77.2	67.9	60.7	54.8
7							90.6	79.9	71.4	64.5
8								91.7	82.0	74.1
9									92.6	83.8
10										93.3

Median Ranks

j	Sample size n									
	11	12	13	14	15	16	17	18	19	20
1	6.1	5.6	5.2	4.8	4.5	4.2	4.0	3.8	3.6	3.4
2	14.8	13.6	12.6	11.7	10.9	10.3	9.7	9.2	8.7	8.3
3	23.6	21.7	20.0	18.6	17.4	16.4	15.4	14.6	13.8	13.1
4	32.4	29.8	27.5	25.6	23.9	22.5	21.2	20.0	19.0	18.1
5	41.2	37.9	35.0	32.6	30.5	28.6	26.9	25.5	24.2	23.0
6	50.0	46.0	42.5	39.5	37.0	34.7	32.7	30.9	29.3	27.9
7	58.8	54.0	50.0	46.5	43.4	40.8	38.5	36.4	34.5	32.8
8	67.6	62.1	57.5	53.5	50.0	46.9	44.2	41.8	39.7	37.7
9	76.4	70.2	65.0	60.5	56.5	53.1	50.0	47.3	44.8	42.6
10	85.2	78.3	72.5	67.4	63.0	59.2	55.8	52.7	50.0	47.5
11	93.9	86.4	80.0	74.4	69.5	65.3	61.5	58.2	55.2	52.5
12		94.4	87.4	81.4	76.1	71.4	67.3	63.6	60.3	57.4
13			94.8	88.3	82.6	77.5	73.1	69.1	65.5	62.3
14				95.2	89.1	83.6	78.8	74.5	70.7	67.2
15					95.5	89.7	84.6	80.0	75.8	72.1
16						95.8	90.3	85.4	81.0	77.0
17							96.0	90.8	86.2	81.9
18								96.2	91.3	86.9
19									96.4	91.7
20										96.6

9. Determine the Weibull slope by drawing a line parallel to the line of best fit that goes through point ß on the Weibull paper. In Fig. 7.4 this was done and the slope was about 1.6. Weibull slope ß gives one insight as to the nature of the distribution of the components as was previously described. The nature of the slope can help problem investigation efforts. Higher Weibull slopes result in less variation in the spread of the failure results, allowing for smaller sample sizes

Failure value, hours	Median rank, %	5% rank	95% rank
171	10.9	0.9	39.3
266	26.4	6.3	58.2
384	42.1	15.3	72.9
512	57.9	27.1	84.7
663	73.6	41.8	93.7
850	89.1	60.7	99.1

Figure 7.3 Comparing the failure value in rank order with the median rank percentage.

required when performing attribute testing to draw conclusions from the data.

10. A desired reliability point can be estimated from reading the Weibull plot. For example, one can determine a minimum allowable failure point (hours, cycles, stress, etc.) that a specified percentage of the population must exceed. For example, if one wants to determine if 99 percent of the population will exceed a performance specification value, they would have to look at the median rank plot. This point will occur on the intersection with the 1.0 percent point on the y axis and the Weibull population line. The data plotted in Fig. 7.4 show that 95 percent of the units will exceed 86 hours of testing and 99 percent of the units will exceed 31 hours of testing. Since these data are the median rank data, it is a "best estimate" for what the true population's life history will be.

When conformance level sampling is used on variable testing, the projected median rank percentage must exceed the desired conformance level *and* all of the units must exceed the test specification; otherwise corrective action should be performed or at least the test sample increased. However, for proper reliability analysis, confidence or error limits should be constructed.

11. For more conservative analysis, one can construct confidence limits for the data. This can be done by using the 5 and 95 or 90 percent rank data in Table 7.2*b* and 7.2*c* or 7.2*d*, respectively. The data should be plotted using the same procedure as described for the median rank tables. Confidence constructs should be drawn with a smooth curve connecting the points. This is shown in Fig. 7.4. From the figure, one can conclude with 95 percent confidence (C95) that at least 90 percent of the population (R90) will exceed 22 hours (see upper curved line in Fig. 7.4). This example illustrates the need for larger test samples where it is crucial to have precise information. Typically either 90 percent rank (C90) or 95 percent rank (C95) data are used to determine the confidence lines.

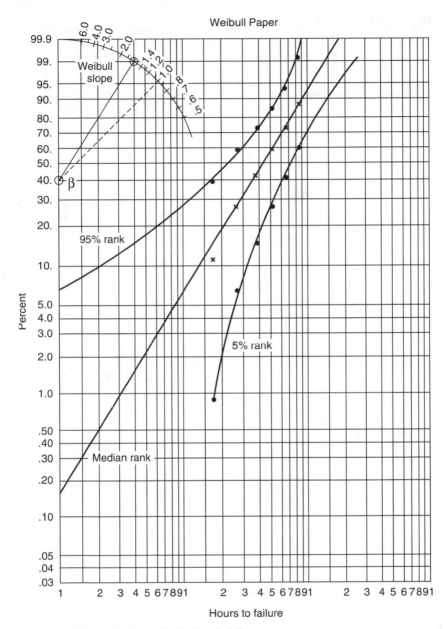

Figure 7.4 A best-fit plot on Weibull probability paper.

TABLE 7.2b   A 5% Rank (Confidence) Table.

5% Ranks

				Sample size n						
j	1	2	3	4	5	6	7	8	9	10
1	5.0	2.5	1.7	1.3	1.0	0.9	0.7	0.6	0.6	0.5
2		22.4	13.5	9.8	7.6	6.3	5.3	4.6	4.1	3.7
3			36.8	24.9	18.9	15.3	12.9	11.1	9.8	8.7
4				47.2	34.3	27.1	22.5	19.3	16.9	15.0
5					54.9	41.8	34.1	28.9	25.1	22.2
6						60.7	47.9	40.0	34.5	30.4
7							65.2	52.9	45.0	39.3
8								68.8	57.1	49.3
9									71.7	60.6
10										74.1

5% Ranks

				Sample size n						
j	11	12	13	14	15	16	17	18	19	20
1	0.5	0.4	0.4	0.4	0.3	0.3	0.3	0.3	0.3	0.3
2	3.3	3.0	2.8	2.6	2.4	2.3	2.1	2.0	1.9	1.8
3	7.9	7.2	6.6	6.1	5.7	5.3	5.0	4.7	4.4	4.2
4	13.5	12.3	11.3	10.4	9.7	9.0	8.5	8.0	7.5	7.1
5	20.0	18.1	16.6	15.3	14.2	13.2	12.4	11.6	11.0	10.4
6	27.1	24.5	22.4	20.6	19.1	17.8	16.6	15.6	14.7	14.0
7	35.0	31.5	28.7	26.4	24.4	22.7	21.2	19.9	18.8	17.7
8	43.6	39.1	35.5	32.5	30.0	27.9	26.0	24.4	23.0	21.7
9	53.0	47.3	42.7	39.0	36.0	33.3	31.1	29.1	27.4	25.9
10	63.6	56.2	50.5	46.0	42.3	39.1	36.4	34.1	32.0	30.2
11	76.2	66.1	59.0	53.4	48.9	45.2	42.0	39.2	36.8	34.7
12		77.9	68.4	61.5	56.0	51.6	47.8	44.6	41.8	39.4
13			79.4	70.3	63.7	58.3	53.9	50.2	47.0	44.2
14				80.7	72.1	65.6	60.4	56.1	52.4	49.2
15					81.9	73.6	67.4	62.3	58.1	54.4
16						82.9	75.0	69.0	64.1	59.9
17							83.8	76.2	70.4	65.6
18								84.7	77.4	71.7
19									85.4	78.4
20										86.1

System Reliability

When determining the required reliability of a component, one must determine the required reliability of the system because if one component fails, the whole system fails unless backup systems have been included in the process. To determine the needed reliability of a component for a specific failure criterion interval (e.g., 500 hours, 1 million cycles, etc.), one can use the following equation:

TABLE 7.2c   A 95% Rank (Confidence) Table

95% Ranks

					Sample size n					
j	1	2	3	4	5	6	7	8	9	10
1	95.0	77.6	63.2	52.7	45.1	39.3	34.8	31.2	28.3	25.9
2		97.5	86.5	75.1	65.7	58.2	52.1	47.1	42.9	39.4
3			98.3	90.2	81.1	72.9	65.9	60.0	55.0	50.7
4				98.7	92.4	84.7	77.5	71.1	65.5	60.7
5					99.0	93.7	87.1	80.7	74.9	69.6
6						99.1	94.7	88.9	83.1	77.8
7							99.3	95.4	90.2	85.0
8								99.4	95.9	91.3
9									99.4	96.3
10										99.5

95% Ranks

					Sample Size n					
j	11	12	13	14	15	16	17	18	19	20
1	23.8	22.1	20.6	19.3	18.1	17.1	16.2	15.3	14.6	13.9
2	36.4	33.9	31.6	29.7	27.9	26.4	25.0	23.8	22.6	21.6
3	47.0	43.8	41.0	38.5	36.3	34.4	32.6	31.0	29.6	28.3
4	56.4	52.7	49.5	46.6	44.0	41.7	39.6	37.7	35.9	34.4
5	65.0	60.9	57.3	54.0	51.1	48.4	46.1	43.9	41.9	40.1
6	72.9	68.5	64.5	60.9	57.7	54.8	52.2	49.8	47.6	45.6
7	80.0	75.5	71.3	67.5	64.0	60.9	58.0	55.4	53.0	50.8
8	86.5	81.9	77.6	73.6	70.0	66.7	63.6	60.8	58.2	55.8
9	92.1	87.7	83.4	79.4	75.6	72.1	68.9	65.9	63.2	60.6
10	96.7	92.8	88.7	84.7	80.9	77.3	74.0	70.9	68.0	65.3
11	99.5	97.0	93.4	89.6	85.8	82.2	78.8	75.6	72.6	69.8
12		99.6	97.2	93.9	90.3	86.8	83.4	80.1	77.0	74.1
13			99.6	97.4	94.3	91.0	87.6	84.4	81.3	78.3
14				99.6	97.6	94.7	91.5	88.4	85.3	82.3
15					99.7	97.7	95.0	92.0	89.0	86.0
16						99.7	97.9	95.3	92.5	89.6
17							99.7	98.0	95.5	92.9
18								99.7	98.1	95.8
19									99.7	98.2
20										99.7

$$R_c = 1 - \frac{1 - R_s}{n} \qquad 7.3$$

Where R_c = required reliability of component for specified failure criteria interval

R_s = required system reliability for specified failure criteria interval

TABLE 7.2d   A 90% Rank (Confidence) Table

90% Ranks

	Sample size n									
j	1	2	3	4	5	6	7	8	9	10
1	90	68	54	44	37	32	28	25	23	21
2		95	80	68	58	51	45	41	37	34
3			97	86	75	67	60	54	49	45
4				97	89	80	72	66	60	55
5					98	91	83	76	70	65
6						98	92	86	79	73
7							99	93	87	81
8								99	94	88
9									99	95
10										99

SOURCE: Table 7.2a, 7.2b, 7.2c, and 7.2d (revised) reprinted with permission of General Motors Research Labs.

n = number of components (or subsystem) in total system being analyzed

Assumptions:

1. Assume that R_c is a high number. If the accuracy comparison term,

$$\text{Accuracy comparison term} = \left[\frac{n(n-1)}{2} \right](1 - R_c)^2 \qquad 7.4$$

is smaller than the last decimal place of desired accuracy, then these calculations can be considered accurate. Otherwise this equation is not accurate to use.

2. The reliability of each component is independent.

3. If a component fails, then the whole system fails (this assumes that no backup systems exist for the components being analyzed).

This equation was derived from the fact that the system's ability is the product of the reliability of each individual component since each component fails independently and no backup systems exist.

Example   There are 15 subsystems in a computer that behave independently and do not have backup systems to compensate for failures. If one system fails, the whole system will be inoperative. If the required reliability of the whole computer system after a severe-usage durability test lasting 600 hours is 0.985, what is the required reliability of each subsystem?

solution   From Eq. 7.3,

$$R_c = 1 - \frac{1 - 0.985}{15} = 1 - 0.001 = 0.999$$

From the accuracy comparison term (Eq. 7.4),

$$\left[\frac{15(15-1)}{2}\right](1-0.999)^2 = 0.000098$$

Since 0.000098 is much smaller than 0.999, the results are accurate.

Parallel Systems

Systems that have backup capability are considered to be in parallel. Parallel systems are common in aviation and military electronics as well as engine control systems. These units have the capability to function almost completely should a failure occur in an electrical subsystem. It is also common to have parallel systems in manufacturing processes where the cost of downtime is prohibitive relative to the cost of having a backup system. Chemical manufacturers frequently use backup pumps when they are down so that their process still operates.

Design Verification Planning and Reporting

Developing a well-planned test and product verification plan early in the program is critical for a project's success. A design verification plan and report (DVP&R) is shown in Fig. 7.5 for a manual window regulator made by Chrysler Corporation. It lists the procedure or performance standard as documented in Chrysler's engineering standards. For the first item listed, this is PF-933. Then a brief description of the test is listed such as "Laboratory life cycle durability test." The acceptance criteria are specified as "functional after 20,000 cycles." The target requirement is the probability of meeting the acceptance criteria at a specified confidence level, which is, in this case, 90 percent. For example, if Weibull analysis were used, and they wanted to have 95 percent confidence with the data, they would have to plot the 5 percent rank line. Then they would use that plot to extrapolate the reliability. If the desired reliability were 90 percent with a 95 percent confidence level, they would have to determine where the 5 percent rank line crossed the 90 percent failure point. This information would be listed as $R = 90$ percent, $C = 95$ percent under target requirements. The person, department, supplier, or outside contractor responsible for running the test is listed, along with the time that the testing began and was completed. The sample size and type of sample is listed along with timing and results. A section for notes is also included.

Planning for Reliability Testing

At the beginning of a product development program, the reliability goals must be established at a specified confidence level. When a com-

CHRYSLER MOTORS — DESIGN VERIFICATION PLAN AND REPORT

DWG NUMBER: 123-8801   DEPT: 3530   PG 1 OF 2
COMPONENT/ASSEMBLY: MANUAL WINDOW REG.   P/N: N.A.   UPG NO: 12B07   PLAN DATE: 2-4-86   PLAN ORIGINATOR: J. SMITH
APPLICATIONS: S-BODY   ODD BOX: ACME, INC.   SOURCE: ACME, INC.   CONCURRENCE: T. JONES   MANAGER APPVL: R. GREEN
MY 1988   REPORT DATE: 8-6-86   REPORTING ENGR: J. SMITH

ITEM NO	PROCEDURE OR STANDARD	TEST DESCRIPTION	ACCEPTANCE CRITERIA	TARGET REQUIREMENTS	TEST RESPONSIBILITY	TEST STAGE	SAMPLE QTY	SAMPLE TYPE	TIMING START	TIMING COMPL	SAMPLES TESTED QTY	TYPE	PHASE	ACTUAL RESULTS	NOTES
1	PF993	LABORATORY LIFE CYCLE DURABILITY TEST.	FUNCTIONAL AFTER 20K CYCLES.	R: 90%	ACME / DEPT.3530	DV / PV / CC	6pr / 6pr / 1/yr	B / D / E	7-7 / 6-87 / 8-87	8-1 / 7-87 / N.A.	6pr	A	I	R:89%	TOOLED PROTO SAMPLES DUE 8-18. ALL SAMPLES RAN 30K CYCLES W/O FAILURE.
2	PF993	ABUSE LOADING.	FUNCTIONAL. NO YIELD AFTER 220 in.LBS.	P: 90%	ACME	DV / PV	6pr / 6pr	B / D	7-7 / 6-87	7-18 / 7-87	2pr	A	I	P:81%	ONE SAMPLE YIELDED AT 210 in.LBS.
3	PF993	CRANKING EFFORT.	MAX EFFORT NOT TO EXCEED 30 in.LBS.	P: 90%	ACME	DV / PV / CC	3pr / 6pr / 6pr	A / B / C	6-20 / 7-7 / 6-87	6-27 / 7-18 / 7-87	3pr	A	I	P:97%	ALL SAMPLES MET REQUIREMENT. MEAN EFFORT = 22 in.LBS., STD DEVIATION = 4 in.LB.
4	PF993	CORROSION EVALUATION.	FUNCTIONAL AFTER 48 HR SALT SPRAY.	R: 80%	ACME	DV / PV	6pr / 6pr	B / C	7-7	7-10	6pr	A	I	R:82%	
5	PF993	COUNTERBALANCE SPRING LABORATORY LIFE CYCLE DURABILITY.	25K CYCLE MIN LIFE W/ <20% TORQUE LOSS.	R: 90%	ACME	DV / PV / CC	24 / 24 / 1/day	B / C / D	6-23	7-25	24	B	I	R:86%	TWO SAMPLES FAILED PREMATURELY AT 18.7K & 23K CYCLES.
6	PF993	CHELSEA P.G. ENDURANCE.	30K MILES VE FOR DV, 2500 MI VE FOR PV & CC.	R: 75%	VEH. ENGRG	DV / PV / CC	3pr / 3pr / 3pr	B / C / D	9-86 / 6-87 / TBD	1-87 / 7-87					P.G. TESTING TO BEGIN WHEN TYPE B PARTS ARE AVAILABLE.

Legend

PROCEDURE Specify the governing Test Procedure or Standard	**TEST DESCRIPTION** Provide a brief description of each test.	**ACCEPTANCE CRITERIA** Specify test targets and/or pass/fail criteria, e.g., cycles, miles, volts, minimum value, no failure, etc.	**TARGET REQUIREMENTS** State required Reliability or Probability of meeting acceptance criteria at 90% Confidence, e.g. R90 C90, P80 C90, etc.	**TEST STAGE** DV = design verification, PV = production validation, CC = conformance	**SAMPLE TYPE** A = prototype (hand made), B = prototype (tooled), C = program level, D = full volume production, E = production	**SAMPLES TESTED** List quantity tested, sample type, and design phase, e.g. I, II, etc.	**ACTUAL RESULTS** List results in terms of Reliability or Probability as appropriate, e.g. R85 C90, P70 C90, etc. **NOTES** Describe or elaborate on unique criteria, results, etc.

Figure 7.5   A design verification plan and report for a manual window regulator. (*Courtesy of Chrysler Corporation.*)

plex system such as a transmission or turbojet engine is being validated, the Weibull slope will probably be low. Thus, one should develop a test plan which conservatively determines sample sizes based on a Weibull slope of 1.0.

After the product test program begins, failures will typically occur. Additionally, as these failed components are redesigned, the Weibull slope may change. When failures occur due to the failure of a component or subsystem, all of the systems tests do not necessarily have to be repeated. Instead, in some industries, it is common practice to redesign the failed component or subsystem and then validate that component on a representative bench test. The bench test must simulate the system test for that component or subsystem and take into account any possible interactive effects between the component and system. The redesigned component's reliability must exceed the reliability goals for the system at the specified confidence level.

This approach is valid only when the design changes to the failed component or subsystem will not affect the durability of the rest of the system (i.e., there are no significant interactive effects). The reasoning behind this approach is that the system's reliability is determined by the reliability of the weak links in that system. By redesigning those weak links to exceed the durability requirement, the durability of the whole system is improved. However, some industries such as electronics and some military applications, prefer to quantify the reliability. They calculate the systems reliability by multiplying the reliability of the individual components (calculations take into account back-up systems).

Components that have back-up systems may not need to be validated to the same confidence level. For example, a critical component may need to be validated to R95, C90. However, if that same component is designed with a back-up system, it may sometimes be prudent to save both test and product development time by validating it to R95, C50. To determine 95 percent confidence level (C95), one uses the 95 percent rank (confidence) table (Table 7.2c). For C90 one uses the 90 percent rank (confidence) table (Table 7.2d). Table 7.2a is used to determine the median rank order which is a 50 percent confidence level plot (C50).

Test Phases

Reliability testing can be broken down into three phases: reliability development, design verification, and product validation:

1. *Reliability development* is concerned with identifying problem areas and evaluating the effectiveness of design improvements. During this phase all test failures are documented and corrective action is taken to improve the design. Thus, all failure-prone aspects of a design are identified and fixed.
2. *Design verification* is concerned with testing a product to determine and quantify the inherent reliability of a design. The reliability is quantified in terms of a life measurement for a specified duty cycle. Commonly, one of two types of tests are used in this phase— evaluation and comparison testing.
   a. *Evaluation testing* evaluates how a product will perform in the field with customers based on a knowledge of customer duty

cycles. This requires a knowledge of customer usage patterns and the ability to reproduce such usage in a test program.

  b. *Comparison testing* is used to compare how a new product compares with an existing product's performance under a set of prescribed test conditions. Although the duty cycle of a test does not directly reflect customer duty cycles, it is known that the test is sufficient to simulate field problems based on previous test and product experiences. Usually comparison testing is performed with evolutionary design changes or when a lot of knowledge about product performance exists.

3. *Production validation* is testing performed to assure that no adverse changes have been introduced into a manufacturing process from earlier prototype processes.

Summary

Having a good system of documentation for design standards, design approaches/methodology, test methods, lab procedures, warranty reviews, along with competitive benchmarking, improves the long-term labor efficiency of an engineering organization. Early involvement with marketing, manufacturing, purchasing, and suppliers improves the success of a product. Performing design FMEAs, design reviews, and reliability analysis on a design verification plan and report helps to improve the design and organize the testing process.

Bibliography

American Society for Quality Control Automotive Division, *Statistical Process Control Manual,* ASQC, Milwaukee, WI, 1986.

Brunner, F. J., "Application of Reliability Technology in Vehicle Development," SAE Paper 871956, Society of Automotive Engineers, Warrendale, Pa., 1987.

Chrysler Corporation, Test Sample Planning, Chrysler Corporation.

Johnson, L. G., *The Statistical Treatment of Fatigue Experiment,* Elsevier Publishing Company, Amsterdam, 1964.

Kapur, K. C., and Lamberson, L. R., *Reliability in Engineering Design,* John Wiley & Sons, New York, 1977.

Lispon, C., and Sheth, N. J., *Statistical Design and Analysis of Engineering Experiments,* McGraw-Hill Book Company, New York, 1973.

Meeker, William Q., and Hahn, Gerald J., *How to Plan Accelerated Life Tests,* American Society of Quality Control—Statistics Division, Milwaukee, Wis., 1985.

Supplier Strategies

Suppliers should be an integral part of the planning process. Early supplier involvement is a crucial factor to assure that a cost-effective product is manufactured on time and consistently meets requirements. Suppliers can be a valuable resource for identifying value improvement and cost reduction opportunities with new and carry-over components. They can also identify methods for identifying improvements in their customers' internal operating practices and procedures. All of this, however, is predicated on utilizing capable suppliers and developing partnerships with them. Partnerships are long-term agreements which mutually benefit both companies, and suppliers' input is sought early in the design cycle of the new product. Methods for assessing suppliers' potential effectiveness and for developing partnerships are discussed later in the chapter.

Suppliers are most likely to commit their resources and efforts to customers that are receptive to resolving problems in a constructive manner, have assurances that they will maintain their current business with their customers if their performance is satisfactory, are involved up front in the planning process, have a significant portion of their business with a specific customer, and are paid on time. Therefore, companies should be interested in developing internal systems and procedures which support these objectives.

A company can develop a brief training seminar to teach employees how to work with suppliers to help improve the constructiveness of those interactions and assure that consistent policies and procedures are being followed. The seminar might include topics such as policies and procedures for dealing with suppliers, defining organizational responsibilities by department function, constructive problem solving, and, finally, introducing the importance and benefits that can be derived from working with suppliers. This can generate a uniform approach so that suppliers are given a consistent message from all areas of the company.

Another approach of paramount importance is to minimize the supply base so that a company becomes a more significant portion of a supplier's business. This improved leveraging should assure better quality assurance, service, support, and sometimes even greater price concessions. There has been a move among original equipment manufacturers to reduce their suppliers as shown in Fig. 8.1.

Source Selection Criteria

Determining supplier capabilities can be quite an elaborate process. Many approaches can be used. There are approximately four key business elements to consider:

1. *Administrative (financial, purchasing, materials management)*
   - Financial stability and resources
   - Management stability and capability
   - Costing system and controls
   - Materials planning and delivery scheduling systems
   - Purchasing systems and supplier selection strategies
2. *Quality Assurance*
   - Preventative planning system
   - Quality control procedures
3. *Manufacturing*
   - Manufacturing engineering capabilities
   - Manufacturing management practices
   - Productivity improvements, measurements, and controls
4. *Engineering*
   - Design engineering systems and testing capabilities
   - Research and development for new and emerging technologies

Company	Before consolidation	Number on August 16, 1991	Percent change
Xerox	5,000	500	− 90%
Motorola	10,000	3,000	− 70%
Digital Equipment Corp.	9,000	3,000	− 67%
General Motors	10,000	5,500	− 45%
Ford Motor Company	1,800	1,000	− 44%
Texas Instruments	22,000	14,000	− 36%
Allied-Signal Aerospace	7,500	6,000	− 20%

NOTE: These companies count their suppliers differently. Some include service and support suppliers, while others include only direct manufacturing suppliers.

Figure 8.1 Supply base consolidation of Original Equipment Manufacturers. (*Revised from the* Wall Street Journal, *8/16/91.*)

These can be assessed either by formally auditing suppliers or more simply by discussing their performance based on experience that company personnel have had with them. There are pros and cons to each of these approaches depending on resource requirements and application.

Another approach to supplier selection is to ask other business contacts who have had experience with suppliers in a specific industry for their recommendation. This method can save a lot of time and resources but cannot yield the benefit of the audits and the industry contact may have a criterion for assessing a supplier's capabilities different from one's own company.

Performing Supplier Audits

Benefits and liabilities

Auditing suppliers offers an opportunity to perform an objective assessment of their capabilities. It can also provide a mechanism to identify opportunities for improvement. However, there are some problems associated with the audits. First, they require a significant time and resource commitment to perform them. Second, if the audit is not performed by well-trained personnel, it can cause misleading information and lead to poor purchasing decisions. Finally, if a company is a small portion of a supplier's business, the supplier may not be willing to devote the time required to allow an audit and may not be willing to take action based upon the results. This is an unfortunate circumstance when alternate purchasing options are limited and are even less desirable.

Preparing for the audits

Before performing an audit, the supplier should be sent a letter discussing the nature and scope of the audit. During the evaluation, the auditor should be complimentary wherever possible and show an appreciation for the supplier's strength and for sharing their time. The audit should be approached in a constructive manner so that they understand the purpose is to help them improve their business management methodology. The customer should communicate that they understand that changes take time to implement; however, they are looking for suppliers who aggressively pursue the changes and are making serious efforts at implementing them. This can help put the supplier personnel more at ease and can help create an effective partnership. However, if a large consolidation strategy is in effect, it can be a difficult situation.

There were four categories of audits mentioned earlier. These topics will now be discussed in detail. The audits should be performed by trained specialists in their respective fields.

Administrative (Financial, Purchasing, Materials Management) Audits

Financial concerns

It is important to do business with financially strong companies because they will be more able to make the necessary investments to remain competitive and invest in a good quality assurance program. Also, it will be unlikely that they will go out of business suddenly, which can jeopardize their customer's order and production schedules. Before analyzing a supplier, one should perform a background check by reviewing a Dun and Bradstreet credit report of the company. Some of the signs of concern would include late or slowness in payments and payments that are past due. One would also want to note how late the payments were. If there are any overdue payments, one must look at the magnitude of the payments to assure it is a significant amount. An overdue payment may be attributed to a company that was unhappy with a product or service performed and the dissatisfaction issue remains unresolved. Therefore, if such information is not available in the report, further investigation would be needed. This review is a cursory check, and more analysis is recommended even if everything appears to be OK. Customers can also ask their suppliers for bank references. The banks can be contacted and will reveal whether a company's loan is a secured or unsecured loan. Unsecured loans indicate that the bank has confidence in the business.

The customer should then request a review of the supplier financial statements. The statements should be independently audited. If they have not been audited, the accuracy of such statements can be questioned. Many suppliers will not be receptive to sharing this information with their customers. To overcome this, the customer can try to inform them that they are not interested in determining their margins as much as in establishing the financial condition of the company. Also, by using a partnership approach combined with long-term agreements, they may be somewhat more receptive if they understand that they will be viewed more favorably as candidates for a long-term relationship and will receive more business in the future. However, many companies will still have limited success at obtaining this information.

By analyzing six key ratios from the supplier's books, one can gain an understanding of the company's financial situation. The ratios must be analyzed individually and then looked at as a group in order to gain a better understanding of the company and how it relates to other companies in the industry. The ratios must be compared with other firms in the same industry in order for them to have any meaning. These ratios can be compared to the results of other suppliers in the industry or to either Dun and Bradstreet ratios (which are calculated for many industries), the Federal Trade Commission's "Quarterly Financial Report," or Robert Morris Associates' "Annual Statement Studies." Smaller suppliers who are willing to cooperate are ideal candidates for this analysis because they lack the diversity of bigger companies whose data are confounded with other diverse businesses.

The six key ratios include the quick ratio, asset turnover, inventory turnover, debt to capital, capital expenditure, and times interest earned. Each one measures different aspects of a company's financial performance. A hypothetical income statement and balance sheet is shown in Figs. 8.2 and 8.3, respectively. These will be used to show how these ratios are calculated.

The quick ratio. Also called the acid test ratio, the quick ratio measures a firm's ability to meet its short-term obligations without selling off inventory. Inventories are considered to have the least liquidity of current assets; therefore, they are taken out for this analysis. Generally, the higher this ratio, the better. Too high means that the firm may be underutilizing its financial resources, which would be of concern to an investor but less so to a buyer.

Hypothetical Income Statement for USA Stamping Corp., Inc.: Income Statement for the Year Ending December 31, 1993

(Millions of dollars)

	1993	1992
Net sales	$29.70	$30.50
Costs and expenses:		
Labor and materials	25.00	25.20
Depreciation	1.00	.90
Selling	.35	.34
General and administrative	.36	.33
Rent	.42	.42
Earnings before interest and taxes	$ 2.57	$ 3.31
Less interest expense	$ .66	$ .47
Earnings before taxes	$ 1.91	$ 2.84
Taxes (at 34%)	.65	.97
Net Income	$ 1.26	$ 1.87
Dividends to common stockholder	$ 1.06	$ 1.47
Addition to retained earnings	$ .20	$ .40

Figure 8.2 Hypothetical income statement.

Hypothetical Balance Sheet for USA Stamping Corp., Inc.: Balance Sheet for the Year Ended December 31, 1993

(Millions of dollars)

Assets	1993	1992	Liabilities and stockholders' equity	1993	1992
Cash	$.50	$.55	Accounts payable	$ .60	$ .30
Marketable securities	0	25	Notes payable	1.00	.60
Accounts receivable	3.50	3.15	Accrued wages	.10	.10
Inventories	3.00	2.15	Accrued taxes	1.30	1.20
Total current assets	$7.00	$6.10	Total current liabilities	$3.00	$2.20
Net plant and equipment	$13.00	$10.70			
Total assets	$20.00	$16.80	Bonds	$5.00	$5.20
			Long-term loans	3.00	.60
			Total long-term debt	$8.00	$5.80
			Stockholders' equity	$ .50	$ .50
			Paid in capital	1.00	1.00
			Retained earnings	7.50	7.30
			Total stockholders' equity	$ 9.00	$ 8.80
			Total liabilities and stockholders' equity	$20.00	$16.80

Figure 8.3 Hypothetical balance sheet.

$$\text{Quick ratio} = \frac{\text{current assets} - \text{inventory}}{\text{current liabilities}}$$

For the sample balance sheet shown in Fig. 8.3, this is equal to $(7.00 - 3.00)/3.00 = 1.3$. This compares favorably with the industry average, which is 1.1.

Asset turnover.   This is a measure of how effectively a firm is utilizing its assets. If the ratio is high, it indicates that a firm's assets are being used effectively to generate sales. However, it could also be an indication that there has not been recent capital investment in the company, which can greatly affect future efficiencies and, ultimately, long-term competitiveness. If this ratio is too low, it can mean an inefficient utilization of assets.

$$\text{Asset turnover} = \frac{\text{sales}}{\text{total assets}}$$

For the USA Stamping Corp., Inc., the ratio is calculated (using Figs. 8.2 and 8.3) as follows: $29.70/20.00 = 14.9$. This compares similarly with the other firms which average 14.6.

Capital expenditure ratio.   This is used to determine if a company is spending a proper amount of money on capital expenditures to assure long-term profitability. This ratio can help determine if a company is reducing capital investments in order to remain profitable during the current period. It can also show if a company is investing for future growth opportunities. However, sufficient capital investment does not tell the whole story. One must also look at the areas in which the firm is investing. If they are in markets that do not show much possibility of being profitable, the investments are unwise. However, in addition to looking at this and other ratios, one must evaluate the total business picture when performing this analysis. For example, suppose a company invested heavily in automation but did not try out the machinery properly or maintain it well; under such a scenario, it could end up being more expensive to run a facility than if automated equipment was never purchased.

$$\text{Capital expenditure ratio} = \frac{\text{capital expenditures}}{\text{net sales}}$$

For the example shown, this would be $= (13 - 10.7 + 1.00)/29.7 = 0.11$. Capital expenditures sometimes can be determined by looking at a company's statement of changes in financial position. Unfortunately, it is sometimes difficult to obtain such information. This was calculated by adding the change in plant and equipment from 1992 to 1993 and adding 1993 depreciation.

The inventory turnover ratio.   This measures how quickly a firm turns over its finished goods. Inventory should include raw material, work in process, and finished goods inventory. This ratio is improved by practicing just-in-time purchased material deliveries, reducing manufacturing cycle times, work in process, and set-up times. Generally, the lower this ratio the better. However, low ratios can be caused by an overcommitment of manufacturing capacity and can mean that not enough safety stock is on hand to assure that customer delivery dates are met.

$$\text{Inventory turnover} = \frac{\text{cost of sales}}{\text{average inventory}}$$

In 1993 this was $(29.7 - 2.57)/[(3.0 + 2.15)/2] = 27.1$. The industry average is 4.8. USA Stamping's turnover is above this value. It appears that they have made more progress at reducing inventories than their competition, but their inventory has increased since the previous year. The reason for this should be verified during the site audit. Determining the average inventory cost can require more analysis if inventories vary seasonally. In such cases, one would need to see monthly or quarterly inventory results. In this example, averaging the beginning and ending inventory is sufficient. The cost of sales was estimated by subtracting earnings before interest and taxes from net sales.

Debt to capital. This measures a supplier's borrowing capacity. From a buyer's point of view, lower is better because the less debt, the more a supplier can borrow to have a steady cash source and hence the less likely an insolvency situation may arise.

$$\text{Debt to capital} = \frac{\text{total debt}}{\text{total debt} + \text{total equity}}$$

In the example, this was $(3.00 + 8.00)/20.00 = 0.55$. The industry average was 0.68, which is favorable for USA Stamping from a financial stability perspective, since the supplier has additional borrowing capacity should a recession occur.

Times interest earned (TIE). TIE measures a firm's ability to meet its annual interest expense. From a customer purchasing standpoint, lower is better because the company is not burdened with high interest payments.

$$\text{TIE} = \frac{\text{earnings before interest and taxes}}{\text{interest expense}}$$

In 1993 this was $2.57/0.66 = 3.9$. Since, the industry average is 2.8, this compares favorably since lower is better.

Management stability and capability

A management audit can evaluate a supplier in the following areas:

- *Management stability and turnover* is important for consistency of direction and can be an indication of the level of nonproductive activities (frequently referred to as politics) and management competency.

- *The human resource department* should be reviewed for its
   Fairness in hiring practices.
   System that monitors employee turnover. This would include exit interview records and evidence that efforts were made to improve the situation when turnover was high.
   System to assure employee training and development of their skills to expand their usefulness.
   An employee suggestion system that rewards employees for their suggestions which improve safety, quality, or productivity, reduce product costs, or for new product ideas. These policies can contribute to a more effective work force by assuring a qualified work force, job satisfaction, and a well-trained, experienced work force.

- *Safety policies* include
   Safety training system for all employees

Plant safety practices and safe guards

Accident and injury recording and tracking system, with comparison to both OSHA and industry averages.

Good safety practices reduce employee absenteeism, turnover, and reduce medical insurance premiums.

- *Strategic business plans* should include a directive indicating the markets and businesses that will be pursued and should have both a 3- to 5-year strategic vision and a one- to 2-year detailed plan with specific goals, assigned responsibilities, and timing.

- *The business improvement plan* can be a part of the business plan; however, it should include plans to improve the operating systems and efficiencies of all operating aspects of the company in support of total quality management (TQM) including finance, engineering, manufacturing, quality assurance, sales, materials planning, purchasing, etc. It can also include a longer term strategic vision with detailed shorter term objectives and tactics.

A system to periodically monitor progress toward the goals.

A budget and reward system which supports the goals.

Costing systems and controls

Part of the financial audit should review the costing system and controls. It would assess

- The quoting system cost breakdown and the accuracy of the assumptions. It should include the following:

  1. Material costs based on the bill of materials, associated material weights, and raw material waste.
  2. Costs based on valid routings including material handling, setups, and applicable machine overhead.
  3. Fixed overhead is based on units of production such as machine hours, product cycle time, or total labor hours. The costing system and assumptions should accurately reflect real costs. A plant's cost should not be unreasonably increased due to poor overhead assumptions. If a productivity improvement occurs or a product becomes outsourced, some accounting approaches would raise the price of the existing product being manufactured in a plant due to overhead allocation methods—that accounting system has deleterious effects on the long-term competitiveness of the plant.

- Material usage reports should be published at regular intervals.

- Manufacturing productivity or labor efficiency reports should be regularly distributed.

- Inventories should be physically counted by a method called *cycle counting,* which periodically counts inventories with varied frequencies based on dollar volumes. Cycle counting uses the Pareto principle, in which typically the top 60 percent dollar items are counted 10 times a year, the middle 30 percent 6 times a year, and the bottom 10 percent are counted annually. Variance reports should be issued by part number. This avoids looking at total numbers on an annual basis, which can neglect vast errors on individual products (see Fig. 8.4). This is a greatly simplified, exaggerated example, but it does show how vast errors between records and physical counts can exist, while a gross report may not reveal the problem. As Fig. 8.4 shows, the inventory records for part number 62945 are 41 percent high, while part number 56712 is 23 percent low, but the net total shows that there is an accurate inventory reporting system.

- Scrap reports should be distributed by part number with defect codes listed in percentages for the purpose of performing corrective action.

- Material usage, productivity, inventory discrepancy, and scrap reports should include variance reports. The variance limits should be established so that the vital few problems can be identified for improvements within resource limitations. The limits should not be so tight that corrective action is taken too frequently and the discrepancy is within common variation, because if this is done, administrative resources are being used unnecessarily. However, the variance report limits should not be so loose that significant problems occur unnoticed. One method of determining effective variance limits is to develop statistically based control limits.

- Quality costs should be monitored in terms of prevention, appraisal, internal failures, and external failures.

- Scrap reports and quality cost reports should have goals to reduce those costs.

Part number	Book inventory, $	Actual inventory, $	Error percentage
56712	100,000	130,000	−23%
62945	72,000	51,000	+41%
38479	60,000	50,000	+20%
44143	210,000	195,000	+ 8%
31754	29,000	20,000	+45%
34408	130,000	142,000	+ 6%
83367	110,000	146,000	−25%
Total	731,000	734,000	− 0.4%

Figure 8.4 Inventory reporting mistakes of reporting total numbers.

Materials management and delivery scheduling system

It is important to review the material management and production scheduling system to assure that on-time delivery performance is effective. This system would include

- Using a material requirements planning (MRP) system, which utilizes a bill of materials to schedule components
- Using a just-in-time and/or Kanban inventory control system (where appropriate)
- Goals that exist to reduce inventory via process improvements
- Sufficient safety stock to meet customer orders
- The ability to increase capacity due to changes in customer schedules
- Using capacity limitations and constraints to maximize plant productivity
- Running daily or weekly scheduling reports and making appropriate adjustments
- A scheduling system that accounts for lead time requirements and manufacturing capacity
- A system that tracks and reduces lead times
- Monitoring on-time delivery performance and taking corrective action as appropriate
- Auditing shipments periodically to verify part counts
- Storing inventory in the correct location and labeling the material properly as determined by periodic audits
- Daily reports with information on raw material inventory, work in process (WIP), and finished goods inventory
- A material handling system that prevents damage and stores the material safely
- Using a first-in, first-out (FIFO) inventory system for inventory stock rotation.

Purchasing systems and supplier selection strategies

- Quoting procedures exist.
- Source approval visits and reports are used to assure that capable suppliers are used which can meet quality, delivery, and cost objectives.

- Presourcing is used when appropriate to assure that products are jointly developed in a cost-effective manner.

- When possible, long-term agreements are sought to assure an uninterrupted supply in the event that material shortages or capacity limitations are encountered.

Quality Assurance Audit

The quality assurance system should be reviewed to assure that the products are manufactured consistently and meet customer requirements. If a company is certified to meet the ISO 9000 series, most of the following items will be practiced. ISO 9000 certification of a company's quality and engineering process assures its effectiveness for the European Economic Community. The ISO certification process is fairly rigorous and reliable. However, many companies do not have ISO certification. All systems should be well documented in the quality control manual. An on-site review should verify that procedures are being followed. The following list is a good one to review during the audit.

Preventative Planning

Administrative management practices

- Quote the package feasibility reviews before issuing them to customers.

- Develop advanced planning procedures utilizing an interdisciplinary teams input to review customer requirements and even include the customer. These meetings should discuss:

  Problem histories with similar products
  Capability studies with similar products
  Concerns about possible problems with the current product
  The functional and process-related characteristics of the product
  Mutual identification of critical characteristics
  Value improvement suggestions

  It would be most beneficial if these meetings were initiated by the customer for nonstandard products. For more complex products, they should occur before the quotations are issued. This will be more easily performed after the supply base is consolidated.

- Project management to assure that gages are qualified and that capability studies are performed before the product is launched.

- The use of process flowcharts.

- The use of failure mode and effects analysis.
- Housekeeping.
- Employee training and development for both new hires and existing employees.
- Employee participation in problem-solving teams.
- Performing periodic self-audits of both quality assurance systems and manufacturing processes.
- Having improvement plans to improve process capability and scrap as is needed.
- Periodic visits to customer facilities are made to identify product improvements.
- Traceability of the finished product to raw material lots is possible.
- Records are saved according to requirements.
- Lot traceability to the raw materials exists.
- Internal self-audits are performed and procedures which are not being followed are documented and corrected. Management monitors this regularly.

Quality Control Procedures

Engineering and document control

- System to assure that the latest customer blueprints and related support documents are being utilized, perhaps requiring a signoff by affected area as needed.
- Procedures to assure that engineering changes are incorporated only after they are requested in writing.
- Written deviations are required from customers if product is out of specification but deemed usable before releasing it

Inspection and measuring equipment

- Calibration procedures are documented which also define acceptance limits, specify linearity checks, and explain what to do if a gage is found to be out of calibration.
- Traceability to a recognized standard such as the National Institute of Standards and Technology (NIST).
- Gage repeatability and reproducibility studies are performed with corrective action taken if results are unacceptable.

Statistical and analytical problem-solving methodology

- Perform process capability studies on critical characteristics for new products.

- Perform corrective action if the process does not meet the C_{pk} goal.

- Monitor process capability to identify changes and process improvement priorities.

- Designed experiments are performed to solve problems using statistically valid tests where appropriate.

Purchased material controls

- An adequately staffed receiving inspection function exists.

- Material can be certified from suppliers if capability is demonstrated. Material certifications which include inspection and/or test data accompany shipments and are reviewed by the inspection department.

- Supplier audits are performed when benefits can be derived from such audits.

- Suppliers utilize statistical process controls (SPC).

- Written corrective action with preventative control measures is required for all nonconforming material received.

In-process controls

- Setup approvals are documented and samples are retained at the operation.

- Process sheets are used and the settings verified.

- In-process inspection is performed according to the inspection instruction sheets.

- Visual aids are used where appropriate.

- SPC is used for in-process controls on significant control characteristics.

- The control charts are properly interpreted and corrective action documented for out-of-control conditions.

Final product verification

- An independent audit is performed to assure product quality.

- Reworked or sorted product is reinspected before shipping authorization.
- Packaging and labeling procedures are documented and followed.

Nonconforming product

- Nonconforming product is properly identified with the defect documented.
- A properly labeled quarantine area exists.
- Appropriate corrective action including verification and preventative measures are taken to correct both internally found and customer-identified nonconforming materials

One method to assure the integrity of the audit is to randomly select approved finished product and measure characteristics according to either the blueprint or the inspection instructions. Some suppliers have implemented systems which appear to be impressive based on a review of their documentation; however, their products do not meet specifications. A random parts audit either from products received or from a supplier's finished goods inventory can verify the accuracy of the paperwork and procedural disciplines.

Manufacturing Audits

Manufacturing or process engineering

Manufacturing practices should be reviewed to assure that a supplier maximizes manufacturing efficiency and good manufacturing practices established for each job, and is continuously finding ways to improve operations.

Review the supplier's capabilities and performance with regard to:

- Tooling and/or process design capabilities (they should at least have access to or a partnership with a reliable nearby source which assures a proprietary competitive advantage).
- Performing studies to try to optimize and define processing parameters.
- Using computer integrated manufacturing (CIM) systems (where appropriate).

Manufacturing management practices should demonstrate that documented systems exist which assure that:

- Preventative and predictive maintenance systems are established and utilized.

- They maintain an inventory control system for perishable tools and equipment replacement components.

- Time motion studies are performed on high-volume assembly operations.

- Process sheets specify the machine settings to be used during production.

- Tool operation sheets list all tools used and the machine cams, speeds, and feeds that are to be used (when appropriate).

- Controls of tooling, equipment, and gage drawings are being practiced.

- Setup equipment lists are utilized.

- Flexible manufacturing possibilities are sought when new equipment is purchased.

Productivity improvements

A supplier's goals and achievements should demonstrate that they continuously set goals to achieve:

- Value improvements or cost reductions
- Inventory reduction
- Setup time reduction
- Total process cycle time reduction
- Improvements in productivity at manufacturing productivity bottlenecks
- Monitoring and control systems which assure that the system is working

Engineering Audits

It is important for certain kinds of suppliers to have their engineering research, development, design, and testing capabilities demonstrated to assure that their designs can meet or exceed customer requirements.

Design engineering and testing capabilities

Some of the things to be reviewed would include:

- Test facilities as appropriate for the products that they manufacture
- Analytical design capabilities for that product line such as

Computer-aided design (CAD) capabilities

Computer-aided engineering (CAE) capabilities: finite elements analysis (FEA), tolerance stack-up, simulation software

Weibull analysis

- Having documented engineering standards

- Documenting test procedures and other standard operating procedures (SOPs)

- Utilizing design FMEAs

- Documenting or using design guides and handbooks

- Involving manufacturing at the onset of projects to utilize the benefits of concurrent engineering

- Utilizing value engineering principles

- Procedures and records which indicate that appropriate corrective action is taken when design flaws are encountered

- Validation testing is completed before officially implementing changes and releasing new products (as appropriate)

Research and development on emerging technologies

The supplier should be continuously looking at ways to improve the value of products by either reducing costs without impairing quality or improving product performance without adding unnecessary costs. This can be done by

- Adding new features

- Improving product quality and reliability

- Reducing manufacturing costs

- Selecting new and less expensive materials

- Looking at new applications for emerging technologies

The audits should be performed by qualified personnel. When the audits are performed initially, there will be a learning curve for those new to the system. The Pareto principle should be used to determine which suppliers should be initially audited and to what extent. Since many organizations will have limited resources, it is recommended to prioritize suppliers and commodities to be audited.

There may be two categories of suppliers:

1. A full-service supplier with design capabilities

2. A commodity manufacturing supplier

Some commodity supplier's may not need to be audited for its engineering and manufacturing design capabilities. This approach is desirable to keep the product overhead costs down with suppliers who manufacture products which are standard parts or designed by their customers.

Requesting an Improvement Plan

After submitting the audit report results to a supplier and discussing the issues, an improvement plan should be requested. It should be submitted by the supplier in writing. Suppliers and customers will benefit by formalizing an improvement plan because this makes it easier to monitor progress. Customers are also convinced that a supplier is serious about improving operations when a well-thought-out plan has been received. I developed the format shown in Fig. 8.5. It is in the form of a Gantt chart. It outlines the activities to be performed, the person responsible to oversee that task, the rate of completion, and the completion date. The rate of completion is useful to monitor progress toward the goal. For example, perform 3 gage R & R studies per week or train 30 employees per quarter in SPC, etc. This format is useful for suppliers to monitor their progress on a monthly or quarterly basis. The customer must keep in mind that it can take several months for a supplier to get the various parts of their organization to buy into the improvement strategy if it is going to be sustained. It also may take some time to implement the changes, and there may be some items which were more difficult to implement than originally anticipated. It is therefore in the buyer's best interest to communicate the importance of developing an effective improvement plan with the company's top management and ask them to endorse the plan. This will make it easier for supplier's middle management to effect change resulting from top management support.

Other Supplier Strategies

It is a good idea for the customer to assure that supplier's bills are paid on time. Some companies believe that it is advantageous to age their payables in order to generate cash for operations. Suppliers learn to adjust for this by increasing their profit margins on quotations. They may also be more reluctant to devote resources to assist customers voluntarily unless specifically requested to do so.

Hidden costs

Production quality and on-time delivery are important factors in making purchasing decisions. Many hidden costs can be traced to poor quality and late deliveries from suppliers. Hidden costs due to

Quality Improvement Plan

Quality improvement plan item	Month due	Team member responsible	Rate (if applicable)	1992												1993											
				J	F	M	A	M	J	J	A	S	O	N	D	J	F	M	A	M	J	J	A	S	O	N	D
1. QIP meeting all departments	–	G. LaVigne / R. Fryman	All departments 1 mtg/month	X	–	–	–	–	–	–	–	–	–	–	–	–	–										
2. Organize present Q.A. manual	2/92	R. Fryman		X	O																						
3. Write company quality policy	1/92	R. Fryman		O																							
4. Training																										
0 Develop material and classes	3/92	G. LaVigne / P. Stansbury / R. Fryman		X	–	O																					
0 Develop SPC program	3/92	G. LaVigne / R. Fryman		X	–	O																					
0 Implement training	2/93	P. Stansbury / R. Fryman				X	–	–	–	–	–	–	–	–	–	–	–	O									
5. Update Q.A. manual																										
0 Write procedures	12/92	R. Fryman		X	–	–	–	–	–	–	–	–	–	–	O												
0 Review and sign-off	3/93	R. Fryman					X	–	–	–	–	–	–	–	–	–	–	O									
6. Write Q.P.S. manuals																										
0 Tooling standards and procedures	9/92	R. Knorr		X	–	–	–	–	–	–	–	O															
0 Failure history similar / Parts to new product	7/92	R. Knorr		X	–	–	–	–	–	O																	
0 Eng. change sign-off procedures	8/92	R. Knorr		X	–	–	–	–	–	–	O																
0 Material specs., standards, procedures	9/92	J. Eggert		X	–	–	–	–	–	–	–	O															

NOTE: X Start date
0 Scheduled completion date
● Task completed
– Efforts continuing

Figure 8.5 Quality improvement planning Gantt chart. (*Courtesy of the Molding Company, a Division of Premix, Inc.*)

poor quality include receiving inspection, extra material handling required to move defective material, rework, reduced productivity when components cannot be assembled, warranty costs, additional administrative personnel required to resolve these problems, and lost sales due to dissatisfied customers. Hidden costs due to late deliveries include assembly-line shutdowns, administrative costs associated with expediting products, holding cost of additional safety stock, and extra material handling costs associated with rushing components to the assembly line.

Recommended contract clauses

To assure that suppliers appreciate the implications of these hidden costs, purchase contracts should be written which include clauses that require suppliers to pay all out-of-pocket costs associated with poor quality and late shipments. Additionally, plants can issue a blanket administrative charge associated with all defective material returns and all expedited orders that are caused by suppliers. One can also charge penalty costs to suppliers that have late shipments, over- or undershipments, or have rejected material on a periodic basis. Contracts should also include clauses that allow a customer to randomly audit a supplier's process, require customer notification of a process change, meet customer's documented quality control requirements, use SPC to control critical characteristics (or 100 percent inspect them), and adjust prices based solely on raw material and labor cost indexes.

Early supplier selection

For outsourced products that are complex and are deemed a high priority for supplier involvement, it is recommended that presourcing the product should be performed. This can be done by having the buyer call an interdisciplinary team meeting with engineering, manufacturing, and quality assurance to discuss possible sources to quote. All team members must sign an approval form which indicates the suppliers who will be allowed to quote the component.

Before submitting the quotation, a kickoff meeting can be held with suppliers, either individually or having them all in one room. They should be told the functional aspects of the products and the general specifications and performance standards. They should be encouraged to meet with engineering to indicate other ways of achieving the design objectives or if desirable product features can be added. It is important to maintain confidentiality with each supplier and not share information with a different supplier. If a breach of confidentiality occurs, suppliers will be reluctant to offer creative suggestions and proprietary technical expertise with future quotations resulting from a soured relationship. Once the quotes are in, the team can meet again and discuss the pros and cons of selecting different sources.

Supplier-customer partnership meetings

Once sources have been selected, those suppliers are a part of the design team. Cost increases should not be allowed for design changes unless special circumstances dictate so because they quoted the finished product. Periodic interdisciplinary team meetings called partnership meetings should be held to discuss the product's status from a design, quality, and manufacturability standpoint. Engineering will share test results. Quality assurance should require that critical characteristics are verified statistically or in some other appropriate manner before pilot lots are run by manufacturing. Suppliers should be required to verify agreed-upon characteristics or specifications with a representative manufacturing process before production launch to allow time to correct any problems that are encountered. The first production shipment should include a certification report which shows test data, Weibull analysis, statistical and gage capability studies, lab test results, dimensional layout, etc., as is appropriate to assure that all requirements can be achieved by the selected design and manufacturing process.

In addition to having improved quality, these meetings allow for alternate design approaches. Early supplier involvement can allow their design input to allow for process-driven designs. Digital Equipment Corporation used this approach with their plastic supplier, Alliance Precision Plastics, to reduce the cost of a housing for the VT 1000 from $100 per unit to $30 by reducing the number of parts and designing a product that was easier to manufacture quickly. The net savings are anticipated to be $21 million over the life of the product.

Single sourcing

Single sourcing has the advantage of reducing supplier variation in the manufacturing process and the cost savings achievable through higher volumes. Single sourcing makes troubleshooting manufacturing and warranty problems less difficult as a result of the reduced variation. Additionally, there is direct accountability and responsibility for resolving problems. There are, however, some risks associated with this strategy. A supplier can have significant leverage over a customer if resourcing a product requires a long or expensive test program, or takes a long time to move and set up the equipment. A customer can get around this difficulty by utilizing a backup source whose product has already been approved by their engineering group.

This also protects the customer in the event that an unforeseen event occurs such as a fire or natural disaster. This approach increases tooling, testing, and administrative expenses as a result of the duplication of efforts. An alternate strategy which reduces a supplier's leverage is to indicate that unsatisfactory performance or inadequate cooperation will limit their ability to obtain new business in the future as a result of a dissatisfied party in the commodity approval sign-off.

Approved commodity list

For products which are more of a commodity type or which are less complex and can be manufactured by a variety of manufacturers, a commodity approval list can be developed. This list should include a set of suppliers who have the endorsement of purchasing, manufacturing, quality assurance, and engineering. Periodically, these lists should be reviewed by these organizations to either add or delete suppliers for consideration of new business.

Supply base commodity review

It is important to periodically review the number of suppliers required to satisfactorily assure a reliable supply source for the commodities, while maintaining competition between suppliers and sufficient business volume to assure purchasing clout within those suppliers. The management and buyers must determine the "ideal number" of suppliers required for a given commodity. Then they should develop a plan to assure that the number of suppliers used for that commodity matches the ideal number.

Value improvements for existing products

Suppliers can also be an excellent source for identifying value improvements or cost savings, and product improvements. Buyers should encourage suppliers to review their products and applications to see if product simplifications can be made, operations eliminated, or alternate materials used. In some cases a supplier may have a lot of slack time in the operation which can be used to perform subassembly work. One injection-molded plastics supplier noticed that their customer performed three assembly operations on their assembly lines before it was assembled onto other components. Each operation took about 7 seconds and required three operators. In the supplier's facility they molded two components in 65 seconds. This operator could load and inspect the parts in less than 15 seconds. They offered to perform the three assembly operations in their facility on both components for a nominal fee. As a result, their customer eliminated three operators on their assembly line, reduced the length of the assembly line, and reduced total product cycle time by 21 seconds in the plant. Suppliers should be encouraged to visit customers' facilities and visit with customers' engineers at least annually. They can then submit their value improvement proposals to a designated committee coordinator for review. Each proposal can be tracked on a log sheet to assure that action is taken. Suppliers should be encouraged to participate by acquiring new business or sharing a portion of the cost savings.

Bibliography

Brigham, Eugene F., *Fundamentals of Financial Management,* 4th ed., Dryden Press, Chicago, 1986.

Chrysler Corporation, *SQA Guide to Quality System Requirements,* Chrysler Corporation, August 1991.

General Motors Corporation, *Targets for Excellence,* General Motors Corporation, June 1987 and September 1991.

Manufacturing Process Flow and Productivity Analysis

When planning for a new product, one should always review existing processes to determine if there are methods which can improve productivity and reduce manufacturing costs. This can be done by reviewing many aspects of the manufacturing process. The review should determine if productivity can be improved by reducing labor content, the amount of plant space required to manufacture the product, process cycle time, manufacturing down time, inventories, operator slack time, and non–value-added operations. Increasing production capacity and improving assembly-line balance and design for manufacture are other methods that can be reviewed to improve productivity. To start this process it is useful to draw a process chart which shows the sequence of all operations, the process cycle time, the productivity or rate of the operation, the amount of work in process, and the production line's process cycle time. A process chart of this nature is shown in Fig. 9.1, which summarizes these items.

Labor content can be reduced by increasing automation, improving assembly-line balancing, or improving the operation's production capacity.

Suggestion System Rewarding Efficiency

A general philosophy that needs to be ingrained in production personnel is to "eliminate waste" or "non–value-added activity." They should be trained to look at ways of improving their areas or making them more productive. When they have discovered a possible opportunity, they can submit a suggestion to their supervisor or the human resource department. Some companies, who train their employees well, offer lifelong employment, empower production operators to create and implement change themselves, have realized enormous benefits.

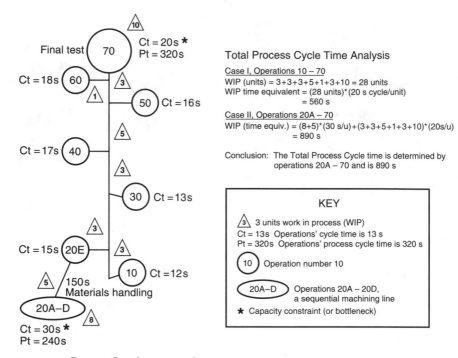

Total Process Cycle Time Analysis

Case I, Operations 10 – 70
WIP (units) = 3+3+3+5+1+3+10 = 28 units
WIP time equivalent = (28 units)*(20 s cycle/unit)
= 560 s

Case II, Operations 20A – 70
WIP (time equiv.) = (8+5)*(30 s/u)+(3+3+5+1+3+10)*(20s/u)
= 890 s

Conclusion: The Total Process Cycle time is determined by operations 20A – 70 and is 890 s

KEY

$\triangle$ 3   3 units work in process (WIP)
Ct = 13s Operations' cycle time is 13 s
Pt = 320s Operations' process cycle time is 320 s

(10) Operation number 10

(20A–D) Operations 20A – 20D,
a sequential machining line
★ Capacity constraint (or bottleneck)

Figure 9.1 Process flowchart example.

The suggestion system should not only identify an improvement opportunity, but also require the employee to offer a possible solution to a problem—this will reduce the number of "unreasonable" suggestions. The suggestion then becomes reviewed and the operator should be rewarded in some manner. However, if the idea eliminates their operation, the operators should not have to worry about losing their job. The system must be established to assure job security for all employees, with additional security for those who have made suggestions which have reduced labor content or improved productivity in the past. Otherwise, the "reward system" could reward an operator who submitted a good labor-reducing suggestion by laying him or her off in the event of severe economic misfortune. Under such a scenario, production personnel would not volunteer information which would yield a counterproductive reward system. The pervasive philosophy should instill the work force with the understanding that their suggestions will increase their job security because they will improve the operating efficiency of the plant, which improves the likelihood that the plant will remain competitive in the face of international competition.

A possible suggestion system would require an initial response within 5 working days and would have the originator of the suggestion explain the suggestion along with any recommended improvements or solutions to a problem. A reward system would be needed to reinforce the suggestions to encourage participation. The reward could be in the form of a free dinner, free T-shirts with the company logo, monetary rewards, etc.

Key Process Efficiency Issues

There are several disciplines that need to be discussed to better understand the issues involved in the process efficiency study. They include time motion studies, quick-changeover strategies, process flow analysis, lean production–total cycle time reduction, and production capacity constraint improvement.

Time Motion Studies

Time studies are performed on operations to maximize labor productivity and to better understand how labor is being utilized. The method for collecting the data is to lay out the operations that need to be performed on a product and then indicate the sequence that tasks must be performed. This can be done by performing a precedence task matrix (Fig. 9.2). Each row and column lists the task to be performed by a number. The sequence is the same in each row and column. Then, where they intersect determines what the sequence of tasks must be. A + 1 indicates that the item in the column goes after the item on the row. A − 1 means that the item in the column goes before the item on the row. A 0 indicates that there is no sequential requirement between the two tasks. In Fig. 9.2, task 4 might be to screw in a housing onto a track and task 3 might be to weld the track onto the frame. One has to weld the track onto the frame before screwing on the housing because the housing blocks access with the welders. The precedence task matrix shows where column 4 meets row 3. A + 1 is listed in that box and it signifies that task 4 (screw in housing) must go after task 3 (weld track onto frame). This analysis dictates the con-

\	1	2	3	4	5	6
1	0	+ 1	+ 1	+ 1	+ 1	+ 1
2	− 1	0	0	+ 1	+ 1	+ 1
3	− 1	0	0	+ 1	+ 1	+ 1
4	− 1	− 1	− 1	0	+ 1	+ 1
5	− 1	− 1	− 1	− 1	0	0
6	− 1	− 1	− 1	− 1	0	0

NOTE: A + 1 means that the task in that column goes after the task in that row. A − 1 means that the column goes before the task in the corresponding row.

Figure 9.2 The precedence matrix.

straints for sequencing tasks when balancing the line. The industrial engineer uses this to determine the assembly sequence of performing assembly tasks. Currently, this is usually performed by computer analysis from data input by industrial engineers.

A methods sheet describes all of the elements required to perform those tasks at that operation. The engineer then breaks each task into *elements*. An element is a subset of an operation such as move left 6 in, hold, lift 4 ft, etc. There are standard times used to determine an element. Figure 9.3 is a time motion survey form for one operator station on an assembly line for a consumer product. It has seven categories for standard elements: gets, hand, places, one hand, two hands, back and hip, and miscellaneous. The hand and back and hip elements are called *transports*. One hand and two hand are classified as precision motions. These motions are concerned with assembling products that generally require locating a tab or pin from one surface into a slot or hole on another. Miscellaneous accounts for specific and awkward movements such as wire cutting with pliers, or twisting one's body 45°, etc.

Each element is broken down into distances. For example, one can transport something with a hand motion. If it is a 6-inch transport, it will take 0.34 min/100, or approximately 0.20 s (the unit one-hundredth of a minute is used, which is equal to 0.60 s). However, if something has to be transported by more than 24 in, the additional motion would have a back and hip time added to it. Under the column of elements, there is L.H. for left hand and R.H. for right hand. Look at operation number 9: the left hand is releasing the unit, which is a place class 2 (full release), it takes 0.14 min/100 to perform, while the right hand is setting aside the hammer, which is an 18-in transport, 0.50 min/100 and a class 3 place down and release. The 0.14 min/100 operation is circled because it is an overlapping operation and does not affect the time of element 9 operation, which is 0.94 min/100. All of the 10 steps in this operation added together take 14.47 min/100.

However, when operators practice the job, their speed will become faster by a process known as the *learning curve*. The industrial engineer divides this by a factor of 1.22 to account for this yielding a cycle time of 11.86 min/100 (7.12 s) at this station. The assembly line's cycle time is 12.52 min/100, which is greater than the assembly operation and yields a slack time of 0.68 min/100. The slack time is the difference between the assembly line's cycle time and the station or operation's cycle time. If the station's time were greater than the line's time, the operation would be overloaded and the tasks would either have to be redistributed or the assembly-line cycle time increased. A perfectly balanced line would have no slack time. Generally speaking, slack time is undesirable unless the slack is

MOTION TIME SURVEY

DRG. NO. _____ PT. or GR. _____ STUDY NO. _____

OPERATION _Place Riser and Reservoir Cover to unit_ SHTS. — SHT. NO. _____

DATE 9-15-88 OBSERVER _____

STANDARD TIMES

#	ELEMENTS	L.H. / R.H.	TRANSPORTS	GETS / PLACES	MISCELLANEOUS	TOTAL TIME IN MIN/C
1	GET NEW UNIT, TRANSPORT / SET ASIDE FINISHED UNIT	.75		.74		1.49
2	PLACE TO WORK AREA / GET RISER TUBE	.15 / .34		.20 / (44).92		1.99
3	GET RISER COVER / MOVE UP & HOLD	.31/.34/.41/.52		.90		1.95
4	PLACE RISER COVER 'H HOLD / TO RISER TUBE	1.35 out		.93		1.98
5	GET ASSEMBLY FROM RIGHT HAND / GIVE ASSEMBLY TO LEFT HAND	.34/.34		.18/.14		1.00
6	PLACE ASSEMBLY ON TO RESERVOIR / GET HAMMER	.42 / .42		(18).44+.2007 Slowdown.3 z	30.30	3.08
7	GET UNIT & HOLD / MOVE UP & HOLD	(21).50		.18		.68
8	HOLD / STRIKE WITH HAMMER TO SEAT				.68	.68
9	RELEASE / SET ASIDE HAMMER	.50		(14).44		.94
10	DRIFT / GET FINISHED UNIT	.50		.18		.68

Note: Circled numbers are overlaps which do not affect Total time

After Learning Curve ✕ 1.03⅔ 14.47 / 11.86

Line Cycle time = 12.54

Slack time = 0.68

DEFINITIONS

GETS
- A. CONTACT – Control is attained by laying hand or finger(s) on part.
- B. GRIP – Control is attained by closing fingers on part.
- C. SLIDING GRIP – Where part must be drawn away from surface on which it lays or may disturb.
- D. DOWN, GRIP AND LIFT – Part usually in pile or container, with no tendency to tangle.
- E. DOWN, GRIP, LIFT AND SEPARATE – Part usually in pile or container, with slight tendency to tangle, or where two or more parts must be separated.
- F. DOWN, GRIP, LIFT AND UNTANGLE OR SHAKE – Part usually in pile or container, with bad tendency to tangle, or two or more parts must be shaken loose to obtain one part.

PLACES
1. DROP RELEASE – Part pushed or dropped into location.
2. FULL RELEASE – Relinquish control by opening fingers.
3. DOWN AND RELEASE – Use when a prepositioned part is placed in location, with one move similar to insert or align preceding release.
4. PREPOSITION, DOWN AND RELEASE – Same as 3 except part has to be prepositioned.
5. STRAIGHTEN, DOWN AND RELEASE – Use when a prepositioned part is placed in location, with two moves such as straighten and down preceding release.
6. PREPOSITION, STRAIGHTEN, DOWN AND RELEASE – Same as 5 except part has to be prepositioned.

MISCELLANEOUS

Blind Positioning – 1 hand ... .27 / 2 hands ... .29

Get up or Sit Down – Chair ... 3.33

Inspect or Select ... .30 / .58 / .90

Press Air Valves or Levers ...

Operate Foot Pedal

Step on pedal and step on pedal ... .90 / .45

Move foot down and up ... .95

Cut Light Wire – Pliers ... .44

Heavy Wire – Pliers ... .68

Cut with Scissors – 1st Snip ... .68

Each Add. Snip ... .30

Hammer – 1st Blow ... .21

Each Add. – Deliberate ... .49

Each Add. – Rapid ... .28

Twist with Fingers – 1st Twist ... .42

Each Add. Twist ... .44

Tightening Twist ... .88

Palm ... 1.23

Unpalm ... .30

Figure 9.3 Time motion study for a consumer product. (Courtesy of *Black and Decker*.)

183

needed for ergonomic considerations, e.g., the operator has to rest to avoid excessive fatigue or strain in a demanding operation. The tables used account for fatigue with objects that do not have excessive weight. Additionally, the more overlap between the right hand and the left hand, the better. In practice a line can be considered to be well balanced if the total slack time for all of the operations on an assembly line is less than 5 percent. Periodically, all assembly lines should be audited for a review to identify methods to improve line balance, simplify operations, automate tasks, and speed up the line.

The ideal left-hand, right-hand element analysis would yield 100 percent overlap between hands. To identify possible improvement opportunities in this regard, some analysts plot both the right- and left-hand motions on two-handed process charts (Fig. 9.4). This shows when each hand is performing one of the following operations: operation, transport, delay, inspect, and hold. This chart will help one identify those operations where unbalanced assignments between the right and left hand exist. This can also be used in conjunction with foot motion analysis if considerable foot motion and pedal work is required. Sometimes it may be necessary to videotape the operations to collect the data to accurately break down operations.

It should be noted that this type of analysis is more cost-effective to perform for repetitive, high-volume production with shorter cycle times and long product lives. An operation description sheet lists the task to be performed by each operator at each station on the assembly line.

There are several principles to apply when performing time motion studies. These principles can be broken down into four categories: human factors, workplace considerations, time conservation, and ergonomic considerations. They are briefly discussed below.

Human factors

1. Hand motions should be smooth and continuous; hence, sudden stops and changes in direction should be avoided.

2. All movements and transports should have the shortest possible distances.

3. Maximize the utilization of both hands and feet to perform productive work. Foot pedals can be used for fixturing and moving products.

4. Body motions should be distributed according to the capabilities of the body members and the weight should be evenly balanced.

5. Minimize lifting, carrying, and exerting forces whenever possible; this can frequently be done by using automation and/or power tools to perform these tasks.

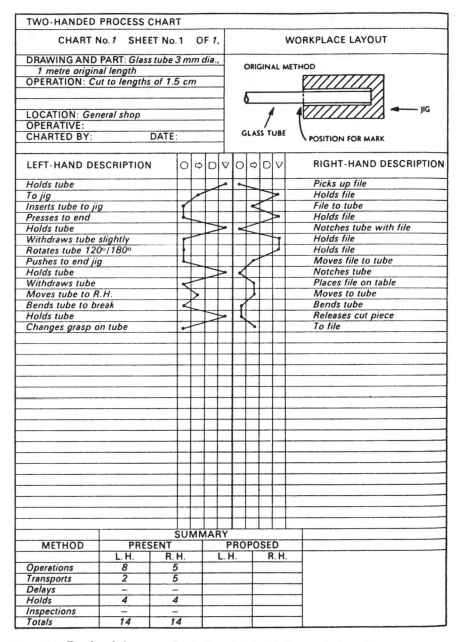

TWO-HANDED PROCESS CHART										

CHART No. *1*   SHEET No. 1   OF *1,*   WORKPLACE LAYOUT

DRAWING AND PART: *Glass tube 3 mm dia.,*
1 metre original length
OPERATION: *Cut to lengths of 1.5 cm*

LOCATION: *General shop*
OPERATIVE:
CHARTED BY: DATE:

ORIGINAL METHOD

GLASS TUBE   POSITION FOR MARK   JIG

LEFT-HAND DESCRIPTION	○	⇨	▢	▽	○	⇨	▢	▽	RIGHT-HAND DESCRIPTION
Holds tube									*Picks up file*
To jig									*Holds file*
Inserts tube to jig									*File to tube*
Presses to end									*Holds file*
Holds tube									*Notches tube with file*
Withdraws tube slightly									*Holds file*
Rotates tube 120°/180°									*Holds file*
Pushes to end jig									*Moves file to tube*
Holds tube									*Notches tube*
Withdraws tube									*Places file on table*
Moves tube to R.H.									*Moves to tube*
Bends tube to break									*Bends tube*
Holds tube									*Releases cut piece*
Changes grasp on tube									*To file*

SUMMARY				
METHOD	PRESENT		PROPOSED	
	L. H.	R. H.	L. H.	R. H.
Operations	*8*	*5*		
Transports	*2*	*5*		
Delays	*–*	*–*		
Holds	*4*	*4*		
Inspections	*–*	*–*		
Totals	*14*	*14*		

Figure 9.4 Two-handed process chart. (*Reprinted with the permission of the International Labour Organization.*) [*Reference 7b, p. 164.*]

Workplace considerations

1. The height of the assembly operation should be designed to accommodate a person who is standing or sitting without any bending.
2. Utilize fixtures to locate and hold tools.
3. Use quick-action clamping and fixtures where possible and design for quick tool changeovers.
4. Material handling should be as close to the point of use as possible to minimize human transport requirements.

Time conservation

1. Any hesitations or rest periods with any limb can be opportunities for additional work. However, one must account for possible fatigue factors.
2. Design the work area to allow for quick changeovers, tool changes, and utilize quick action clamps at clamping and fixturing operations.

Ergonomic considerations

1. Minimize unnecessary bending either with the back or knees; assure that a safe posture is an objective of the workstation design. This can be done by designing the workplace to have adjustable seat heights or floor heights. A forward-facing posturing with the head slightly forward is a recommended approach.
2. Minimize the transmission of tool or machinery vibration to the operator to avoid some of the negative side effects such as "white finger."
3. Design the motion so that there is an equal weight distribution to minimize muscle strain and fatigue due to awkward motions.
4. Feed the station with a magazine whenever possible to minimize transport motion and unnecessary lifting.
5. Assure that the work area is well lit, clean, and has adequate hearing and eye protection available.
6. Design safety into the operation by using safety guards, requiring both hands to hold down a button to operate a press, etc.
7. Minimize employee exposure to repetitive motion injuries wherever possible. One method of doing this is by rotating work assignments in jobs that are more likely to induce repetitive motion injury. An employee's job satisfaction will typically be improved when work assignments are rotated.

Improving line balance

On almost any assembly or sequential processing line there is room for improving the line balance and improving the assembly process. It is therefore an iterative process. The process should be reviewed on a periodic basis to identify improvement opportunities. One method is to have an industrial engineer audit the process. Another is to video-tape the line, map out its operations, and give the operators a chance to perform all operations, in the form of a rotation, so that they are familiar with all operations on the line. After the rotation is completed, solicit their suggestions. This method generates numerous improvements, because each operator is a specialist in his or her work area and has the whole shift to come up with ideas for improvements. Some companies empower the operators to develop the best method. Additionally, by rotating assignments there will be many viewpoints that can be used and considered. A rotation also gives them an appreciation for the whole process so they can identify methods to integrate the manufacturing process better. Operator rotation has the added benefit that the manufacturing line will not suffer adverse consequences should absenteeism occur. The lean production or demand flow approach requires that each operator know how to perform the task before and after its operation so that they can fill in if the line speed is reduced and remove unnecessary laborers to keep the line well balanced. Finally, one can compare differences between shift operators and utilize the best methods to become the recommended approach.

When designing a new manufacturing line, it is invaluable to solicit operators' input for the improvement opportunities in material handling, work area layout, ergonomic considerations, and other productivity improvements. Material should be placed in a WIP storage area which is as close as possible to the point of consumption in order to avoid unnecessary material handling. Also, where possible, design a process flow so operator handling and loading is minimized, because loading and unloading as well as material handling does not add value to the product. They are, however, necessary to perform some manufacturing processes, but such efforts should be minimized.

Time motion studies offer the opportunity to reduce labor cost per unit on products by minimizing slack time during assembly operations. They also try to maximize the utilization of all limbs. As a result of improved efficiency, it also can reduce the floor area required to assemble a product by combining and eliminating stations so the assembly line can be shortened. By using less plant space, the fixed overhead of the plant, as it applies to a product, is reduced.

Quick-Changeover Strategies

Reducing setup or changeover times can benefit an operation in several ways:

1. Reduces machine downtime
2. Reduces work-in-process inventory requirements
3. Reduces scrap
4. Improves ability to respond to changes in production schedules
5. Allows for inventory storage reduction

By developing quick-change strategies, one can reduce the time required to set up a machine. Machine setups typically do not add direct value to the product, since products are not being manufactured during setups. Therefore, it is desirable to minimize the time required to set up a manufacturing process.

Quicker tool changes can sometimes allow work-in-process inventory to be reduced since the buffer requirements relating to changeovers can be reduced for subsequent operations. Suppose, for example, that a machining line has 20 machining stations, and at station 10 the carbide tool is worn and needs to be changed or scrap will be manufactured. It currently takes 40 min to change over the tool, so the foreman typically keeps a bank of about 60 min of production to allow for the tool changeover without affecting subsequent production processes. Additionally, after inserting the tool, several adjustments have to be made until an acceptable product is manufactured so that several parts may have to be scrapped. A quick changeover approach would have the tool premeasured in a fixture which is easy to remove and change. The new tool can be changed in 2 min and the first pieces machined with the new tool will be acceptable. The work-in-process inventory required to bank the product can now be reduced to 5 min and no scrap is generated during the tool change.

Having a quick changeover capability allows for more flexibility in production scheduling because changeover costs are greatly reduced and the machine utilization efficiency will not be greatly affected. The costs are lower, relating to reduced downtime and reduced setup labor costs.

Performing quick changeovers involves three basic steps:

1. Advanced preparation
2. Performing setup tasks
3. Setup approval

Each is discussed below.

Advanced preparation

Also known as external setups, *advanced preparation* involves preparing before the changeover begins, while the machine is still running production. It involves getting the equipment and tools ready at the operation before starting to perform the change. Some key principles to apply include

1. Do all possible preparation work while the machine is still manufacturing product.
2. Utilize a setup checklist to obtain all necessary items before initiating the job.

A good example of this would be in a stamping operation, where one would have the hoist, the new die nearby on a stand, all equipment and tools needed to remove and replace the dies available according to a changeover checklist, and raw material stock. The changeover personnel would be ready at the press prepared to change the die over as soon as the production order is completed. This eliminates unnecessary downtime that would normally occur while waiting for the other die to arrive when the changeover begins. The die would already have been reviewed by the tool room at the end of the previous run to assure that the die did not need any repairs. In injection molding a similar approach would be used with the addition that the plastic raw material or resin would already be dried in advance since this usually takes several hours to perform. Predrying the resin prevents the factory from wasting machine time unnecessarily. This general approach can be used in many other industries. To assist the setup personnel, a checklist of all tools, fixtures, gages, inserts, machine process setting sheets, and any additional requirements is used to assure that all equipment is ready before the changeover. The molding company, which is a Division of Premix, Inc., and is a company that has good quality systems, uses a process sheet to assist their setup efforts. A sheet such as the one shown in Fig. 9.5 is used to preprogram their molding machines during a changeover. The data are entered in advance and the machine settings can be downloaded with the press of a button and the regrind settings can be set. In Fig. 9.6, H&W Screw Products, which has successfully implemented a TQM approach, uses a Davenport tool layout sheet to help their setup personnel obtain all of the proper cams and perishable tooling for their machine setups (Davenport is their screw machine equipment manufacturer).

Setup tasks

Also known as internal setups, *setup tasks* are concerned with designing equipment to reduce the time required to perform the changeover.

```
THE MOLDING COMPANY, DIVISON OF PREMIX, INC.   SET-UP SHEET

    TYPE: TP            DATE: 07/02/91
CUSTOMER: M.F.C.C.                    MATERIAL: SANTOPRENE
PART NO.: C90RC9200                     SERIES: 101-73
PART NAME: ROLLER                     PROJECT:
MOLD NO.:                             BATCH NO.: PIC042-05
REV NO.:                              DATE MFG.:   /  /
NO. CAV S: 4                           STATUS: S
STANDARD CLCLE:                   ACTUAL CYCLE:   22
COLOR: BLACK
PART WT.:   0.10
SHOT WT.:   0.50


SET-UP FOR PRESS: 58

BARREL: NOZ. SET: 420   ACT: 420      MOLD: STAT.SET: 100   ACT: 110
        FRN. SET: 430   ACT: 430            MOV.SET: 100   ACT: 105
        MID. SET:       ACT:                   CORE:   %
        BAC. SET: 423   ACT: 423              MELT: 390

TIME: INJ. HIGH: 4 SEC.       INJECTION TIME: 1 SEC.
       LOW  HOLD: 5 SEC.    SCREW RETRACTION: 6 SEC.
         COOLING: 16 SEC.          CURE TIME:   16SEC.
      CLAMP OPEN:    SEC.
    DECOMPRESSION:    SEC.
    EJECTOR COUNT: 1#

PRESSURE: INJ. HIGH: 400 PSI.    SCREW: FEED: 1.5
          LOW HOLD: 400 PSI.           CUSHION: 0
              BACK: 0   PSI.            R.P.M.: SL
             CLAMP:     PSI.      REGIND MIX: 25%
           STUFFER:     PSI.           DRYER: N/A

PACKING:   TYPE: BULK              EQUIPMENT:
        BOX SIZE:                 NO. LAYERS:   0
    PARTS PR. BOX:   0          PARTS PR.LAYER:   0


    SETUP COMMENTS
    --------------


    DO NOT OVER PACK, OR GATES WILL START TO BLOW OUT.
    OPERATOR MUST WATCH FOR PARTS STICKING. TO TOP MOLD.   RAN
    GOOD.



    PART COMMENT
    ------------


    USE PART C19RC9100   OVER PACKING WILL CAUSE DEEP GATES
```

Figure 9.5   Process setup sheet. (*Courtesy of the Molding Company.*)

The basic principles to apply to reduce the time required to actually perform setup tasks include

1. Standardize the tooling to make common components and change-over tasks between machines and processes.

2. Design equipment to have common locating fixtures and pins which reduce the number of adjustments required to change over a job.

DAVENPORT LAYOUT SHEET

PART # _221_

MATERIAL _35/64 R 12L14_

TOOL LOCATION _80_

RPM _1500_

GEARS DRIVER _32_ DRIVEN _32_

CYCLE TIME _4.45 SEC_

ENGAGE GEAR _30_ WITH _60_

	FORM	TURN/DRILL	TOOLS REQUIRED	
1	CAM RISE DOVETAIL	TYPE OF FEED STOP TO BE USED	5 COLLETS SIZE	35/64 R
		☒ 2763-10-SA SPOT AND FACE	5 PUSHERS SIZE	35/64 R
	B.L. 1/8	☐ 2810-SA CAM RISE	PICKOFF COLLET SIZE	35/64 R
		☐ 2904-10-SA 1/8	DOVETAIL	1
			CR FORM	
2	CAM RISE SHAVE	CAM RISE 5 MM DRILL	SHAVE	1
			DRILLS SIZE	5 MM
	B.L. 7/32 SPECIAL CAM	B.L. 1/4 CAM	DRILLS SIZE	5/16 SPOT
			DRILLS SIZE	3/16
			REAMERS SIZE	1 BROACH
3	CAM RISE	CAM RISE 5 MM BROACH	TAPS	
			SAWS	
	B.L.	B.L. 7/32 CAM	KNURLING WHEELS	
			THREAD ROLLERS SIZE	
4	OVERHEAD CAM RISE M10X1MM THREAD ROLL 5/32 CAM	CAM RISE 3/16 DRILL	l FFT HAND BACK DRILL	
		B.L. 1/4 CAM	CUT OFF CIRCULAR OR BLADE SIZE	5/64
5	CUT OFF	TYPE OF PICKOFF CAM TO BE USED	BURNISH ROLLS	
		☐ EARLY		
	CAM RISE 1/4	☒ C32 or C45 CAM RISE		
		☐ LATE FOR BACK DRILL		

REMARKS M10 X 1
MAJOR DIA MAX 9.974 (.3926)
MIN 9.794 (3855)
P.D. .363/.367

INSPECTION NOTES

GAUGES REQUIRED

PLUG GAUGES SIZE

RING THREAD GAUGES M10 X 1

OTHERS

Figure 9.6 Setup checklist. (*Courtesy of H&W Screw Products.*)

3. Use quick-disconnect and spring-loaded clamps and hoses when possible. Alternatively, design clamps and screws so that they can easily be inserted and have only one turn required for sufficient clamping. There are several methods for doing this, as is shown in Fig. 9.7, including a combination of pear-shaped holes. Combining this with a U-type washer makes it easier to install

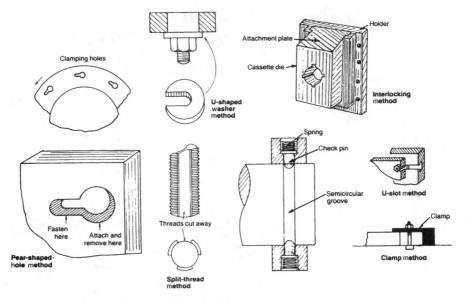

Figure 9.7 One-touch clamping methods. (*Reprinted with permission of the Productivity Press.*) [*From p. 110 of Ref. 1.*]

and remove a top plate quickly. Another approach is to use a bolt and boss with slots machined off so that they can fit all of the way into the boss and begin clamping as soon as the turning begins. Since less thread engagement occurs, bigger bolts and bosses may be needed.

4. Alternatively, use power tools instead of wrenches to speed up the time required to tighten bolts and other fastening devices.

5. Establish setup instructions and procedures to standardize methods and maximize the setup efficiency based on methods analysis results.

6. Use preprogrammed cartridges where possible to download setup parameters.

7. Use several preset graduated adjustments or fixtures or use several limit switches that can be quickly turned on and off to eliminate the need for performing setting adjustments.

8. Perform time motion studies on setups that are frequently performed or involve a critical process in which a small amount of downtime is very costly.

9. Assign personnel full time to help perform changeovers.

10. Train all employees involved in proper methodology and help them understand the importance of doing the tasks properly.

An example of this in the stamping industry is to have all dies set in a die shoe which closes to a common shut height. Additionally, changeover time can be further reduced by having common locator stops (or plates) that support the die in two planes. Roller tracks, which allow for dies to come on and off to a specified position, can also speed up this process. Quick-disconnect clamps are also used to shorten the setup times.

Injection molding component manufacturers are concerned with the above items, and they also utilize a quick changeover material loader which has three hoppers and two driers. One hopper is for the existing material that is currently running at the press, the other is for the material that will be run, and the third, smaller hopper is for the purging compound. Injection molders also use quick-disconnect hose clamps to connect water fittings quickly. In machining industries, tool change times can be reduced by utilizing fixtures which locate the tool so that the setup is correct without requiring any readjustments. The tool insert is measured to the correct height in the fixture so that it will go into the machine to the correct height for machining the product. An analogy to this is the difference between cassette tapes and reel to reel. The older style reel-to-reel tapes require that a person must put the tape reel and a blank reel on the machine. Then they have to thread the tape onto the blank reel and then start the tape. This may take about 30 s to perform. However, this same person can load a cassette into a cassette player in less than 3 s (one-tenth as much time), resulting in a difference of 27 s. Twenty-seven seconds is not a lot of time, but die changeovers that used to take more than 2 h can now be performed in under 2 min. When one looks at the lost machine time and the additional personnel utilized, the savings can be substantial. Computer numerical control (CNC) and injection molding machines as well as heat treat equipment have preprogrammed databases that can reduce the time to program the operating parameters.

Setup approval

Setup approval involves running the job and sampling the product to determine if it conforms to specifications. It can also include verification techniques to assure that all machine settings are properly set, all bolts tightened, etc., to assure that the process settings are correct and the machine will operate safely as well as prevent tool damage due to carelessness.

Frequently, adjustments may need to be made until the product is in conformance. A setup approval is used to determine if the quality criteria sheet has been met. Additionally, a troubleshooting guide should be established to assure that the adjustments are made in the most efficient manner. Once there is sufficient confidence with the setup methods, the process should run and only be stopped if a problem is encountered during verification.

A strategy is to try to convert a setup task into a preparatory one. For example, suppose a company reduces the time required to set up a machining operation by designing fixtures with preset insert heights; they would change the setup and adjustment task to one that is performed during setup preparation. Sometimes videotapes of setups are taken with a timer in the lower corner of the video screen. The results are reviewed by operators, job setters, and management to help them understand improvement opportunities. By making the setups easier to perform, the operators can participate, which reduces their nonproductive idle time. It also makes it easier to train new and temporary employees.

Another strategy is to design the setup equipment to *eliminate adjustments after the installation* of the new tools. This can be done by premeasuring perishable tools such as insert heights, punch and button diameters, and also designing jigs and fixtures with stops to locate tool positions precisely. Other approaches include using several limit switches at preset locations or inputting appropriate settings onto a computer that locates tool positions.

Quick-changeover features should be given strong consideration when purchasing new manufacturing equipment because of the resulting productivity improvements over the life of the product. However, one does not need to spend a fortune. Only those modifications that are necessary to perform quick setups should be implemented. A manufacturing facility should develop the ability to design and manufacture equipment add-ons and modifications to better service their own needs. Frequently, outside tool and equipment sources have a broader customer base and will design modifications that will appeal to many. These would not necessarily appeal to a plant's specific needs, and specific modifications will likely cost more. Additionally, special modifications performed by a manufacturing facility will give their plant a competitive advantage which will not be sold to competitors.

While planning new products, setup checklists should be developed because the benefits that accrue during the product life cycle will usually exceed the nominal administrative managerial costs. To reduce management time dedicated to such a task, these checklists can be developed by the job setters (changeover personnel) and operators. The effectiveness of a setup time reduction program can be monitored by reviewing setup times for each job and tracking performance.

When prioritizing quick-changeover capital investment expenditures, one must first determine the cost of machine downtime as well as the projected reduction in setup time, the number of setups to be performed annually, and the holding costs of inventory that can be eliminated by improving setups and tool changes. These costs should be compared with the capital costs required to modify the machinery. Those with the greatest return on investment and savings should receive highest priority for conversions.

Techniques for improving changeover times were developed by Shigeo Shingo. As an outside consultant, in 1970 he reduced the setup time for a 1000-ton press at Toyota from 4 h to $1\frac{1}{2}$ h in 6 months primarily by improving advance preparation. Three months later Toyota management insisted that he develop a technique to reduce this to 3 min. He initially thought that this was an "unreasonable request." However, in 3 months he was able to achieve this goal by converting setup tasks to advanced preparation tasks, adding fixtures, and changing clamping techniques.[1]

This illustrates three important concepts. One must try to *convert setup tasks to advanced preparation tasks.* Management and engineering should develop equipment and technology which will allow for tasks to be performed more rapidly as in the case of modifying bolts to allow them to be inserted and tightened more rapidly. Finally, it is imperative to *change mindset barriers* to achieve tasks that are important to improve processes and designs which ultimately will improve customer satisfaction, improve durability, or reduce cost.

Total Productive Maintenance

An important part of a lean production process is to have a high degree of machine availability or uptime. This means that a system must be established to assure that machine breakdowns are minimized. For that reason, preventative and predictive maintenance systems were established to improve machine uptime or efficiencies so that machine costs and plant overhead costs, as applied to a product, do not have to be unnecessarily high.

A total productive maintenance program can have several elements including breakdown maintenance, preventative maintenance, predictive maintenance, data collection and storage, spare parts inventory control, and performance tracking. Each of these issues will be discussed further. The goal of a total productive maintenance program is to minimize the combined costs of maintenance administration and labor, replacement components, and downtime, etc.

Breakdown maintenance consists of fixing machines after they break down. It is most cost-effective in the following situations:

- The process has on-line spares that can be immediately utilized.
- Machinery can be quickly repaired.

- Excess capacity exists.

An aspect of breakdown maintenance is to have a contingency plan for a power loss, alternate coolers, etc., so that a company is prepared should a disaster strike.

Both preventative and predictive maintenance utilize instruction sheets and visual aids. The instruction sheets will specify that machines are checked according to a maintenance checklist at specified intervals. The list will explain

- The type of inspection
- The check or monitoring to be performed
- The acceptance criteria
- The frequency of performing that task
- The general action to take if an inspection fails the criteria.

Visual aids should accompany the checklists in the form of drawings which show the machines' check and lube points. The aids can also show standards for acceptance which can include pictures or actual sample components showing various degrees of wear (this allows for ease of training new personnel).

Preventative maintenance involves inspecting places in the machinery to look for wear points and other important characteristics which can impact the machinery's performance, along with routine maintenance such as oiling, lubing, calibrating sensors, checking bolt torque, belt tensions, etc. It would include the following:

1. A good maintenance instruction sheet will specify:
   - Visual wear inspection checkpoints.
   - Lube points, along with the amount and type of lubrication.
   - Other checks to be performed such as belt tensions, sensor calibrations, and pressure checks.
   - The acceptance limit or standard for acceptance.
   - The frequency of performing each check.
   - Who will perform those checks.
   - Brief instructions on what to do if the check determines an unacceptable condition exists.

Such a checklist is used by SKF Bearing Industries in their Bremen, Indiana, facility. They have implemented an effective total productive maintenance system. Figure 9.8a is a checklist for their operators to use. Figure 9.8b is a visual aid that is used to clarify the inspection and checkpoints so that it is easier to train the operators and help them locate each item. Amoco Chemical Company, which is effectively implementing TQM, has a very good reputation for provid-

			1 OIL CHAINS	2 GREASE PILLOW BLOCK	3 GREASE SUPPORT WHEEL BNGS.	4 GREASE REAR SEAL	5 GREASE FRONT SEAL	6 DRAIN WATER TRAP	7 FILL AIR LINE LUBRICATOR	8 CHANGE BLOWER FILTER	9 CHECK & OIL RETORT DRIVE GEAR BOX	
OPERATOR	DATE		WAY OIL	2 STROKES BEARING GREASE #2		6 STROKES HIGH TEMP. GREASE	3 STROKES HIGH TEMP. GREASE	AS NEEDED	SPINDLE OIL	AS NEEDED		
			2 TIMES PER WEEK	WEEKLY		2 TIMES PER SHIFT	EVERY SHIFT		AS NEEDED			

Figure 9.8a   Preventative maintenance checklist for operators. (*Courtesy of SKF Bearing Industries Co.*)

ing their polypropylene customers with excellent technical support. They also have implemented an effective maintenance system. Figure 9.9 is an example of part of their written procedure for maintaining a melt flow analyzer, which is a crucial part of their laboratory work. The procedure specifies daily, weekly, quarterly, and annual checks to be performed. It also describes corrective maintenance procedures (not shown).

2. Molds and die maintenance would include a production report of any problems observed during the run that would accompany the tool along with the last shot or piece after it was pulled from production. Every time a run is over, the tool and last shot (or piece) are reviewed for wear and damage according to a tool checklist. (See Fig. 9.10, which is an example from an injection molding operation.) It prompts the maintenance person to review issues with the tools as well as the last shot. Critical tool characteristics are measured to monitor wear. Changes in the process capability are noted from SPC data and corrective action is performed as appropriate. For longer running jobs, molds or dies are pulled and reviewed at specified intervals. The number of cycles run and all work are recorded on a database for that tool number.

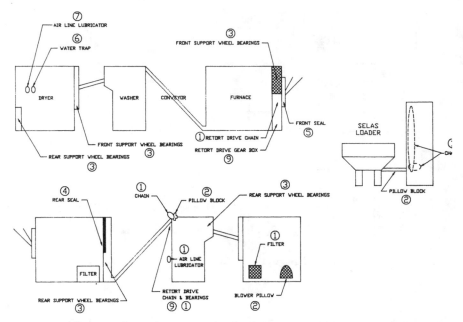

Figure 9.8b Preventative maintenance visual aid. (*Courtesy of SKF Bearing Industries Co.*)

Predictive maintenance is concerned with monitoring equipment to replace components before failures occur. Some of the monitoring includes

1. Measuring the resistance of electric motors to monitor insulation breakdown or arcing due to carbon dust buildup. Changes in the power consumption of a motor can also be an indication of problems.

2. Checking hydraulic or pneumatic pressure readings to determine plumbing, valve and pipe flow rates as well as pump efficiencies and whether any significant deterioration is developing in those systems. This way valve and pipe problems can be addressed before they become significant.

3. Checking corrosion of pipes and pressure vessels to assure strength and heat transfer characteristics are maintained.

4. Utilizing a vibration monitor to determine changes in characteristic signals in rotating equipment to identify bearing failures and other potential problems.

5. Using ultrasonic monitoring to discover cracks in machine components, pipes, pressure vessels, etc.

6. Recording infrared signals to identify potential wiring and electric panel problems, as well as switch gear failures.

AMOCO CHEMICAL COMPANY
CHOCOLATE BAYOU PLANT

Laboratory Standard Operating Procedures

Amoco Chemical Company
Chocolate Bayou Laboratory

Method No.   CB-LSOP-4.10.005
Date   3-13-91
Issue No.   A1
Issued By   RAG
Approved By LRC/

PREVENTATIVE MAINTENANCE PROCEDURES
FOR TINIUS OLSEN MELT FLOW RATERS

Scope

Specific routine maintenance is required on Tinius Olsen Melt Flow
Raters to insure equipment is kept in optimum analytical operating
condition.

Summary

This procedure itemizes the daily, weekly and quarterly routine
maintenance work necessary to insure Tinius Olsen testing equipment is
kept mechanically clean, calibrated and in conformance with
manufacturer specifications and laboratory testing requirements.

Procedure

Section A: Routine Maintenance of Tinius-Olsen Melt Flow Raters

1.   Daily

a.   Check pistons visually for straightness, free movement of
collar, cleanliness, and foot wear. If piston is gummed
up, clean it with chore girl copper mesh. If it cannot be
cleaned with chore girl, then clean it in warm soap bath.
If the foot is worn or bent, replace it.

b.   Visually check the follower arm assemblies for dirty
contacts, loose or bent arms. Clean dirty contacts with
pencil eraser to remove carbon build-up. Tighten loose
arms with their Allen set screw and straighten or replace
any bent arm.

Page 1 of 5

Figure 9.9   Preventative maintenance procedures for laboratory equipment. (*Courtesy of Amoco Chemical Company.*)

7. Monitoring oil and coolant temperatures because of the impact that a relatively small increase in temperature can have on a lubricant's viscosity and the time for viscosity deterioration.

8. Analyzing oil and coolant to determine if contaminants are in the oil, the viscosity is breaking down, or if there are problems with the machinery.

I. MOLD CONDITION REVIEW

Part No.: _____   Description: _____   Mold No.: _____

I. Mold condition ✓ (check mark) verifies acceptable condition. An "X"
   indicates an unacceptable condition and requires comments. Check for
   the following:

Cavities/Cores

No burrs on parting lines_____
Clean   _____
Blemishes   _____
Rust   _____
Clear Water Lines   _____
Vents Clean & Sharp   _____
Comments:_____
_____

_____

Slides

Worn   _____
Broken Springs   _____
Heel Blocks   _____
Horn Pins   _____
Stops   _____
Flush Screws   _____
Hydraulics(if applic)_____
Comments:_____

_____

Ejector Pins/Blades/Screws

Bent   _____
Worn   _____
Broken   _____
Chipped   _____
Comments:_____

_____

_____

Ejector Plates

Bent   _____
Hobbed   _____
Stops   _____
Springs   _____

Comments:_____

_____

_____

Mold Plates/Frame

Bent   _____
Hobbed   _____
Rust   _____
Water Leaks   _____
Clear Water Lines   _____
Leader Pins   _____
Leader Pin Bushings   _____
Sprue Bushing   _____
Interlock   _____

Comments:_____

_____

Core Pins

Pin Diameter   _____
Pin Broken/Cracked   _____
Pin Clean & Sharp   _____
Comments: _____

_____

_____

Page 1 of 2

Figure 9.10   Mold maintenance checklist.

9. Scheduling a machine recondition or rebuild if significant changes
   in a process's capability is noted.

10. Reconditioning or rebuilding machines and equipment at speci-
    fied intervals and capitalizing the budget so that there is money
    appropriated to support those activities. The schedules are based
    on utilizing historic replacement data to predict failures in cer-
    tain components. The intervals are determined by evaluating the
    cost of replacing a component before the probable end of its useful

life vs. the cost of downtime. However, adjustments to this schedule can be made based on capacity considerations.

Data collection and storage is an important part of any total productive maintenance program. Records of all inspections and repairs are recorded in a database along with the number of machine cycles or parts manufactured. Periodically, a review is performed to determine if any components are replaced excessively or how often they should be replaced before a breakdown will occur to assist predictive maintenance analysis. Excessive repairs are also reviewed to see if improvements can be incorporated in the tooling's and machinery component's design. Frequently this requires communication with the tooling and equipment source.

Spare parts inventory control is performed by cataloging each tool and replacement part in an inventory database. It will also involve monitoring the frequency of use, determining the order and delivery time for each component, and establishing the required level of safety stock to assure that repairs will not be delayed due to replacement shortages. The advantage of this approach is that certain components will not be overstocked, which adds to corporate inventory costs. Additionally, downtime relating to spare parts shortages will be minimized. Keep in mind that one has to account for bulk discounts when determining the "optimal" spare parts inventory requirement. A similar approach should be used for perishable tooling such as inserts, punches, etc.

Performance tracking monitors the effectiveness of a preventative maintenance program. This is usually done by tracking the unscheduled downtime as a percentage of scheduled running time for each machine and the total plant. Where feasible, operators should be trained to maintain their equipment to expand their job scope and to reduce maintenance personnel's responsibility.

Machinery Improvement

Improving machinery is a necessity for a manufacturer who wants to obtain a competitive manufacturing advantage. Such manufacturers have the capability to design and manufacture improvements to their machines but do not share this information with their equipment builders, who would incorporate the improvements and sell the machines to competitors in the industry. This approach allows for a firm to gain a competitive manufacturing advantage with their proprietary manufacturing technology. A company who has this capability continuously seeks ideas from operators and other personnel on how processes can be improved. They also develop a life cycle cost database to determine which components need to be redesigned to reduce maintenance and repair costs. This approach allows a company to minimize tooling costs by modifying existing equipment to manufacture new products.

Process Flow Analysis

Material flow analysis shows how components are processed and assembled (or, alternatively, in process industries, how chemicals are mixed and produced). The purpose of performing process flow analysis is to identify ways to

1. Reduce material handling and associated costs

2. Reduce work in process inventory

3. Decrease unnecessary or nonproductive operations

4. Decrease the amount of plant floor space used

5. Commonize operations

6. Reduce the amount of labor required to perform an operation

There are many approaches that can be used to identify these opportunities.

String diagrams, or trip frequency diagrams, are used to count the frequency of movements of material or equipment to analyze the aggregate motion of a process. One plots the distance traveled as well as the number of motions or material that moves on the diagram. By reviewing the process one can gain an understanding of how to reduce the number of material movements and the distance traveled for the products. The net benefit is to reduce both material handling costs and plant floor space utilized. Figure 9.11 shows a string diagram that was used in conjunction with group technology analysis to change the plant layout from a department to a manufacturing cell layout.

Material flow diagrams are used to determine methods to improve the process layout and reduce material handling and storage. This is illustrated in Fig. 9.12a, the original method for machining a cylinder head, and Fig. 9.12b, the improved method after changing the plant layout and material transfer techniques. The analysis for improvement was performed by using a flow process chart.

Flow process charts are used to analyze a process and determine the nature of each operation (e.g., operation, transport, delay, inspect, storage), the distance traveled, and the time to perform each task. This type of chart was used to analyze the material movement used in machining the cylinder head. After analysis the flow of the process was improved, and the improved method is documented on the process chart as is shown in Fig. 9.13. The process performed three

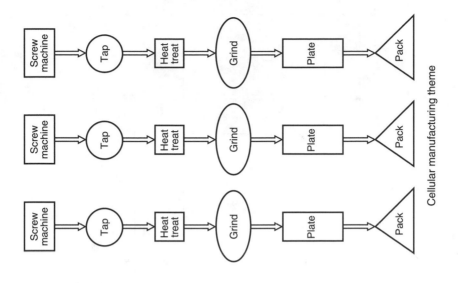

Cellular manufacturing theme

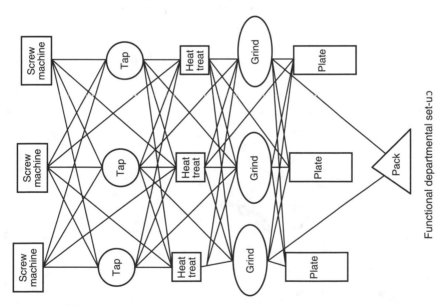

Functional departmental set-up

Figure 9.11   String diagram.

operations, 15 transports, two delays, and one storage operation. This analysis demonstrated to the engineer that there might be opportunities to improve material handling or transport operations. By plotting the activity, if excessive material storage or material transports or delays exist, it becomes readily apparent with this charting method and improvement opportunities can be easily identified.

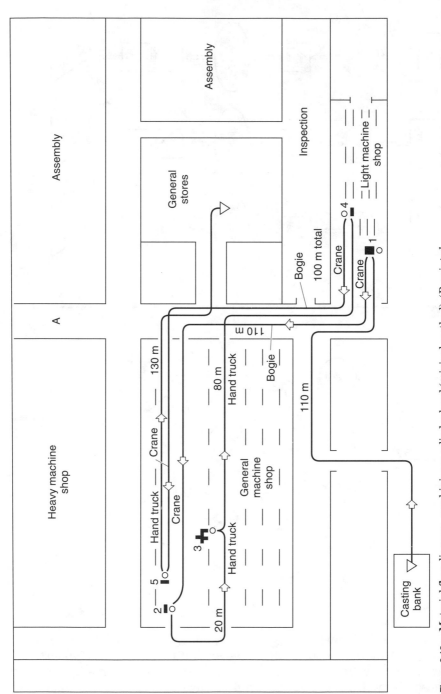

Figure 9.12a Material flow diagram, machining a cylinder head (original method). *(Reprinted with the permission of the Industrial Labour Organization.) [Reference 7a, p. 130.]*

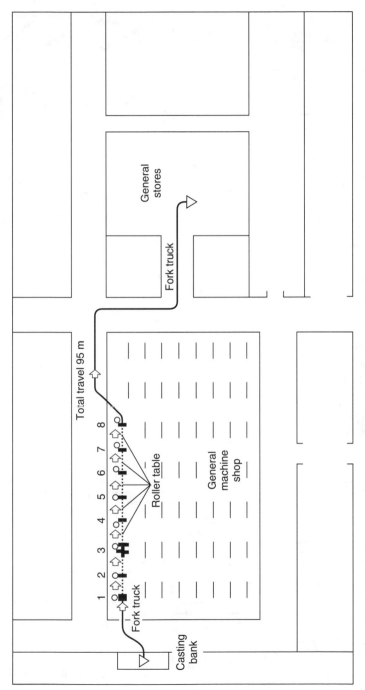

Figure 9.12b Material flow diagram, machining a cylinder head (improved method). *(Reprinted with permission of the Industrial Labour Organization.) [Reference 7a, p. 135.]*

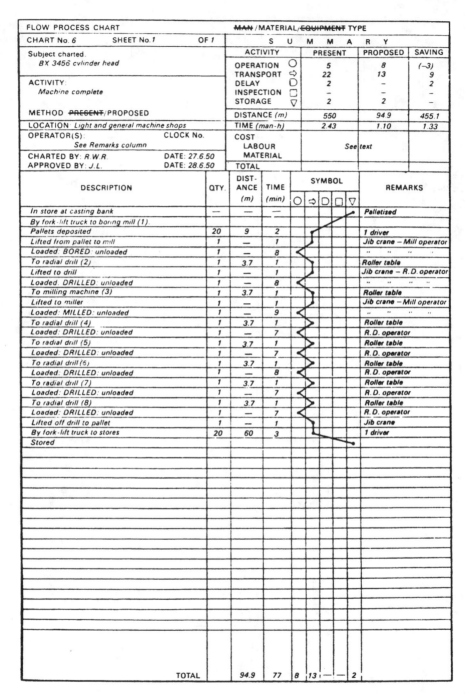

FLOW PROCESS CHART				~~MAN~~ /MATERIAL/~~EQUIPMENT~~ TYPE				
CHART No. 6		SHEET No. 1	OF 1	**S U M M A R Y**				
Subject charted:				ACTIVITY		PRESENT	PROPOSED	SAVING
BX 3456 cylinder head				OPERATION ○		5	8	(−3)
				TRANSPORT ⇨		22	13	9
ACTIVITY:				DELAY D		2	−	2
Machine complete				INSPECTION ☐		−	−	−
				STORAGE ▽		2	2	−
METHOD ~~PRESENT~~/PROPOSED				DISTANCE *(m)*		550	94.9	455.1
LOCATION: *Light and general machine shops*				TIME *(man-h)*		2.43	1.10	1.33
OPERATOR(S):		CLOCK No.		COST				
See Remarks column				LABOUR		*See text*		
CHARTED BY: *R.W.R.*		DATE: *27.6.50*		MATERIAL				
APPROVED BY: *J.L.*		DATE: *28.6.50*		TOTAL				

DESCRIPTION	QTY.	DIST-ANCE *(m)*	TIME *(min)*	SYMBOL					REMARKS
				○	⇨	D	☐	▽	
In store at casting bank	—	—	—						*Palletised*
By fork-lift truck to boring mill (1).									
Pallets deposited	20	9	2						*1 driver*
Lifted from pallet to mill	1	—	1						*Jib crane — Mill operator*
Loaded: BORED: unloaded	1	—	8						" " "
To radial drill (2)	1	3.7	1						*Roller table*
Lifted to drill	1	—	1						*Jib crane — R.D. operator*
Loaded: DRILLED: unloaded	1	—	8						" " "
To milling machine (3)	1	3.7	1						*Roller table*
Lifted to miller	1	—	1						*Jib crane — Mill operator*
Loaded: MILLED: unloaded	1	—	9						" " "
To radial drill (4)	1	3.7	1						*Roller table*
Loaded: DRILLED: unloaded	1	—	7						*R.D. operator*
To radial drill (5)	1	3.7	1						*Roller table*
Loaded: DRILLED: unloaded	1	—	7						*R.D. operator*
To radial drill (6)	1	3.7	1						*Roller table*
Loaded: DRILLED: unloaded	1	—	8						*R.D. operator*
To radial drill (7)	1	3.7	1						*Roller table*
Loaded: DRILLED: unloaded	1	—	7						*R.D. operator*
To radial drill (8)	1	3.7	1						*Roller table*
Loaded: DRILLED: unloaded	1	—	7						*R.D. operator*
Lifted off drill to pallet	1	—	1						*Jib crane*
By fork-lift truck to stores	20	60	3						*1 driver*
Stored									
TOTAL		94.9	77	8	13	—	—	2	

Figure 9.13 Material type flow process chart for machining a cylinder head. (*Reprinted with the permission of the International Labour Organization.*) [Reference 7a, p. 134.]

Network diagrams, or critical path analysis, are used to analyze many different situations. They are used to identify the critical path operations, which if delayed, delay the production of the finished product. Operations which are not on the critical path, if delayed, would not affect production results as long as the delay is less than the slack time. For example, in Fig. 9.14 a product takes 16 days to manufacture. The critical path is operations 2–4–6–9–10. Operations 1 to 5 take 7 days to produce until they are combined into operation 6. However, operations 2 to 4 take 9 days to manufacture, which leaves operations 1 to 5 an extra 2 days of slack time to produce products should a delay occur. The project manager would focus efforts on improving the productivity of operations along the critical path to reduce the time required to manufacture a product. Network analysis is more commonly used in planning new products and for products which require long lead times. This technique can be useful for analyzing a company's product development process for ways of reducing the time taken to develop new products.

Group technology utilizes similarity between parts and their operations to develop common processes. It allows the processes to be converted from a departmental organization to a cellular one by rearranging the plant layout. The benefits include

1. Reduced work-in-process inventory.

2. Reduced material handling costs.

3. Reduced total process cycle times.

4. Reduced setup times through commonality of fixtures and methods; also it is easier to justify capital expenditures on quick-change technologies resulting from higher usages.

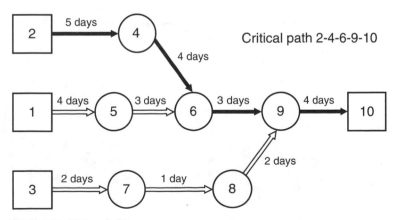

Figure 9.14 Network diagram.

5. Reduced tooling costs resulting from commonality.

The approach to take is to map out the processes for a set of relatively similar products and determine if a plant can be rearranged to allow for an improved material flow for the common processes. One can map the processes for commonality as shown in Fig. 9.15.

When reviewing the process map, one can look for commonality that can be used to develop a common manufacturing cell design. For certain products, the cell will be used for only a portion of the operation. In some cases one can work with one's own or the customer's engineering department to generate common specifications on products so that they can be processed in a similar manner. For example, using Fig. 9.15, one might try to see if part numbers 105 and 791 can be induction-hardened instead of through-hardened. This would allow for the cells to be located near the induction-hardening operations. One would also try to get one's own or the customer's engineering organization to standardize designs so that they can have common tool inserts, machine boring and bushing orientations, punches, etc. This will further reduce tooling costs. When planning new products, one should investigate standardization of components and seek to utilize grouped technology wherever possible because of the cost savings and economies of scale that can be derived from using such components.

In general the methodology used to improve process flow and reduce unnecessary downtime is to

1. *Eliminate* unnecessary operations or elements. This gets rid of wasted machine utilization and direct labor. This can be done by reviewing component tolerances specified vs. the application.

2. *Combine* operations and elements by utilizing the slack time inherent in the current manufacturing process, and grouping tech-

Process	Shape code: Part no:	1 105	2 210	1 345	1 423	1 619	2 827	1 635	1 791
Mill		1		1		1			1
Rough turn		2	1	2	1	2	1	1	2
CNC machine		3	2	3		3	2		3
Drill			3		2		3		4
Through harden		4							5
Induction harden			5	4	3	4	4	2	
Rough grind		5	6	5	4	5	5	3	6
Tumble		6	7	6	5		6		7
Wash			8	7			7	4	8
Pack		7	9	8	6	7	8	5	9
Other									

Figure 9.15 Process mapping for group technology.

nologies. Also, combine products that require similar movements and can utilize common tooling and fixtures.

3. *Rearrange* operations, elements, or process flow to reduce material handling and inventory. Improving ergonomics can also improve productivity.

4. *Simplify* processes and equipment changeovers by using either group technologies or quick-changeover strategies.

The Lean Production–Demand Flow System

The lean production–demand flow system was developed by Toyota Motor Company over a 20-year period. Eiji Toyoda, Taiicho Ohno, and Shigeo Shingo have made major contributions to the development of this system. After implementing this process successfully in its factories, Toyota demonstrated the system to its suppliers and trained them in its methodology. It took Toyota about 10 years to develop and implement it with its suppliers.[1,2]

Minimize manufacturing cost

The goal of the lean production system is to maximize profits by *minimizing manufacturing costs*. The reasoning is that the marketplace determines the product's selling price according to its demand. The only way that profits can be increased by plant personnel is by reducing manufacturing and administrative costs. This is shown in the following equation:

$$\text{Sales price} - \text{manufacturing costs} = \text{profits} \qquad 9.1$$

Eliminate waste

The way to reduce costs is to eliminate waste. There are nine common causes of waste in a manufacturing organization:

1. *Overproduction*   Manufacturing products before the orders are due for shipment or when no orders exist.

2. *Waiting*   When employees or machines are standing idle due to slack time, are waiting for machine repairs, material to be delivered, have no work to perform, etc.

3. *Transportation*   Material handling of any form.

4. *Processing method*   All processes can be improved, and sometimes unnecessary processes are performed on a product.

5. *Inventory*   This includes raw material, work-in-process, and finished goods inventory.

6. *Wasted motion*   Any operation in which person or machine moves limbs or equipment in a manner that is not required to perform the operation.

7. *Defective products*   Any product which cannot be used or must be repaired.

8. *Inspection to catch defects*   As opposed to inspecting to prevent defects. Also inspections which are performed unnecessarily due to the nature of the process. It should be noted that inspection, when properly applied, adds value because of the information that it communicates to production personnel to prevent scrap and customer return problems. It also avoids losing dissatisfied customers by implementing preventative quality inspection methods.

9. *Inefficient administrative procedures*   Many administrative methods can be streamlined to reduce paperwork requirements and improve the responsiveness to the plant's needs.

To summarize, the goal is to reduce cost. The method is to reduce or eliminate waste in areas such as inventory, downtime, slack time, defects, etc., and to reduce the time that it takes to process a part once an order arrives.

Manufactures only to customer demand

Lean production manufactures products *according to customer demand and minimizes finished goods inventory requirements*. It does, however, require a *relatively predictable order schedule*. This allows a manufacturer to minimize safety stock, in finished goods inventory, that is associated with erratic customer order schedules. In order to be able to respond rapidly to changes or surprises in customer orders, the system minimizes the total process cycle time, which is the time that it takes to manufacture a product once an order is received. This allows for one to have a lower safety stock inventory, hence less "waste" and lower costs. The total process cycle time is reduced by eliminating both work-in-process inventory and improving material handling and operations.

A flow process

The manufacturing process is set up according to a *flow process*. A flow process utilizes a batch size of one. Work-in-process inventory is minimized or eliminated, and material flows from one operation to the next with minimal material handling and wherever possible, without requiring the operator to physically move it. The transfers should be automated. The material should be delivered to the point of use. Each operation should be as close as possible to the next operation and allow operators to be in close proximity to each other. This allows for operators to be able to assist each other more easily. Operations such as clamping and unclamping do not add value; hence, they are automated wherever possible in a manner which will not slow down the process. The production rate is determined by the demand schedule.

A balanced line

Depending on customer orders, the line speed is either increased or decreased. However, corresponding with this change, workers are either added or removed from the line to allow for good balance and eliminate slack time. All operations are run at the same rate and sequenced so that excess material is not stored in between operations. Processes with excess capacity are sequenced to perform with the line speed so that in-process inventory is not developed. Eliminating work in process exposes quality problems readily so that they must be addressed immediately and permanently resolved. Otherwise, inventory banks can hide some quality problems, and they will periodically repeat themselves while manufacturing costs will be increased. In the event of a slower line speed, the operator who normally attends that process may operate additional machinery to fill up the slack time. Also, if the line speed is increased, temporary workers will be hired to meet production requirements. This way, when production demand decreases, only temporary workers are discharged and the permanent workers remain employed.

In certain situations a work-in-process inventory can be built up if it can eliminate a shift of operators or overtime pay. This might occur because of a significant difference in productivity at a bottleneck operation. This would be done only if it is most economical to perform production in that fashion, or if current manufacturing technology makes shutdowns expensive, such as a molding process which takes time to stabilize the mold's wall temperature and requires some raw material to be lost when purging the barrels during a changeover. It frequently would be prohibitive to invest capital in more sophisticated molding equipment which would allow for a more rapid changeover and waste less material.

Quick changeovers

Setup operations do not add value; hence, quick-changeover strategies are practiced. This also allows for additional flexibility to react to changes in the anticipated production schedule and to keep lot sizes small.

Well-trained personnel

Production operators know how to perform the job in front of them and the job behind them. This enables them to assist each other should a problem exist or if an operator is having difficulty keeping up with the production process. This also fosters teamwork. When the line speed is reduced and operators are eliminated from the line, it is first determined whether they can be used elsewhere; if not, they may perform nonroutine machine maintenance or repairs, or they may practice ways of improving the production process, reducing setup times, improving line balance, painting the plant, or receiving additional training. If all else fails, they can read the newspaper or a book. However, extensive efforts are made to assure that permanent employees are not laid off. This results in a loyal, committed work force. When the line speed is increased, temporary workers are assigned to assist the operations and the line is rebalanced. However, the line speed is gradually increased so that the temporary employees can be properly trained. Processes are designed to be easy by using locating fixtures, and preset cartridges when setting up the equipment. An operator who demonstrates slack time at an operation receives the production supervisor's attention and is given an improvement priority in order to eliminate that form of labor waste.

Highly automated system

Lean production systems tend to emphasize automation. It is generally less expensive to automate for the life of a product than to have a human operator, who receives hourly wages along with medical and retirement benefits, run machines. Generally, one operator will operate several machines. Further coverage is possible when the machinery is highly automated and has problem detection and correction capabilities.

Inspecting to prevent defects

Inspection is performed for the purpose of preventing defects as opposed to detecting them. When a defect or potential defect is discovered, the operator and management work together to correct the problem and assure that the cause of the defect is eliminated so that the preventative corrective action taken will assure that the defect will never occur again. When a defect is discovered, a system exists to visually display a problem to other personnel and management. An example of one method is a light board with each machine listed that is easily visible to all people in the plant. It would flash a light next to a machine name or number should a problem exist.

Independent verification of quality

The system is designed so that an operator inspects his or her own work, and the work performed from the previous operations. For example, after a stamping operation, the next operation may have a fixture to load the part onto. This fixture will be able to detect any missing holes caused by broken punches so that later operations which need those holes will not be the source for detecting those defects. Such an approach allows for 100 percent verification of product quality at the source. Other methods encourage the use of in-line automated gaging and testing equipment immediately after the point of manufacturing. However, since the goal is to minimize long-term manufacturing costs, a determination is needed to see if process controls can be used more economically than automatic gaging and testing. This is needed because a defect that goes by undetected early in the process can be repetitive and cause many units to be either scrapped or reworked and the customer order can be delayed.

The Kanban inventory control method

Inventory is controlled on the floor with a Kanban card. This card communicates the part number and name, how much product needs to be manufactured by a specified time, where it should be made, and where the products should be sent. The production control personnel assign a Kanban card to the operator, and they only manufacture the amount specified during the allotted time interval. Otherwise, overproduction waste would be generated, causing a material storage problem. The Kanban system has the assembly-line personnel communicate to the component manufacturing area that it is time to manufacture more components once the reorder point or safety stock cushion has been reached in the assembly-line component inventory (a safety cushion may be needed if production schedules fluctuate erratically). Kanban systems are best to use when there is a repetitive production process or the manufacturing operations performed are similar. Kanban serves as a method of improving the material control while simultaneously reducing administrative overhead relating to material management.

Transforming a plant to a lean production operation

Once the management has decided that they want to implement a lean production manufacturing system, there should be several phases of emphasis:

1. The first phase is to *address wasted motion*. By improving assembly-line balance and assuring that operators' slack time is minimized

and cost savings can be achieved without investing capital. In essence these savings are free (excluding management time). Labor personnel are instructed to stand erect and not look artificially busy during the slack time of an operation, so that their supervisor can notice it. The supervisor must then make it a priority to see how work responsibility can be reassigned so that labor can be used more efficiently.

2. After completing phase 1, both the management and employees should *improve material flow.* This can be done by reorganizing the plant to encompass a flow process with a batch size of one. It includes grouping similar processes and operations. Additionally material handling should be arranged so that it is at the point of use. The line should generally be synchronized and balanced to manufacture at the rate required to meet the production order at the specified time. This production rate determines the daily cycle time known as *tact time* and is determined by the following equation:

$$\text{Tact time} = \frac{\text{demand per shift}}{\text{one shift's time}} \qquad 9.2$$

If the order exceeds production capacity, the production rate should be synchronized according to the rate of the bottleneck (the slowest operation). Time motion studies should be performed in advance to balance the line for different order requirement scenarios. The process of balancing the line for several different line speeds assumes repetitive orders or similar processes and operations for high-volume production products with a reasonably long life cycle; otherwise the administrative efforts could not be justified.

If production capacity is limited, efforts should focus on improving productivity at the bottleneck. This includes utilizing obsolete and less efficient machines to improve the capacity. The value added of the whole line, which includes machine productivity, is limited by that one bottleneck. Hence, a slight cost penalty at the bottleneck operation can be used to improve the productivity of the assembly line. The cost penalty is usually offset by the reduction of the allocated plant and machine overhead cost of the product on a per unit basis. Sometimes it will be most economical to build a work-in-process inventory before the bottleneck operation by running operations before the bottleneck, on one or two shifts and running the bottleneck operation around the clock and during breaks.

3. *Automate the manufacturing process.* Material should flow from one process to another without requiring the operator or assembly-line worker to transport the material or perform assembly work.

There are several levels of automation: (*a*) Tasks that are performed by direct labor personnel are replaced by a machine. (*b*) The machine has the ability to detect defects and potential problems with the manufacturing process so that production personnel can address them. (*c*) The last phase of automation is one in which machines cannot only detect problems, but can also correct them without human intervention. This phase can require a significant amount of capital investment.

Inventory requirements should be reduced *only after improvements have been implemented* and can demonstrate that the reduced inventory level is sufficient to assure that production orders will not be jeopardized. The three phases of implementation are outlined. However, every day, all personnel are constantly trying to discover ways to further eliminate waste, improve material flow, and improve automation. The goal is to constantly improve so that work-in-process, purchased material, and finished goods inventory are reduced.

Minimizing total process cycle time

There are several terms that one needs to understand when discussing a demand flow system. They are total process cycle time, lead time, and cycle time. *Total process cycle time* refers to the time it takes to process material in a plant once purchased material is set on the line. Included in this number are the work-in-process inventory that is sitting on an assembly line but is not being processed and the number of operations plus the slack time at each operation. It differs from lead times in that *lead times* also include the amount of time it takes to procure components and raw materials from other companies. *Cycle time* refers to the amount of time that it takes to perform a given operation. In Fig. 9.1 if at operation 70 (final test) a unit takes 320 s to be processed, but every 20 s a new unit has completed testing, then the cycle time for that station would be 20 s, and the process cycle time for operation 70 is 320 s.

In order to meet customer orders promptly, *total cycle time analysis* is used. The goal is to reduce the *total process cycle time,* which is the time it takes to manufacture one product in the plant from the beginning of the process through its completion after the raw material has arrived. An extension of this idea is to reduce the time it takes to manufacture the product starting from the supplier's *lead time.* However, for this discussion, we will focus on the process inside a manufacturing plant.

Minimizing inventory

A driving force behind a demand flow system is to minimize inventory because of its detrimental effect on manufacturing efficiency and cash flow. Inventory hurts a production operation for the following reasons:

1. It uses up cash for operations which could be invested elsewhere in the company. The cash must then come from bank loans, resulting in interest charges.

2. It incurs additional material handling expenses to move material to and from storage areas.

3. It requires additional administrative overhead to manage the inventory.

4. It requires additional plant storage space, which requires additional expenditures for land, brick, and mortar.

5. It requires the purchase of additional material handling bins and shelves.

6. It raises utility expenses for lighting and heating as a result of having additional plant space.

7. It increases total process cycle time because of unnecessary work-in-process inventory.

8. Quality problems become more expensive because more product is exposed until quality problems are encountered. If a company has a well-developed quality assurance system, this effect is not usually as significant.

9. Inventory buffers cover up inept management in the areas of preventative quality assurance, preventative maintenance, and long setup times because the buffers do not readily expose problems in those areas.

10. Engineering changes either take longer to be implemented because existing inventory must be used up, or else they are more expensive because more material must be scrapped to implement a change.

Inventory does, however, serve the purpose of assuring that customer deliveries are made if unpredictable schedules are likely, and protects lines from shutdowns should production problems arise. Inventory should only be reduced when it reduces the total cost of the product. This includes shipping, storage costs, downtime, and lost sales. Improvements that will reduce these costs should be constantly sought. This approach will assure that inventory is reduced cost-effectively.

Accounting—applying fixed overhead

The lean production accounting system is activity-based (this is explained in Chap. 11). It applies fixed overhead based on plant space and the total process cycle time so that production operations reduce their allocated overhead costs if they become more efficient and utilize less floor space. The accounting system makes adjustments for differences in the cost of the machinery as is appropriate. Material costs per product are generally treated as a percentage of machine overhead. Direct labor is treated as a fixed overhead cost and is included in the machine overhead cost. All scrap and rework is handled as a variance; therefore, the system is designed to reinforce goals to achieve zero defects and 100 percent first-time through capability. Because overhead is applied on the basis of total process cycle time and plant floor-space utilization, this system also rewards flow processes for reductions in the time that it takes to manufacture a product and other improvements that use up less floor space. This reduces the overhead cost of those products on a unit basis, and hence increases the profit margins of those product lines.

Prioritizing improvements

The prioritization for improvements is illustrated by the analysis in Fig. 9.1. According to this figure, the total process cycle time from operation 20A through operation 70 is 890 s. Operation 10 and the subsequent work in process until operation 20E takes 60 s and is less than for operations 20A through 20E, which take 320 s. Therefore, any operation in that loop which can be eliminated or combined can reduce the total process cycle time. If work-in-process inventory on the line can be reduced or if operations 20D or 70 can be run faster, the total process cycle time would be reduced by an even greater amount. Suppose that improvements were implemented on operations 20E through 70 and reduced the number of work-in-process units from 15 units to 8. The reduction in the total process cycle time would be 140 s, a 16 percent improvement. If the final test operation 70 could have one less station and be processed in 300 s instead of 320, it would take 20 s out of the total cycle. If, however, the cycle time could be reduced to 18 s, the primary assembly line could be speeded up by 2 s and the total cycle time would be reduced by 50 s (25 work-in-process units times 2 s), resulting in a 5.6 percent gain in production efficiency and reducing the time to process the product to 840 s.

An atmosphere of problem solving

When problems arise in production, operators are not blamed for shoddy workmanship, nor accused of being lazy when production goals are not achieved; instead, the management works with the workers to understand the root cause of the problem so that it can be permanently corrected. This develops an atmosphere of cooperation and results in improved productivity and quality. Causes for the manufacture of defects, such as not having a locating fixture, operator fatigue, and excessive bending, are identified and eliminated.

Gradually phasing in a lean production system

One note of caution is for a company to gradually phase in a lean production–demand flow system and not do it by brute force. If systems and processes are not in a position to support these changes, a lot of undesirable side effects will occur. When a just-in-time delivery is used with suppliers who do not have good production scheduling systems, manufacturing process shutdowns and premium freight shipping charges are inevitable. A second caution is if the supplier's quality control programs are not well developed, the products shipped may not be acceptable. Under such a scenario, the plant will then be forced to make a decision to manufacture a substandard product or shut down the manufacturing process (or assembly line) and not fill customer orders. This illustrates the need to gradually phase in these programs and develop methods to assure that the transition is an effective one.

Hydrogen embrittlement

Reducing manufacturing lead times can lead to hydrogen embrittlement problems. Hydrogen embrittlement is a tensile failure-related material problem, associated with steel products that are first heat-treated and then treated with acid (to clean or prepare for plating or other coatings). If the part is stressed in tension shortly after this process, hydrogen molecules, which are trapped inside the grain boundaries of the steel, migrate out along these boundaries and the part becomes brittle. This can be minimized by adding a bake cycle after the acid treatment or, in the case of some porous coatings, storing the parts in inventory for 2 days before use.

Reviewing lean production—summary

The philosophy is to minimize manufacturing costs by reducing non–value-added operations such as setups, equipment and tool maintenance, material handling, inspection, line imbalance, and inventory storage. Many people misinterpret this to mean that they should cut the staff associated with performing these tasks. However, the real interpretation is to perform only those tasks that improve manufacturing productivity by increasing uptime (in the long run) and improving product quality through a preventative approach. The quality inspection costs can add value by reducing customer returns, warranty costs, and internal scrap. Inspection should be independently performed as close to the point of use as possible. Material-handling costs can be reduced by improving plant logistics, using manufacturing cells rather than batch operations, shortening manufacturing lines, and reducing work-in-process and safety stock inventory requirements. Setup times are reduced by applying quick-changeover principles. The maintenance staff improves uptime if it is effectively managed in a preventative manner. Lean production is flexible enough to accommodate any method, even if it was not discussed, as long as the goal to reduce manufacturing costs is achieved.

Production Capacity Constraint Analysis

Production capacity constraint analysis has many similarities with the lean production approach. The primary difference is that it focuses on improving capacity at bottlenecks, known as *capacity constraints*, and builds inventory buffers before only a few critical bottlenecks. It is less concerned with reducing total process cycle time. Also, less emphasis is placed on perfectly balancing a line because it is deemed more prudent to assign extra resources to the bottleneck to assure that it is productive. It is concerned with maximizing productivity by addressing issues at the capacity-limiting operation (also known as the capacity constraint or bottleneck). The plant focuses its resources on improving production capacity at those bottlenecks by speeding up machines, buying additional capacity, etc.

In practice, a bottleneck may change from day to day. On paper, one bottleneck may be identified; however, an incident such as a machine breakdown or a supply shortage in another part of the process can change it. Therefore, the work-in-process inventory buffers must be sufficiently large to assure that the theoretical bottleneck is protected so that this bottleneck can continually run without material shortages. Also, there must be excess capacity behind a few other critical bottleneck operations so that if a production problem exists, the capacity to rebuild the inventory buffer can be restored. If an operation is delayed or a unit is scrapped before the bottleneck and there is no extra capacity, the productivity for that sequential process is lost. Therefore, a plant has to assure that there is not a material shortage or quality problem before a bottleneck. To maximize the productivity of the line, a bottleneck can be run three shifts and during breaks 7 days a week and be given top priority for preventative maintenance and repair work. Excessive personnel resources should be assigned to operate and maintain this machine. Sometimes the capacity constraint is run on a 12-hour, 4-crew shift to reduce overtime pay. For the process that was shown in Fig. 9.1, one would focus management efforts on maximizing production output on OP 20D, which has a 30-s cycle time. The secondary bottleneck is operation 70, which has a 20-s cycle time and limits the line's productivity during its two shifts of operation.

The capacity constraint approach utilizes the Pareto principle to prioritize improvement efforts. The bottleneck operations will have inventory buffers prior to those operations, but no buffers other than at those vital few operations. The buffer serves to assure that a disruption will not affect the productivity of that manufacturing line if previous operations are down. Operations prior to a bottleneck are run in synchronized manner. If a disruption in production occurs such as machine breakage, the whole line is affected; however, the buffer serves to protect the productivity of the capacity constraint operation. Management would focus its resources on improving the availability or reliability of the line supplying the capacity constraint so that the inventory buffer at the bottleneck operation can be reduced as improvements are implemented. This approach reduces the overall work-in-process inventory by keeping it available at only the vital few locations. Of course, management would also focus its resources on improving the production capacity of those few bottlenecks identified.

Many long assembly lines are set up so that the testing stations earlier in the line have excess capacity and the bottleneck is at the end of the line. The line is then balanced according to the final test cycle time to minimize assembly labor costs. Frequently it is done this way, because the final test equipment is the most expensive capital investment so the number of testing units needed is minimized.

The logic behind capacity constraint management is that the sequential processes' overhead, which includes capital investment, plant, facilities, and direct labor, should be applied on a per unit basis. If a unit is lost from production (due to quality problems, equipment downtime, or material shortages) before or at a bottleneck, the allocation of those overhead costs is increased on the other units produced. Product expenses can therefore be reduced by effectively improving maintenance, reducing tool change and setup times, improving material handling, and increasing productivity at bottleneck operations. One also wants to assure that there is a partial bank of parts that have all possible detectable defects eliminated entering a bottleneck so that all products produced at this capacity constraint are approved. This assures that only usable products are produced, hence maximizing the productivity of the assembly line. In practice, one may frequently find that insufficient sales orders become a bottleneck. However, by using this strategy and reducing changeover times, it can still be beneficial where a nondedicated line is used so that one does not have to expand plant space or open up a new plant if factory orders are increased. This approach can also reduce the work-in-process inventory if it is properly implemented.

When planning new products, bottlenecks should be identified with current processes to prioritize improvement opportunities. However, the concept of improving productivity at bottlenecks should be a continuous one. One should continuously try to improve cycle times at production-limiting operations even after an improvement was recently implemented at a former bottleneck.

Applying constraint theory to product development

Outside of the manufacturing arena, this approach can be applied to reduce product development times by utilizing similar principles in conjunction with critical path analysis and process mapping techniques. Bottlenecks for tasks that are on the critical path should always be reviewed to see if either procedures can be improved or resources can be allocated in a cost-effective manner to speed up the process. Frequently, one must identify internal barriers and those assumptions relating to those barriers to achieve improvements. For example, if it takes a long time to produce component drawings with the current system, one should look at why and determine if more resources are needed. A mental barrier such as "management has both an employment and capital budget freeze on, we can't hire additional drafters or drafting services" should be reconsidered if it is prudent and cost-effective from a total cost standpoint to do so. However, there are frequently many methods that should be first considered to reduce drafting time that do not require the hiring of additional personnel such as assuring that the specifications are clearly defined and correct when submitted, specifying only those characteristics that are important so that fewer characteristics are identified, delegating some design work to the supply base, etc. Constraint theory can even be utilized in a broader scope to overcome constraints of systems, mental barriers, etc.

Summing Up the Decision-Making Process

Lean production and capacity constraint analysis are similar in many aspects: they both make valid points and can be used in conjunction with each other to minimize manufacturing costs. The decision-making process for determining capital investments can be different, and one needs to evaluate which approach will offer the greatest benefit for a specific situation. A comparison of the two methods is shown in Fig. 9.16.

When determining process improvements to reduce manufacturing costs, one must consider many of the following issues:

1. Machine time and tooling cost per unit.
2. Variable labor cost per unit.

Manufacturing issue	Manufacturing Theory	
	Capacity constraint	Lean production
1. Total productive maintenance (TPM)	TPM is recommended. Also assign top maintenance personnel to bottlenecks or capacity constraints.	TPM is recommended. Train operators to perform routine tasks where possible.
2. Work-in-process (WIP) inventory	Assure that bottlenecks have a sufficient WIP buffer before it. Otherwise eliminate WIP in nonbottleneck operations. Continuously improve reliability, suppliers, and quality control, etc., to reduce WIP inventory requirements at bottlenecks.	Minimize or eliminate WIP at all operations. Also minimize receiving and finished goods inventory. Design a flow process with a lot size of one which minimizes material handling and utilizes automated material and point-of-use material storage.
3. Line speed	Focus on maximizing production rates at all bottlenecks. Synchronize other operations with the rate at the localized bottleneck.	Synchronize operations to be in sequence with the customer order schedule or the operation, with the longest cycle time.
4. Quick changeovers	Recommended to utilize quick changeovers at all capacity constraints. Quick changeovers can improve productivity at bottleneck operations.	Recommended—it reduces non–value-added machine time.
5. Prioritizing capital investment	Allocate resources to improve productivity at bottlenecks and problem areas in the synchronous line.	Allocate resources to reduce total process cycle time and floor space utilized. If demand exceeds capacity, invest to improve capacity at bottleneck operation.
6. Line balancing	Balance the line, but assign additional resources to assure that the productivity at the bottleneck will not be disturbed.	Sequence line speed based on order requirements. Simultaneously reduce both the line speed and the number of operators at that operation when production requirements are lower.
7. Quality control	Design quality into the process and assure that only good quality components will be assembled at the capacity constraint operation.	Design quality into the process. Assure that all controls are either at the point of manufacture or at the next operation.

Figure 9.16 Comparison between capacity constraint and lean production theories.

3. Amount of plant floor space utilized

4. Whether the line is dedicated.

5. Whether the lighting and production line for part of the sequential process can be turned off while another section can be run.

6. Whether the sequential production processes are reliable enough to assure that they will run without significant downtime.

7. The holding cost of inventory. This varies and is usually around 20 percent cost of the inventory (which includes value-added costs for work-in-process material).

8. The line speed.

9. The total process cycle time.

10. The number of setups and tool changes performed annually.

To determine capital investment priorities for quick-change tooling investments, the plant must evaluate the machine, tooling, and variable labor costs per unit as well as the number of setups or tool changes that are typically performed. If the machine and variable labor rates are high or if many of the setups and tool changeovers occur when the operators are not on break, it usually is cost-effective to invest to have quick-changeover modifications. If a line can be run on two shifts while the equipment and plant lighting can be turned off on the third shift except for a portion of the line, and the in-process quality controls are very good, it would make sense to bank work-in-process inventory before the capacity constraint and operate the bottleneck for an extra shift. This would reduce the variable labor cost per unit for the previous operations while incurring an additional holding cost for the product that is retained before the bottleneck. In very few situations would it make sense *not* to do this. If, however, the variable labor costs for those previous operations or lighting costs are negligible, if customer shipments are made every few hours, or if there is no place to store the extra inventory, it may make more sense to run the whole assembly operation in a synchronized manner for the three shifts.

When plant management must determine if it has to appropriate capital investment for reducing the total process cycle time or to improve capacity at critical bottlenecks, several factors must be taken into account. Management should consider the amount of floor space, inventory, and production capacity that will be affected by both projects and try to assign costs to each.

Sometimes it is difficult to slow down a sequential processing line and rebalance it by having fewer operators perform more tasks for logistic reasons. Operators will be spending a lot of wasted motion walking between workstations performing various tasks. This non–value-added "operator travel" will result in an inefficiency in the variable labor cost per unit. Depending on the relative weights of the variable labor cost penalty vs. the inventory holding costs as it applies to the plant, at that instant in time, it may not be wise to slow down the line. If the plant has excess floor space which will not be used for another year, it may not be cost-effective to sequence the line until the floor space in the plant is needed for other equipment. The only real cost in such a scenario is the cost of capital for the material that is stored, provided that good indicators exist for machine downtime and in-process quality. When customer orders increase or new products are developed for the factory, the plant management must be aware that options, such as line sequencing to reduce inventory, reducing plant floor space by reducing the length of an assembly line, or increasing capacity at bottlenecks, are available before considering plant expansions or opening up a new facility.

Consideration should be given to determine the effectiveness of the in-process quality control program. If the current approach is to catch defects at the end of the process and a more desirable preventative method has not been implemented, it would be unwise to sequence lines until effective process control training and analysis has been instituted because of the impacts on the production process. The same considerations should be given to assessing the effectiveness of the preventative maintenance program by reviewing the amount of downtime currently experienced. Until a preventative maintenance system has demonstrated success by reducing machine downtime to an acceptable level, one should sequence the line speeds to a few key bottlenecks and store some safety stock. As with any radical change to operating philosophies, one must assure that the plant has prepared for such a change and has a chance to gradually phase it in.

Manufacturers should try to project possible opportunities to increase sales of products that can be manufactured from that line. Sometimes this can be done on dedicated lines by some modifications to existing equipment. Automobile manufacturers such as Chrysler did this by adapting a V-6 engine with many common components from their V-8 lines and running the products on the same assembly line without requiring changeovers. Honda designed flexibility into their new car assembly plant in Marysville, Ohio, to allow for several potential car lines in the future. The cost was higher initially, but if it is spread over several car lines, the long-term cost is anticipated to be lower.

Plant management should train operators to seek ways to improve the process's capacity, reduce both labor and inventory, and revise the layout of the operators' work area for better labor efficiency, ergonomics, and maintenance access. When a new process or a revision to an existing one is being considered, operators' input should be solicited.

The resulting improvements will be well worth the time spent. It will also increase their commitment to their motivation when the process is implemented.

Design for Manufacturing—Concurrent Engineering

Concurrent Engineering, which is also call simultaneous engineering, is encouraging early manufacturing involvement and input into a product's design before drawings are finalized. Proper product team management will emphasize such coordination and consider it as an integral part of the design process. The importance of practicing concurrent engineering is that it prevents late manufacturing-related design changes, thereby reducing both engineering efforts and tooling revision costs. Manufacturing productivity is also greatly improved and product costs reduced.

There are several basic principles that are used when designing a product to make it easy to manufacture:

1. *Minimize the number of parts.* This reduces assembly operations, material handing, purchased material inventory storage requirements, and the number of parts in the system. Whenever possible, *commonize components between product lines.*

2. Design the part so that it can be easily assembled in a *layered fashion*, allowing for easy and ergonomical access to the sub-assembled components by stacking the assembly operations (preferably face up). This makes it easier to assemble and avoids access and interference problems.

3. Make the part *easy to automate in assembly and easy to handle and pick up.* Oily parts are slippery and, hence, are hard to position. Fragile parts break easily. Sharp edges can cause injuries. Sticky backing paper and glues can cause assembly difficulties when not properly addressed in the part and process design. Parts that tangle up with each other cause operator and automation handling problems. All of there conditions should, therefore, be avoided by addressing them at the outset of a new product design.

4. *Mating parts should be easy to insert and align.* Locating pins and holes with chamfers can be used to align mating parts. Manufacturing process variation must be considered to assure that mating parts will fit to required tolerances. Consider using preassembled subassemblies, eg., part with seals molded in, locating pins cast or molded in etc.

5. *Minimize the number of fastening operations* by using parts that snap fit together. Fastening operations require additional tooling, additional parts, and add to the total process cycle time.

6. Parts should be *symmetrically designed* to aid in orientation for automation and prevent misbuilds. If symmetry is not possible, exaggerate the asymmetric condition to avoid a misbuilds possibility and eliminate operator confusion.

7. Whenever possible, design the part so that is *does not require adjustments*. The components and systems should be reviewed to determine if the variation of a characteristic affects a critical finished product characteristic. If it does, this situation must be eliminated. Many quality problems result from improper adjustments of finished items.

Design engineers should also meet with production operators and solicit their ideas to learn about how existing designs can be improved so that the new product will be easier to manufacture.

References

1. Shingo, Shigeo, *A Study of the Toyota Production System from an Industrial Engineering Viewpoint,* Productivity Press, Cambridge, Massachusetts, 1989.
2. Womack, James P., Jones, Daniel T., and Roos Daniel, *The Machine that Changed the World,* Rawson Associates, New York, 1981.
3. International Labour Office (ILO), *Introduction to Work Study,* 2nd ed., ILO Publications, Geneva, Switzerland, 1978.
4. International Labour Office (ILO), *Introduction to Work Study,* 3rd ed., ILO Publications, Geneva, Switzerland, 1978.

Bibliography

Close, Guy C., Jr., *Principles for Motion Improvement, Work Improvement,* Wiley, New York, 1960.
Corlett, E. Nigel, "Design of Handtools, Machines, and Workplaces," in Salvendy, Gavriel (ed.), *Handbook of Industrial Engineering,* Purdue University, Wiley, 1982, pp. 6.9.1–6.9.12.
Costanza, John R., *The Quantum Leap in Speed to Market,* JIT Institute of Technology, Denver, Colorado, 1990.
Goldratt, Eliyahu M., and Cox, Jeff, *The Goal,* North River Press, Croton on Hudson, New York, 1986.
Goldratt, Eliyahu M., and Fox, Robert E., *The Race,* North River Press, Croton on Hudson, New York, 1986.
Ham, Inyong, "Group Technology," in Salvendy, Gavriel (ed.), *Handbook of Industrial Engineering,* Purdue University, Wiley, 1982, pp. 7.8.1–7.8.19.
Kadota, Takeji, "Charting Techniques," in Salvendy, Gavriel (ed.), *Handbook of Industrial Engineering,* Purdue University, Wiley, 1982, pp. 3.3.1–3.3.31.
Kobe, Gerry, "DFMA: Design for Manufacture and Assembly," *Automotive Industries,* March 1990.
Moodie, Colin L., "Assembly Line Balancing," in Salvendy, Gavriel (ed.), *Handbook of Industrial Engineering,* Purdue University, Wiley, 1982, pp. 3.4.1–3.4.15.
Nakajima, Seiichi, Yamashina, Hatime, Kumagai, Chitoku, and Toyota, Toshio, "Maintenance Management and Control," in Salvendy, Gavriel (ed.), *Handbook of Industrial Engineering,* Purdue University, Wiley, 1992, Chap. 73, pp. 1927–1985.
Shingo, Shigeo, *A Revolution in Manufacturing: The SMED System,* Productivity Press, Cambridge, Massachusetts, 1986.
Van Zile, Donald K., and Otis, I., "Measuring and Controlling Performance," in Salvendy, Gavriel (ed.), *Handbook of Industrial Engineering,* Purdue University, Wiley, 1992, Chap. 60, pp. 1575–1584.

10

Tooling Issues, Process Verification, and Continuous Improvement Planning

Equipment and tool purchases are frequently purchased from outside companies. However, it is recommended to have the internal capability to modify equipment after it is purchased in order to obtain a competitive advantage.

Purchase Agreement Considerations

When purchasing equipment, a company should write a contract with clauses to assure that the equipment will reliably perform its intended function by the date specified in the contract. More specifically the contract should have provisions including the following stating that the equipment supplier will:

1. Pay *cost penalties* for unsatisfactory performance if the machine does not meet the specified quality, quantity, reliability, or productivity requirements by the contract's completion date. The purchaser should have the right to refuse the equipment if the contract requirements have not been met. The amount of the penalty will vary depending on the criticality of the process in terms of ability to substitute for it and the size of the machine tool supplier.

2. Have systems for maintaining and *updating engineering drawings* relating to their machines. Each drawing should be reviewed, checked, and signed off by the equipment vendor's engineering organization. The customers will receive copies of these drawings and changes and review initial prints for concept approval.

3. Verify the machinery's performance with a continuous reliability runoff for all equipment. This means that the machine will operate continuously for a specified time frame at the maximum rated loads and speeds around all axes without a failure, breakdown, or disturbance in the production environment. This should be performed at the tool supplier's facility before shipping it to the customer.

4. Meet the specified *reliability requirement*. Reliability or availability is defined as follows:

$$A = \frac{MTBF}{MTBF + MTTR}$$

where A = machine's availability or percentage uptime
     MTBF = mean (or average) time between failures
     MTTR = mean (or average) time to repair

This information can be determined by reviewing data with similar components on existing production systems and performing a failure mode and effects analysis (FMEA).

It is important for a customer to share information regarding all equipment and related component failures with equipment manufacturers so that they can redesign the components and improve the reliability of the equipment. Therefore, a system to enhance this communication should be developed.

5. Perform *statistical process capability studies* (i.e., C_p, C_{pk}) to a specified quality standard on those characteristics that were mutually agreed upon in writing.

6. Provide *training* to the plant personnel on how to use and maintain the equipment.

7. Provide documentation which explains *service and maintenance procedures,* as well as preventative maintenance schedules.

8. Provide a *list of spare parts* and where to order them.

9. Provide *ongoing service support* as requested.

10. Design the equipment to be *easy to access* and repair for a maintenance technician.

11. Design the equipment to be good *ergonomically* for the operators.

12. The customer will review all tooling concepts before approving the quotation.

13. The runoffs are required to be performed at the equipment supplier and then verified at the customer's facility to verify that all quality, productivity, and reliability goals have been achieved.

Contracts for molds and dies should include a specific C_p, and C_{pk} requirement for a mold or die. It should also be targeted away from nominal in a direction which will allow for an improved C_{pk} as the tool initially wears.

When purchasing gaging it is recommended to place a gage repeatability and to reproducibility requirement on the purchase order.

Machine Design Considerations

The machinery should be designed with flexibility to process future models and other applications. Additionally, the tooling should be designed by using standard components wherever possible because this will reduce the tooling cribs inventory and also time-tested, reliable components will be used in the machinery. Quick-changeover considerations should be incorporated into the equipment's design.

Early involvement before designing equipment

Before purchasing a new line of equipment, it is recommended to solicit the operator's input in the design so that improvements can be made on existing processes in areas such as material handling, ergonomics, layout, quality, and efficiency. Once the tooling has been purchased, the plant personnel should be asked to critique the equipment to identify modifications for subsequent machine improvements. It is important to review the personnel's knowledge of maintenance, repair, and operating procedures to assure that they will perform those tasks correctly and efficiently.

Packaging design

The packaging of both purchased and finished goods should be designed to protect the product in the most economical manner possible. It should be tested to simulate possible field conditions. Tests on shaker tables and impact equipment can simulate transportation, loading, and handling on railcars, trucks, airfreight, etc. It should also protect the product from moisture and temperature extremes (as appropriate) for that product and its storage/handling environment.

Process Verification

A company must have good verification procedures to determine the effectiveness of a new manufacturing process. The process verification checklist, shown in Fig. 10.1, is a good guideline for determining how successful the planning and implementation of a new product pro-

___ Procedures—preventative maintenance (manufacturing)

___ Process flowchart (manufacturing engineering)

___ Process sheets—machine running conditions (manufacturing engineering)

___ Procedures—setup (manufacturing engineering)

___ Operation description sheets (manufacturing engineering, engineering)

___ Standard operating procedure assembly process (manufacturing)

___ Standard operating procedures—machinery (manufacturing)

___ Standards—finished product performance testing (engineering)

___ Assembly process and machine operator training (manufacturing)

___ Manufacturing control plan (quality)

___ Inspection instructions—receiving (quality)

___ Inspection instructions in-process (quality)

___ Instructions—final inspection/test (quality)

___ Instructions—setup approval (quality)

___ Instructions—special gage usage and calibration procedures (quality)

___ Protective packaging testing (manufacturing engineering)

___ Machine durability runoff (manufacturing engineering)

___ Operator workstation completed (manufacturing)

___ Time motion studies and cycle time/productivity analysis (manufacturing)

___ Establish activity-based cost standard (accounting)

___ Gage repeatability and reproducibility studies (quality)

___ Process capability studies of significant characteristics (quality)

___ Initial sample 100% verification of all dimensional, lab tests, and performance characteristics (quality)

___ Consumer market test confirmation of pilots (marketing)

___ Supplier capability studies—significant characteristics (quality)

___ Supplier initial sample 100% inspection, lab and test results (quality)

___ Product performance testing verification of pilots (engineering/quality)

___ Durability/reliability tests (engineering)

Figure 10.1   The process verification checklist.

gram has been before the commencement of higher volume production. It assures that machine durability runoffs, process capability studies, motion studies, cycle time trials, cost standards establishment, instruction sheet and other procedural documentation, durability testing, and customer acceptance research have been performed with the production manufacturing process.

Bearing Part Number:				
Process	Control item	Standard	Measuring device	Inspection method
Raceway grind	Raceway diameter	Process standard	Dial gage .001mm	Check inspection
	Raceway o/r	"	Talyrond & O/R gage	"
	Parallelism	"	Offset gage	"
	Offset	"	Offset gage	"
	Race radius size	"	Form Talysurf and "R" gage	"
	Visual	No unusual shoe mark, nick, etc.	Visual	"
Bore grind	Bore size	Process standard	Air micrometer	100% check
	Bore o/r	"	"	Check inspection
	Bore taper	"	"	"
	Visual	No unusual mark, nick, etc.	Visual	"
Superfinish	Waviness	Process standard	Waviness meter	Check inspection
	Visual	No shoe mark, not cleaned up	Visual	"
Ultrasonic wash				
Steel ball Incoming Inspection		Purchase specification		Ball quality information sheet — check
Matching	Radial clearance	Process standard	Radial clearance gage	Check inspection
Cage Incoming Inspection	Component drawing	Component drawing		Inspection in Japan

Figure 10.2 Manufacturing flowchart and control plan. (*Courtesy of NSK Corporation of America, Ann Arbor, Mich.*)

Manufacturing Planning and Analysis

Control plans can be done in a variety of manners. Figure 10.2 shows a *process control plan* that is used by NSK Corporation, which is the world's largest manufacturer of ball bearings. The sheet includes a flow diagram, process description, characteristic to be monitored, inspection standard to refer to, measurement device, and verification method.

DIRKSEN FRONT-END SPREAD SHEET SET-UP OPER. M.P.   INSPECTOR R.G.B. AND J.M.   DATE: 6-29-92

CUSTOMER XYZ CORP.   PART NO. 1000   REV. G   SAMPLE 2   PAGE 1 OF 2 DEPT./MC.# #14

PROC. I.D.	DIMENSION	GAGE	SET-UP OPERATOR FINDINGS HI/LO	LAYOUT INSPECTOR FINDINGS HI/LO	GRR	CAPABILITY 1ST	CAPABILITY 2ND	COMMENTS
1	.885/.865 LENGTH	0-1" MICROMETER	.8840 - .8830	.8840 - .8805				
2	20° ANG. 15°	OPTICAL COMPARATOR	OK - OK	17° - 16°				
3	1/2-14 N.P.T.F.	1/2-14 N.P.T.F. THD. RING GAGE	OK - OK	OK TO GAGE				
4	.02 R MAX.	OPTICAL COMPARATOR	OK - OK	.0120 - .0110				
5	.685/.675 DIA.	0-1" MICROMETER	.6825 - .6823	.6821 - .6818				
6	50° ANG. 40°	OPTICAL COMPARATOR	OK - OK	49°				
7	.710/.690 LENGTH	OPTICAL COMPARATOR	.7057 - .7057	.7032 - .7022				
8	.297/.287 LENGTH	OPTICAL COMPARATOR	.2930 - .2923	.2920 - .2918				
9	.134/.132 LENGTH	OPTICAL COMPARATOR	1.3284 - 1.3278	1.3290 - 1.3288				
10	1.826/1.806 D.A.L.	1-2" MICROMETER	1.8162 - 1.8160	1.8155 - 1.8150				
11	.097/.087 LENGTH [K]	INDICATOR AND STAND	.0921 - .0921	.0923 - .0921	8%	1.87		
12	.055/.045 LENGTH	INDICATOR AND STAND	.0487 - .0487	.0489 - .0488				
13	.640/.630 DIA. [K]	BORE GAGE	OK - OK	OK	5%	1.61		
14	.015 R MAX.	SECTION OF PART & OPTICAL COMPARATOR	OK	.005				
15	.035/.025 LENGTH [K]	INDICATOR AND STAND	.0297 - .0294	.0300 - .0295	5%	1.75		
16	DRILL POINT NOT TO EXCEED .015 DEEP	SECTION OF PART & OPTICAL COMPARATOR	OK	OK				
17	.760/.755 DIA. [K]	HOLE GAGE	OK	OK	13%	1.91		

AUTOMATIC (1)

SAMPLES SUBMITTED TO Q.C.   TIME LAYOUT INSPECTOR INITIAL   SET-UP OPERATOR INITIAL   NOTE TIME OF ANY SAMPLES RE-SUBMITTED

Q.C. APPROVAL TO SET-UP OPER.   10:23 AM R.G.B. AND J.M.   M.P.   CYCLE TIME 40 SEC.
                                 11:45 AM R.G.B. AND J.M.   M.P.

Figure 10.3a The front end spreadsheet is used for both initial process verification procedures and later for all setup approvals. (*Courtesy of Dirksen Screw Products, Inc., Warren, Mich.*)

Dirksen Screw Products, which has a reputation for supplying high-quality screw machine products to its customers in the automotive, faucet, and industrial metering industries, uses a *front end spreadsheet* (Fig. 10.3a) both to verify their manufacturing process capability and to use for all setup approval reports. First they reproduce a "marked drawing" of the part on their CAD system (Fig. 10.3b). All characteristics are numbered sequentially to make them easier to locate on the drawing. The sheet lists the process used to manufacture those dimensions, the characteristic, the gage used, the

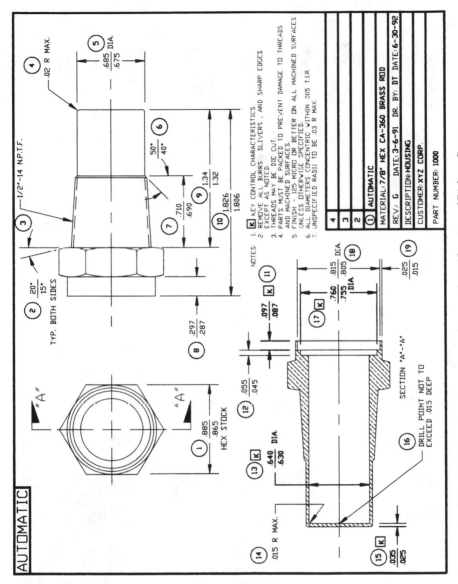

Figure 10.3b A "marked" drawing of a screw machine product. (*Courtesy of Dirksen Screw Products, Inc.*)

layout inspector's readings, the gage R&R (repeatability and reproducibility) results, process capability study results, and any comments (Figs. 10.3*a* and 10.3*b* were modified to maintain proprietary information with their customers.)

The Molding Company supplies quality products of injection-molded thermoplastic and thermoset plastic components to their customers in the automotive, consumer appliance, and electric component industries. Their *control plan* (Fig. 10.4) defines the characteris-

CONTROL PLAN

Part No. _182567-00_ _182567-02_   Part Name _Control Panel_   Rev. _8_   Number of Cavities _2_

Supplier _The Molding Company_

Characteristic	Reason* For Charac.	Frequency/ Sample Size	Analysis Methods	Cpk	Reaction Program For Out Of Control Conditions
1) Material: Premix 1100V-15	1	Every Shipment	Visual	N/A	Contact Supplier/Review MTL. Data tag
2) Length: S/M15.280±.015	1/2	3 shots/2 hrs.	Surface Plt/Height gage	N/A	Adjust Process/Reject & Sort 100%
3) Bow .000 to .030 Twist .000 to .030	1/2	3 shots/2 hrs. 6 parts per box	Surface plate & Pin gage	N/A	Adjust Process/Reject & Sort 100%
4) .110 Dia ±.002	1/2	3 shots/2 hrs.	Gage pin	N/A	Adjust Process/Reject & Sort 100%
5) .112 Dia ±.002	1/2	3 shots/2 hrs.	Gage pin	N/A	Adjust Process/Reject & Sort 100%
6) .2500 Dia ±.002 -.000	1/2	3 shots/2 hrs.	Gage pin	N/A	Adjust Process/Reject & Sort 100%
7) .282 ±.003		3 shots/2 hrs.	Calipers/Gage block	N/A	Adjust Process/Reject & Sort 100%
8) Visual: Checks for cracks, shorts, voids flash, contamination, etc.	2	3 shots/2 hrs. 8 parts per box	Visual	N/A	Adjust Process/Reject & Sort 100%

Submitted by: _[signature]_   /Date _10/26/90_

Approvals: Supplier

Quality Engineering   /Date

Procurement Quality   /Date

Figure 10.4   A control plan. (*Courtesy of the Molding Company, Georgetown, Ky.*)

tic, frequency of inspection/sample size, analysis method, initial process capability (C_{pk}), and reaction plan for out-of-specification or out-of-control conditions. They also have a drawing of the part with the dimensions to be controlled numbered corresponding to the control plan (not shown).

H&W Screw Products manufactures screw machined products and also performs assembly work in a cellular manufacturing setup. They use a *control plan* format that was developed by the Ford Motor Company in their planning process. The plan is a combination of a control plan, process verification spreadsheet, and FMEA (Fig. 10.5). It lists the operation number, the characteristic number corresponding to a marked blueprint (not shown), the tolerance (this is shown on the characteristic matrix, Fig. 10.6), the type of characteristic [e.g., blueprint (BP) or in-process characteristic (IP)], the importance of the characteristic [a number from 0 to 4 (Fig. 10.7a)]. It then performs a process FMEA and lists control factors. These are the primary or significant factors which cause variation of that process. Figure 10.7b is a summary of abbreviations for those factors. The spreadsheet then identifies the control method, sample size and frequency, gage method, gage repeatability and reproducibility results, and the process capability information, C_p and C_{pk}.

Figure 10.6, which is a *characteristic matrix,* shows the operation number and the station that is performing an operation that affects that characteristic. For example: 1) Diameter .268–.272 is affected by operation one in two of the 5 indexing stations in the screw machine: 1-1 and 1-4.

Figure 10.8 is a *tool glossary* used by H&W to summarize the operations performed at each of the five indexing stations in the screw machine. It shows the dimensions on the characteristic matrix that are affected by each operation.

This control plan format is a time-consuming method initially. However, performing a systematic and detailed analysis of each dimension will reduce manufacturing problems for the life of the product by identifying improved control methodology. It will identify those characteristics that require close monitoring and those that do not; therefore, inspection costs can be reduced because some inspection that traditionally has been performed will be determined to be unnecessary.

Figure 10.9 is an inspection instruction sheet that is used by Brighton Tool and Die. It lists the characteristic and tolerance, class of the characteristic (major or critical), whether SPC will be used, sample size and frequency of inspection, and inspection method. It specifies the parts engineering revision level and includes nonconforming material instructions for operators. The bottom of the sheet allows room for operators to record the raw material coil number, meter readings (which can be used to determine the number of parts manufactured), inspection results, and operator's initials. This allows for product traceability to the operator and raw material lot.

Figure 10.10 is an example of *gage usage instructions*. These procedures are needed to help train employees and to standardize the inspection methodology. Figure 10.11 is an example of *laboratory*

PART INFORMATION

PART NAME	Fittings	PART NO.	N/A
DEPARTMENT	Raw	OPERATION NO.	
PROCESS ILLUSTRATION SHEET	DATE		

CONTROL PLAN

REVISION CONTROL

NAME:	Release	DATE:
REVISION DESCRIPTION:		
APPROVAL:		DATE:

■ Represents a revision

OP.	I.D.	CHARACTERISTIC DESCRIPTION (PROCESS & PRODUCT)	TOLERANCE	TYPE	IMPORTANCE P A C	POTENTIAL FAILURE MODE	POTENTIAL EFFECTS OF FAILURE	POTENTIAL CAUSES OF FAILURE	OCC.	SEV.	DET.	R.P.N.	CONTROL FACTORS	TOOL #	CONTROL METHODS	SAMPLE SIZE FREQ.	M/S NO.	Cp	DATE	GAGE DESCRIPTION	GAGE R&R	DATE	REAC. PLAN
1	1	Diameter		BP	3	Oversize	Improper Fit	Improper set-up	1	3	3	9	M, O, & T		Set-up Instruction								QA Pg. 31
								Tool wear							In-Process Inspection	5	45			Chamfer chk 10909 15593 15594	certified annually	11-29-89	
								Gaging error							First piece Inspection	5	S/U						
								Improper P.M.							P.M. Program Training		Daily week						
						Undersize	Improper Fit	Operator error	1	3	3	9	M, O, & T		Set-up Instruction					Chamfer chk 10909 15593 15594			
								Improper set-up							In-process Inspection	5	45						
								Operator error							First piece Inspection	5	S/U						
								Gaging error							P.M. Program Training		Daily week						
								Improper P.M.															
1	2	Inside Diameter		BP	3 ι	Oversize	Improper Fit	Improper set-up	1	3	6		M, O, & T		Set-up Instruction					Plug Gauge P-005 P-022 P-023	certified annually	12-2-89	QA Pg. 31
								Chips							In-process Inspection	5	45						
								Gaging error							First piece Inspection								
								Improper P.M.							P.M. Program training		Daily week						

Figure 10.5 A control plan. (*Courtesy of H&W Screw Products, Inc., Taylor, Mich.*)

PART NUMBER ___M-51062___   CHARACTERISTIC MATRIX

REVISION _____A_____

CHARACTERISTIC	TOLERANCE	0	1-1	1-2	1-3	1-4	1-5				
1) Diameter	.268-.272		xx			xx					
2) Diameter	.194-.199		xx	xx·	xx						
3) Hex Width	.375 + .010	xx	C				xx				
4) Diameter	.301-.316			xx	xx	xx					
5) Angle	90° + 1°		xx			xx					
6) Angle	45° + 1°			xx	xx						
7) Length	.325 + .010		xx			xx					
8) Length	.385 + .010		xx	xx	xx	xx					
9) Note	Chamfer to give 3/4 1 1/4 Incompl THD				xx	xx					
10) Overall Length	.850 + .010		xx	xx	xx	xx	xx				
11) Radius	.050-.060 R					xx					
12) Chamfer	Present		xx	xx		xx					
13) Undercut			xx	xx	xx						
14) Threads	3/8-24 UNF-2A				xx	xx					
15) Raw Material	MS-573	xx									

Figure 10.6 A characteristic matrix, which lists the operations being performed. (*Courtesy H&W Screw Products, Inc.*)

Importance Rating Criteria

0—No effect on product function, processing, or customer satisfaction.
1—Minor impact on product function, processing, or customer satisfaction.
2—Moderate impact on product function, processing, or customer satisfaction.
3—Major impact on product function, processing, or customer satisfaction.
4—Critical characteristic affects customer safety or regulatory requirement.

Figure 10.7a Rating criteria for the importance of a characteristic.

equipment test procedure. It is only one page of a 14-page document. This type of documentation and associated training of operators and technicians should be incorporated into the planning process either when new gaging and equipment are being utilized or new employees are hired.

Assembly Operation Instructions

An *operation description sheet* (ODS) for assembling a window onto a car door is shown in Fig. 10.12. An ODS is used to show assembly-line

---

Control Factor

S: Setup affected—this characteristic is strongly influenced by setup procedures. Proper setup methods will control this cause of variation.

M: Machine affected—the machine affects this characteristic in one of two methods. The first is that only a few machines have the capability to control these characteristics. Therefore, those machine numbers should be specified. The other is that processing parameters vary over time with this machine, and process monitoring should be implemented to control the process.

O: Operator affected—this characteristic is affected by operator skill. Therefore, proper training and screening of operators for this task are needed.

C: Component affected—this characteristic is strongly influenced by the quality of purchased components and raw materials. The control is instituted by good statistical controls at the supplier, receiving inspection and certified material data.

P: Preventative maintenance affected—the characteristic is affected by the maintenance of tooling or equipment. Good preventative maintenance procedures will eliminate this concern.

W: Wear affected. This characteristic is strongly influenced by the wear of tools such as inserts, dies, punches, buttons, molds, etc. Statistically monitoring the product is frequently an acceptable method to monitor wear; however, specifying tool change and sharpening frequencies is another acceptable approach.

F: Fixture/pallet affected. The characteristic is affected by the fixturing and clamping of the product. Designing effective fixturing systems and monitoring fixture/pallet wear for significant wear characteristics are generally acceptable control techniques.

T: Tool design affected. If the tool is designed and made properly, this characteristic will always be produced correctly.

Figure 10.7b Summary of abbreviations for determining significant sources of variation in the finished manufacturing process.

personnel how to perform their assembly task. The ODS in Fig. 10.12 has a drawing of the parts, which are identified by numbers in circles. The dotted lines show where the fasteners will attach the parts after the operation is completed. In the lower right hand corner of the drawing, the circled number corresponds to a part number, description, and quantity used. In the example shown, these are numbers 1, 3, and 4. Number 2 is in a square box with arrows pointing to the window and door, which indicates that in this process these pieces will be joined. If a clamping operation were required for subassembly work, it would be numbered inside a hexagon. In the upper middle, the operations to be performed are numbered and described. It also specifies which fixtures and socket sizes are needed. In the upper right hand corner, the machine torque settings are listed below the corresponding operation item number. The minimum, maximum, and target torque settings are listed. Some companies that use these also have pictorials of how the operator should position his or her body to avoid wasted motion and back problems. The time required to per-

TOOL GLOSSARY

M-51062

TOOL NO.	DESCRIPTION	POSITION	TOOL LIFE	DIM NO. CUT
	Dovetail	1		8, 12 & 14
	Spot-drill	1		2 & 5
	Circular form	2		4,7,8,12 & 14
	Drill	2		2
	Shave	3		4,7,8,13 & 14
	Drill	3		2
	Thread rolls	4		7 & 14
	Combination drill	4		5,7,8,9,10 & 11
	Facing tool	4		1 & 10
	Cut-off	5		10
	Back drill	5		12

Figure 10.8 A tool glossary of the operations performed at each station and the characteristics affected by each process. (*Courtesy of H&W Screw Products, Inc.*)

BRIGHTON TOOL & DIE   INSPECTION REPORT   BT-10?

BTD# 1115		P.O.#		HEAT #		
CUSTOMER:CHRYSLER		PART NO:6100882		B\P DATE06/01/1983	REV.:STD	
PART NAME: WASHER		OPER. STAMP		NEXT OPER.TUMBLE	MACH.	
LAST ISIR DATE: 5-27-192		APPROVED BY: 7KSauryer			DATE:05/27/1992	

OPERATOR INSPECTION INSTRUCTION

ITEM		CHARACTERISTIC	CLASS	SPC	FREQUENCY	INSP. METHOD	
1	X	STOCK DIA..0787 / .110	M		5 - 5000PCS	MICROMETER	
2	X	BURR MINUS STOCK DIA.	M		5-5000 PCS	MICROMETER	
3	X	INSIDE DIA..423 / .437		X	1 - 20000PC	CALIPERS/CHART	
4		OUTSIDE DIA.1.0818/1.1023			1ST PIECE	CALIPERS	
5	X	BURRS,DIE MARKS,CUT-INS, LAMINATED,SERIATED,TRIM ENDS,FLAT,RADIUS	M		5-5000 PCS CONTINUOUS CONTINUOUS	VISUAL/FEEL PART TO PART	

* ACCEPTANCE CRITERIA IS ZERO DEFECTS, ANY DEFECTIVE MATERIAL IS TO BE D.M.N.
** ANY DESCREPENCIES THAT ARE DISCOVERED, CONTACT YOUR SUPERVISOR

COIL #	MET RDG	1	2	5	OPER	COIL #	MET RDG	1	2	5	OPER

*QUALITY OF SAFETY & HOUSEKEEPING*QUALITY OF PRODUCT*QUALITY OF DELIVERY & COST?
W-BURF

Figure 10.9 An in-process inspection instruction sheet for operators. (*Courtesy of Brighton Tool & Die, Brighton, Mich.*)

Johnson Gage Instruction for Internal Threads

1. Check Johnson gage to "go" set master every time the gage is used by rotating the set master one (1) revolution to assure a zero reading on the dial indicator.

2. Load part by collapsing the segment locking screws by applying inward pressure to them.

3. Rotate part 1/2 turn to set in gaging position. (Do not screw part onto the gage.)

4. Rotate part one (1) turn to check for oval threads.

5. Withdraw part by applying inward pressure and removing part from gage.

6. Repeat operation depending on the length of the thread.

7. When using the Johnson gage for S.P.C. follow the above procedures but always take your data from the middle of the part, using the thread pitch diameter segments.

Figure 10.10 A gage usage instruction sheet for a Johnson thread gage. (*Courtesy of H&W Screw Products, Inc.*)

form each operation corresponding to a body position would also be listed next to these drawings.

Operator Workstation

Designing an effective *operator workstation* is important to facilitate ongoing process controls. A well-designed workstation will make it easier for operators to perform inspection tasks and subconsciously communicate the importance of quality to their job responsibilities. They should have adequate lighting and be located as close to the process as possible. They should include a table which contains all of the necessary measuring and test equipment, a board which includes a drawing of the part, inspection instructions, and SPC instructions and SPC sheets so that significant characteristics can be monitored on a control chart. Figure 10.13 is a picture of a workstation which meets all of those criteria. However, instead of hand-plotting the points, they are downloaded electronically into a computer and statistically charted. Computerizing the process saves the employee's time and the computer notifies an employee when an out-of-control condition exists.

In order to verify that every characteristic and specification has been met on the blueprint, an *initial sample inspection report* (ISIR) and an *initial sample lab report* (ISLR) should be performed. Figure 10.14 is a page of an ISIR from Brighton Tool and Die which verifies every characteristic on their customer's print. They measured 6 pieces which were randomly selected from a 300-piece run to verify those characteristics. The ISLR was attached with certifications which showed conformance to the material and heat-treat specifica-

Issued To _J̲I̲_

Method No. CB-LTP-PP-303
Issue No.   A1
Date   3-1-91
Issued By   GMT/SB
Approved By LRC

Amoco Chemical Company
Chocolate Bayou Laboratory

Procedure

<u>Analysis A</u>:   Determination of Flow Rate by Manual Method

The following table is used to select the time interval for this test.

Flow Range g/10 min	Time Interval Minutes
0.15 to 1.0	6
1.0 to 3.5	3
3.5 to 10.0	1
10.0 to 25.0	.5

1. Check to see that the plastometer is at 230 +/- 0.2 deg. C.

2. Check the orifice with the "go-no-go" gauge for specification die dimensions.

3. Clean **cylinder** chamber, piston, and dies with gun patches or a **cloth** and appropriate equipment accessories.

4. Place die into cylinder chamber.

5. Charge approximately 4-6 grams of polymer into cylinder chamber. Powders may be charged in one increment while pellets are done in two. The sample should be tamped down after each addition to prevent the formation of air pockets in the extrudate.

6. Insert the piston on top of the sample (piston weight = 100 gm).

7. Preheat the sample for four minutes.

8. At four minutes, place the 2060 gm weight on the piston.

9. At the 4th minute, hand pressure the weight and piston down so that after 6 minutes the piston will have descended to its calibration mark. (Note: No external pressure besides the 2060 gm load should be applied between the 4th and 6th minutes.)

Amoco Quality

Figure 10.11 A lab test procedure for testing the melt flow rate of a polypropylene resin. (*Courtesy of Amoco Chemical Company, Chicago, Ill.*)

Item	Operation Description	Tool/Fixt #	#				B. Car Line	Body Style
DL	DOOR LINE OPERATION						ZJ/ALL	74
SELECT FROM STOCK						
1 GLASS-		3	85 ILbMin	105 ILb T		
AND			125 ILbMx	ILbMxA		
		4	7 ILbMin	11 ILb T		
2 FROM OUTER SIDE OF DOOR			15 ILbMx	ILbMxA		
POSITION DIVISION BAR ON GLASS BETWEEN INNER &						
OUTER PANEL BELT,LOCATE GLASS REARWARD & UP						
INTO REAR AND UPPER LEG OF DOOR,WORKING LIP						
ON GLASS OVER SHEET METAL						
USING-						
FIBER STICK	90-765-7480					
SECURE DIVISION BAR AT LOWER ATTACHMENT THRU						
INNER PANEL WITH						
3 SCREW-						
USING-						
NUTRUNNER ST STALL PISTOL GRIP 1/4 O.C.C.	87-801-4400					
DRIVER 1/4-D-1/4-2N	93-490-1105					
SOCKET 10MM-6PN-1/4-R (APEX #NIOMMEII	93-869-2445					
SECURE UPPER TAB OF GLASS TO UPPER LEG OF DOOR						
WITH						
4 SCREW-						
USING-						
NUTRUNNER ST STALL PISTOL GRIP 1/4 O.C.C.	87-801-1200					
BIT HOLDER M-480	93-580-0327					
BIT #2 PHILLIPS	93-220-7220					

NCR: C

#GED/ABE	Eng.Gr: 92J480B-D-2.00,2.02		CHRYSLER MOTORS	TC
#GED/ABE	Ref.		O.D.M.T.C PRODUCTION ENG	55
#GE6	Op Cept: x Cont On:		Sect: DOOR BUILD-UP ZJ ONLY	
#GE6	O Port: x Process O Clamp			
			Oper. INSTALL REAR DOOR FIXED GLASS	
ST			Ref. Sht. 92-5201-ZJ - 61.00	
			Qualif. NOTED	
ST			Print Date: 02-17-92 18147	
			Pit Sht	
			Rel Date: 02-14-92 Change	
			KMH	93-5201-ZJ - 61.00
Qualif, Rv Tr	Engineering Change	Date	By	Pr	Apd	MY	PL#	Body	Sheet #

Rv	Itm	Part No.	RI	Qty	P	Part Name
1		55032848	50C	1	C	GLASS ASSY-ENCAPSULATED RR DOOR FIXED
1		55032849	50A	1	C	GLASS ASSY-ENCAPSULATED RR DOOR FIXED
1		55033998	50A	1	C	GLASS ASSY-RR DR STATIONARY S/SCREEN RT
1		55033999	50A	1	C	GLASS ASSY-RR DR STATIONARY S/SCREEN LT
3		06502858	50G	1/1	C	SCREW-HEX FLG HD W/ANNULAR RING RR DR FIXED GLASS
4		00153034	50A	1/1	S	SCREW-UPPER DIV BAR ATTACH

Figure 10.12 An operation description sheet showing how to assemble a portion of window glass onto a car door frame. (*Courtesy of Chrysler Corporation.*)

Figure 10.13 A computerized operator workstation which includes electronic direct-feed gaging, a drawing of the part, inspection instructions, SPC instructions, and nonconforming material instructions. (*Courtesy of H&W Screw Products, Inc., Taylor, Mich.*)

tions. An ISLR also can include certificates of conformance demonstrating that subassemblies passed durability tests. In industries where multiple cavities and dies are used, a sample from each cavity or die is completely verified.

Continuous Improvement Planning

After a product has been manufactured and shipped to customers, the management should focus efforts on continually improving the product. This will help the company remain competitive as the product matures in its life cycle as well as improve profitability by reaping the benefits of lower manufacturing costs, reduced warranty expenses, and higher plant efficiencies. Some of the areas that should be continuously reviewed would include improving manufacturing productivity at bottlenecks (the capacity constraints), reducing total process cycle

BRIGHTON TOOL & DIE INC.

INITIAL SAMPLE INSPECTION REPORT						
CUSTOMER:			PART NUMBER:			BT#1172
B/P DATE:02FE91	CHANGE LEVEL:A		PART NAME:PLUG PITMAN ARM BALL STUD			

REASON FOR REPORT
NEW PART ____ ENG.CHANGE ___ NEW TOOLING X FIRST/LAST PIECE ___ OTHER X

CHARACTERISTIC SPEC	#1	#2	#3	#4	#5	#6
1)FLAT.005 .12 MIN	.005 NOGO	.005NOGO	.005NOGO	.005 NOGO	.005NOGO	.005 NOGO
2)10 DEG. BEND	PASS	PASS	PASS	PASS	PASS	PASS
3) .232 - .242	.240	.240	.240	.240	.240	.240
4) .440 +-.010	.434	.430	.436	.435	.441	.449
5).350/370 MIN..04	.354	.354	.354	.354	.354	.354
6) 1.60 +- .010	1.60	1.5979	1.5992	1.5978	1.5992	1.5982
7) 1/4-28 UNF 2B TH	ACCEPT	ACCEPT	ACCEPT	ACCEPT	ACCEPT	ACCEPT
8).320/.340 DIA.MIN	.354	.254	.354	.354	.354	.254
9) .03 RADIUS	.03	.03	.03	.03	.03	.03
10).24 RADIUS	.245	.245	.245	.245	.245	.245
11).01 MIN. WIRE	PASS	PASS	PASS	PASS	PASS	PASS
12) .02 RADIUS TYP	.02	.02	.02	.02	.02	.02
13) A .010	.008	.009	.008	.009	.008	.008
14).050 TYP	.05	.05	.05	.05	.05	.05
15).03 4 GRV.+-010	.038	.038	.038	.038	.038	.038
16)MATERIAL	NAX FINE GRAIN SEE DAYTON STEEL CERTIFICATION					
17)HEAT TREAT	SEE MATALLURGICAL PROCESSING CERTIFICATIONS					
18)R15N 90.2 MIN	91.5	91.0	91.5	92.0	91.5	91.0
19).352-.361 REF.	.361	.361	.361	.361	.361	.361
	APPROVED BY: *K.Sawyer*					
	DATE: 6-03-92					

Figure 10.14 An initial sample inspection report. (*Courtesy of Brighton Tool & Die.*)

time, improving manufacturing equipment's availability or uptime, reducing setup times, reducing work-in-process material, making more effective use of a machine's nonproductive time or dead time, addressing customer complaints and warranty items, identifying features and product improvements to improve customer satisfaction, improving product value/reducing product costs, and reducing product lead time requirements.

These objectives can be developed by discussing the situations with employees and assigning tasks to them for completion. Sometimes product improvements and cost reductions can be identified with emerging technologies. Methods for improving new product planning methods and reducing product development times can be identified with a program review after each job.

Developing Performance Indicators

Tracking plant efficiency indicators such as labor and material variances, production output, first-time-through capability, unscheduled downtime, and setup times can be useful to identify problems encountered with the manufacturing process as well as opportunities for improvement. Monitoring scrap, rework, and process capability can identify project priorities for the quality and manufacturing engineering organization to investigate.

It is important to develop a set of indicators to monitor the system's effectiveness. Figure 10.15 is a set of quality indicators established by Technimark, Inc., which are used to track performance (the figures were modified to protect proprietary concerns). They monitor plant quality (Fig. 10.15 upper left), which includes scrap and internal QC department rejects and customer returns. They then break down the data into the categories final audit, in-process scrap and rework, and customer returns (Fig. 10.15 upper right). They also analyze the data and establish a Pareto chart of their top five rejects in terms of dollar value. Several plants only chart their top five scrap problems or top five warranty problems because they have limited resources and they feel they achieve better results attacking their five biggest problems effectively than diluting their resources and attacking "all of them," which results in fewer effective solutions. They also break down the cause of the rejects for their five most problematic parts (Fig. 10.15 lower right).

A warranty-customer complaint monitoring system and customer complaint hotline can be used to help prioritize warranty reduction projects. The progress status of these items can be reviewed at regularly scheduled meetings which involves project team members who represent the various disciplines. When selecting projects to work on, the management must prioritize the projects in order to assure that resources have been effectively allocated to address the most important issues.

NSK Corporation of America first reviews their corporate goals (Fig. 10.16a), which includes goals for sales, customer returns, pretax profits, and productivity. Then, they develop goals and objectives for safety and morale, cost, delivery, and quality (Fig. 10.16b). Finally, they

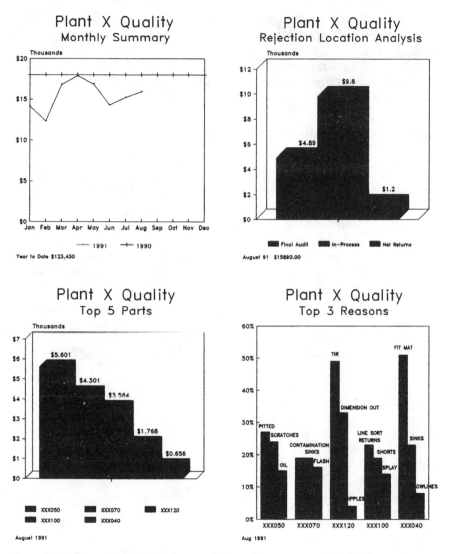

Figure 10.15 Some quality indicators used for performance tracking. (*Courtesy of Technimark, Inc.*)

develop indicators to track performance (Fig. 10.16c). The indicators are prioritized by one, two, and three stars (three being most important). This helps them determine where to focus their efforts when resource conflicts exist. Monitoring performance indicators also helps them establish and prioritize future improvement opportunities.

Jefferson Rubber Works, which is a manufacturer of rubber products for the consumer appliance and auto industries, uses the improvement planning sheet shown in Fig. 10.17 (the author developed this format—a similar format was used in Chap. 8 with the Molding Company). The figure displays 1 page out of an 8-page report. Each goal is listed and numbered. Beneath the goal, all tasks required to achieve that goal are listed; then the timing and assigned responsibility are listed.

Internal Machinery Modification Capability

When a manufacturer has the ability to modify machinery to better suit their own needs they derive several competitive advantages. First, they can better adapt the tooling to suit their plant's needs. Second, they can develop a proprietary process which will give the company an advantage over their competition. Finally, as the machinery is used by production personnel, new ideas will be developed which can improve the process and productivity. Therefore, the concept of continuous improvement can be applied to the machinery.

Bibliography

Chrysler Corporation, *Guide to Quality Systems Requirements for Tooling and Equipment,* TESQA, Chrysler Corporation, Detroit, MI, 1990.

Ford Motor Company—Transmission and Chassis Division, *Dimensional Control Plans: Systematic Approach for Implementing Customer Expectations,* Ford Motor Company, February 1988.

Gevirtz, Charles, *The Fundamentals of Advanced Quality Planning,* Quality Progress, April 1991, pp. 49–51.

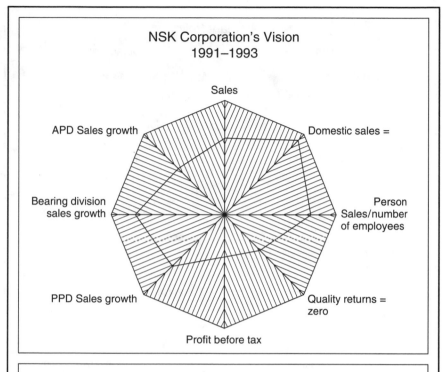

NSK Corporation's Vision
1991–1993

Sales

APD Sales growth

Domestic sales =

Bearing division
sales growth

Person
Sales/number
of employees

PPD Sales growth

Quality returns =
zero

Profit before tax

NSK Corporation Goals

- Continuous improvement of quality
- Continuous improvement of product
- Continuous improvement of operational
- Support and expand our capabilities
- Continuous improvement of service to customer
- Develop people and provide opportunities for growth
- Continuous growth of sales while attaining profit goals
- Improve communications

FY92 Conditions

- Full capacity for all part sizes
  (Several sizes are over capacity and overtime will be necessary)

- Major training effort to be implemented for all employees
- Uncertain economic conditions

Figure 10.16a Continuous improvement planning goals for NSK Corp. Corporate goals.

FY92 Plant Policy

Goals	Objectives

✚ Safety and morale

✚ Safety and morale

1. Continuous safety improvement

    1.1 Eliminate lost time accidents

    1.2 Implement machine safety improvement plan for our equipment

2. Ongoing employee development

    2.1 Upgrade SGA system

    2.2 Introduce training effort for all C/L employees

    2.3 Continue upgrade of succession plan

₵ost

₵ost

1. Improve profitability

    1.1 Improve productivity

    1.2 Reduce scrap/noise

    1.3 Develop cost reduction projects

Delivery

Delivery

1. Achieve engineering capacity

    1.1 Continuous improvement of bottleneck areas

2. Meet production schedule

    2.1 Improve plant scheduling system and component control

    2.2 Develop system for new projects and customers

    2.3 Review setup and changeover procedures

Quality

Quality

1. Continual focus on customer satisfaction

    1.1 Eliminate customer returns

    1.2 Schedule visits to customers

2. Improve plant quality

    2.1 Upgrade X and Z program

    2.2 Introduce Y program

    2.3 Improve SPC/CPK system

3. Utilize cost of quality

    3.1 Develop cost of quality program

Figure 10.16b Continuous improvement planning goals for NSK Corp. Plant goals and objectives.

FY92 Plant Indicators

Item	Indicator	Priority	FY92 Target	Calendar year FY91 target	Calendar year FY91 actual
✚ Safety and morale	Lost time accidents Machine safety improvement SGA activities	*** * **	T-NSK G2 mach Record results	——— 1/dept/shift	
¢ost	Scrap cost ratio Cost/piece Cost savings Inventory turns	*** ** *** *	Record results	———	
Delivery	Output Schedule attainment (production order) PCS/man-hour	** ** ***			
Quality	RMA Scrap pcs. % Noise pcs. % X defects Customer visits	*** * ** *** **		———	

Figure 10.16c Continuous improvement planning goals for NSK Corp. Performance tracking indicators. (*Courtesy of NSK Corporation of America.*)

QUALITY IMPROVEMENT PLAN

Quality Improvement Plan Item	Month Due	Team Member Responsible	Rate (if applicable)	1992 J F M A M J J A S O N D	1993 J F M A M J J A S O N D
1. Train/Retrain SPC I					
(all employees)					
o develop training class	4/92	J. Radel		X — ≡	
o implement training	9/92	J. Radel		X — — — — — — —	— — — O
2. Update QA Manual					
o write procedures	1/93	J. Radel	min. 1/mo.	X — — — — — — — — — — —	O
o approve & signoff	2/93	J. Radel	min. 1/mo.	X — — — — — — — — — — —	— O
(see action plan)					
3. Perform Supplier			min. 1/yr.		
audit/s					
o notify supplier	4/92	E. Toomey		≡	
o schedule audit/s	5/92	E. Toomey		≡	
o conduct audit/s	6/92	J. Radel		≡	

NOTE: X = Start Date
O = Scheduled Completion Date
≡ = Task Completed
— = Efforts Continuing

NOTE: If progress is less than specified by the rate, place an * in the rate box.

Figure 10.17 An improvement planning spreadsheet. (*Courtesy of Jefferson Rubber Works.*)

11

Activity-Based Cost Accounting

It is important to utilize an accounting system which accurately reports real costs. An objective of such a system is to minimize differences between reported accounting costs and "true" costs while minimizing the administrative costs related to obtaining and estimating that data. An optimal system would minimize the total cost of errors (relating to bad decisions) and the cost of measurement. Generally the more complex the system, the more accurate, but it is also more expensive to administer. In practice, the "true costs" are never known, but a good accounting system will generate close approximations.

Problems with Traditional Accounting Approaches

Traditional accounting systems generally account for direct labor or machine hours and then apply a fixed overhead cost to each part produced. Some of the problems with this approach result in inaccuracies in the reported costs, which can affect the profitability of a manufacturing company. These errors arise from differences between products in production volumes, size of the machinery, complexity, setup times, material handling requirements, inspection labor, plant administrative support requirements, floor space utilized, etc.

An example showing inaccuracies relating to production volume diversity can be described as follows. Suppose a plant runs similar products A and B, which are manufactured with similar processes. Product B has a long production run time of 30 days, while product A has a shorter run lasting 2 days. The current accounting system prices both products equivalently. However, this does not take into account the differences in setup costs when amortized on a unit basis. Suppose it takes 4 h to set up each of these products, and the setup costs in terms of machine downtime and skilled labor are approximately equal to the cost to run the machine. Therefore, the equivalent machine cost per setup would be 4 machine-hours. If the machine costs are $100 per hour, the actual equivalent machine costs for job B (which runs for 30 days) would be $72,400 (720 h run time + 4 h to set up the job × $100/h machine rate). The cost to run job A would be $5,200 (48 h running time + 4 h setup multiplied by $100/h). Traditionally, the plant applies a $.01 price per unit overhead to cover setup costs. This does *not* include engineering overhead, inspection labor, administrative scheduling, and order costs. The traditional accounting system would have both products, A and B, receiving equal costs, while the actual costs amortized over the run relating to setup costs would be 1.083 for product A (the shorter running job) and 1.006 for product B (the longer running order) (Fig. 11.1). This difference is $0.077 per unit. If a $100 administrative ordering cost was considered for each order, the cost of product A would be 1.104 and for B would become 1.007, a $0.097 difference. If the unit costs $2.00 to manufacture including raw materials, this results in a 4.0 percent hidden loss for product A due to errors in the cost assumptions and a 1 percent additional profit from product B. In a very competitive industry where profit margins are below 10 percent, this can be significant.

A problem arises when this manufacturer estimates costs for their products, in that they will quote higher than true costs for high-volume products and lower than actual costs for low-volume products. As a result, this plant will find that they win a disproportionate amount of bids for low-volume jobs (which are less profitable) and win fewer for higher volume. This will ultimately reduce the plant's profitability.

Accounting Issues to Address

Problems relating to *differences in machine sizes* should be accounted for because typically larger machines use up more electricity and the

Job	Run time, h	Setup time, h	Production rate, #/h	Traditional machine costs/unit	Real machine costs/unit	Administrative costs/unit
A	48	4	100	$1.01	$1.083	$0.021
B	720	4	100	$1.01	$1.006	$0.001

NOTE: (1) Machine costs equal $100 per hour. (2) Administrative time per order equals $100. (3) Setup costs are approximately equivalent to machine running costs; both costs include direct labor.

Figure 11.1 Comparison between traditional accounting costs and real costs.

components that need replacement are more expensive because they are larger. Larger machines (such as a 750-ton press) are typically more expensive than smaller machines (such as a 75-ton press); therefore, the depreciation costs are higher. Finally, larger machines use up more floor space.

When setup times vary significantly, the cost differences can be substantial. Suppose on a 5-spindle screw machine, two jobs each run for 3 days (72 h). Job A can be set up in 1 h, and job B takes 11 h. Assuming the setup costs are equivalent to the hourly machine rate and the machine produces the same number of parts per hour, the machine costs per unit for job A are (72 + 1)/number of units manufactured. However, the machine rate for job B is (72 + 11)/the number of units manufactured. The difference in the true machine costs per unit will be (72 + 11)/(72 + 1), or a 13.7 percent machine cost differential.

If the machine rates of two products are well known, but one requires additional material handling due to problems with the plant layout, the accounting system will not flag this as being a costly issue and the management may not have sufficient economic justification to invest capital to improve the situation.

Suppose one product has a lot of critical characteristics that require more controls and inspection efforts than are typically used, then that product will be undercosted and the plant's general overhead will be unnecessarily burdened.

One plant ordered a newly automated manufacturing line. This line used up more floor space than the previous line used to manufacture that type of product. The plant then had to expand its floor space to accommodate this addition. However, the accounting system did not apply the plant overhead to this line and did not truly estimate the cost of running this line. The plant heating, cooling, lighting, maintenance, and brick and mortar expenses were all increased, and these costs were treated as general plant overhead, raising the costs of other products improperly.

Applying Corporate Overhead

When corporate overhead is applied to a product, it is important to estimate actual engineering costs. The higher volume jobs typically should have a lower expense per unit than the lower volume jobs. If these costs are allocated in a manner which does not account for this, the company will have higher costing high-volume jobs and lower costing low-volume jobs. A similar accounting issue exists if a product did not require a lot of engineering design costs because a lot of carry-over components were used, while another product required substantial amounts of design time because it utilized new components. The overhead needs to be applied accordingly. Otherwise, the engineering design group will not appreciate the costs of designing new components as opposed to using carryover components.

Another problem arises when a company elects to source a component or product from an outside company, instead of manufacturing it in house. For the corporate management to determine that it is less expensive to manufacture the component at an outside supplier, several items must be taken into account. The plant's costs may include corporate overhead in their price, while the supplier's costs do not. Additionally, if the supplier designs a component, the company has to realize that corporate costs still may be used to test the component and the company's engineering labor is used to coordinate and review design activities with that supplier. One company determined that a profitable plant would improve its margins by outsourcing one product line which was about 10 percent of its total dollar sales. The plant subsequently reduced its machine content and direct labor force accordingly. However, the staff levels and plant size remained the same. When the plant bid on jobs, it was less competitive because corporate and plant overhead costs remained the same but were allocated over fewer product lines (purchased components did not have to adjust for corporate overhead). The plant received fewer new jobs, while some older jobs were being retired. The plant was no longer profitable as its utilization decreased and its fixed overhead per unit was increased. The corporate management never effectively corrected this. Eight years later the plant was closed primarily due to mistaken assumptions in accounting practices.

Activity-Based Cost Accounting and Cost Drivers

The way to avoid the inaccuracies mentioned is to develop a more accurate accounting system which accounts for the significant variables as they apply to that plant and product line. Such a system would economically account for the critical factors that can be used to determine the cost accurately and would be based on the manufacturing activities related to producing that product. These critical factors are called *cost drivers*. The drivers vary depending on the plant and manufacturing process used. Some typical drivers include

- Setup time
- Number of setups
- Material handling time
- Engineering time

- Administrative time
- Machine size
- Amount of floor space utilized
- Inventory storage space
- Machine time
- Direct labor time
- Inspection labor time
- Machine maintenance and tooling cost per amount of running time

An accounting system does not need to track all of these drivers to assure reasonable accuracy. A good system would utilize the Pareto principle to track the most important drivers that are required to achieve the desired accuracy. This is what an activity-based cost accounting system achieves. The management must determine how much accuracy is required to have an effective system (e.g., should the costs be accurate within 1 percent or is 5 percent all that is required). However, when making this determination, they must appreciate that additional costs will be required to achieve more accurate figures. The objective is to attempt to minimize the sum of the costs of establishing and maintaining such a system and the costs of making bad decisions. Generally speaking, the more drivers used, the more accurate the costing system; however, it also becomes more expensive to administer.

Cost drivers can be approached in two ways. One is by time or hours, while the other is by the number of transactions (Fig. 11.2). When the driver is measured by the amount of time, the assumption is that the time usage of the driver differs between products. When the driver is measured by the number of transactions, it assumes that the cost effect of that transaction or event is similar between products (Fig. 11.2).

It is important to appreciate the costs associated with not having an accurate accounting system. The costs of distorted accounting figures include

Amount of time	Number of transactions
Setup hours	Number of setups
Material handling hours	Number of times handled
Material ordering hours	Number of times ordered
Part number administration hours	Number of part numbers maintained

Figure 11.2   Different approaches in accounting for cost drivers.

- When bidding competitively, winning more low-margin jobs and winning fewer high-margin jobs than would occur with a more accurate cost system.

- Marketing products that are misleadingly profitable while not marketing other products that would have been profitable.

- Making bad product decisions such as increasing the number of options or variations of a product, but not accurately accounting for costs relating to program management, engineering development, administering drawing and engineering standard changes, administering more parts in the system and at service centers, additional material handling, additional inventory, additional setups and changeovers, etc.

The costs to administer such a system include administrative resources relating to obtaining the cost standards through studies, the cost of inputting the data, and accounting labor relating to monitoring and administering the system. Costs are also temporarily increased when a company is in a transition phase to train plant personnel on activity-based accounting, information systems' programming and support, and administrative resources required to implement the transition from the current database. The costs to utilize such a system can be aided with computer-integrated manufacturing systems. In such systems the plant floor personnel can input information such as setup time, the number of setups, number of units manufactured, downtime, etc. This would help to establish a cost baseline as well as identify variances.

Considerations When Selecting Cost Drivers

In order to determine which drivers should be used in the accounting standard, one must review the following three items:

1. Find out *how much a cost driver relates to a percentage of total product costs*. For example, if setup times are short and runs are long for all products in a stamping plant and never amount to more than half a percentage of the product costs, setup time and frequency would not be a good choice for a driver. In this instance, machine costs are typically 20 to 40 percent of the products cost so machine time would be a good choice for one of the drivers.

2. Find out how closely it *relates to another driver* so that two or more drivers can be combined. For example, if each setup in a plant takes approximately 4 h, give or take 30 mins, the number of setups performed could be a good driver. Now suppose that another factor is to schedule that job, and that task uses up $500 of administrative services. The administrative charge per order could be combined with a

fixed setup charge relating to 4 h of setup time. The driver would be the number of changeovers, but it would be defined to include setup machine time plus associated administrative overhead charges relating to processing an order. Another example of grouping drivers is to combine hourly machine costs and hourly direct labor wages into one driver categorized as machine rates.

3. *Determine the diversity ratio for a given driver.* The diversity ratio is a measure of how much a driver varies between product lines. The diversity ratio is a ratio of the relative proportions between the driver and divergent product lines. The highest number goes in the numerator. Suppose that the quickest job to set up takes 1 h, while the slowest takes 6 h. The diversity ratio is 6/1, or 6. Another example, suppose that a 75-ton press is the lowest tonnage in the plant with an hourly machine cost of \$30, and a 1000-ton press is the highest with an hourly machine cost of \$60; the diversity ratio for machine time between the two presses is 60/30, or 2.

The potential error that can be established by using a driver can be calculated by multiplying the diversity ratio by the percentage that a driver relates to the total product cost. In the previous example, if machine time varies as a percentage of total product cost between 20 and 40 percent, depending on raw material costs, but is typically around 30 percent, and the machine size diversity ratio is 2; then the total variation can be calculated by

$$0.20 \times 2 = 0.40, \text{ or } 40\% \text{ of the total product costs}$$

$$0.40 \times 2 = 0.80, \text{ or } 80\% \text{ of the total product costs}$$

Hence, the variance is between 40 and 80 percent, but is typically around 60 percent (0.30×2). If the total accuracy of the data required must be greater than 3 percent, the data would suggest that it would be wise to have a cost driver relating to machine size (unless data collection and monitoring costs are prohibitive).

It is important to document all of the assumptions used to select various drivers, because, if those assumptions change, it will be easier to revise the costing system and identify problems before reported costs become inaccurate. The database should be revised as standard times change. For example, if setup times were reduced by a combination of machine modifications and improved setup procedures, the setup costs should be reduced accordingly. Similarly if the plant layout was improved for better material flow, material handling costs should also be reduced.

The cost system should have cost standards verified on a periodic basis to see if the assumptions and standards remain valid. An exam-

	Part number		
	456789	326780	234175
Setup costs, $	460.00	800.00	225.00
Setup costs/unit, $/unit	Depends	Depends	Depends
Component overhead, $/unit	0.43	0.91	0.29
Machine overhead, $/unit	8.34	12.87	4.65
Purchased material costs	16.71	6.52	3.94
Total (without setup)	25.48	20.30	8.88

Definitions

Setup costs   All costs incurred every time a job is set up. It includes administrative scheduling, machine downtime, setup personnel, and production labor. It also includes the order processing cost, which includes the administrative labor, overhead, and paper costs required to process an order. It costs approximately $75 per order. (This number changes with lot size.)

Setup cost/unit   This is calculated by dividing (the setup cost per order) by the order size. It therefore varies by the lot size scheduled with each order filled.

Component overhead   The engineering, inspection, and technical support costs regarding the manufacture and support of that product.

Machine overhead   The hourly cost to run the machine including direct labor, depreciation, maintenance, and repair costs (including support personnel salaries from those departments), plant lighting and heating for the area used up by the machine, perishable tooling expenses. Material handling expenses are also included.

Purchased material costs   The cost of all purchased components and raw material, and packaging material.

Figure 11.3   An example of an activity-based cost system.

ple of an activity-based system which defines each term is illustrated in Fig. 11.3.

Summary

Having a more accurate accounting system will help plant personnel focus on issues that can drive costs down, such as reducing material handling by improving plant layout and reducing setup costs. A reward incentive system such as a profit-sharing system can help the plant personnel cooperate at reducing true costs, instead of improving reported costs by taking advantage of inaccuracies in the accounting system.

It is important to establish which drivers are important when planning new products so that the management can focus on areas where costs can be improved and understand actual costs. The cost standards must be estimated upfront and then verified during trial runs.

Bibliography

Cooper, Robin, "The Rise of Activity Based Costing Part One through Four," *Journal of Cost Management for the Manufacturing Industry*, September 6, 1988.

12

Value Analysis

Value analysis or, as it is sometimes referred to, value engineering is a technique that is used to identify methods of performing the intended functions and uses of a product for the lowest possible total cost. The technique originated with Lawrence Miles, of the General Electric Company, who formally developed it in 1947. As an electrical engineer at GE, he complained to his boss that they were paying too much for parts. His boss then arranged to have him work with the purchasing department to improve the situation. During World War II, due to material shortages, he initiated many material substitutions in products which did not impact functionality. Afterwards, working in purchasing, he developed this technique.[1,2]

Value analysis, which is usually performed most effectively with interdisciplinary teams of between 3 and 7 people, results in utilizing substantially fewer components while maintaining product features. The team members usually include representatives from marketing, engineering, manufacturing, purchasing, quality, and sometimes suppliers. The cost savings, which often are between 15 and 25 percent,[1,2] result from material changes and lowering the number of parts, which reduces the number of assembly operations and associated administrative burdens. Value analysis is used to reduce the cost of a product while maintaining the quality, durability, reliability, and maintainability of a product.

Cost reduction projects frequently emphasize the effort to reduce the cost of a product, but frequently the quality and reliability effects of such decisions are, unfortunately, overlooked and creative design alternatives are not investigated.

Value analysis can be grouped into five phases: information gathering, function analysis and feature costing, innovation phase (identifying alternatives), prioritizing and determining opportunities, and follow-up and implementation.

Information Gathering

To perform value analysis, one must first have good background data for the project. The following information will be useful: market research and price sensitivity information, plant scrap and repair concerns, and customer complaints.

Market research can identify any new features that can easily be added to the product which can enhance customer satisfaction. Price sensitivity information can tell the team how much sales volume can be increased by various reductions in the selling price. This can be used to establish sales projections after value analysis changes have been incorporated in order to optimize profits.

Scrap and repair information as well as warranty information are used to know which designs must be improved.

Part of performing the quality function deployment (QFD) process involves performing competitive analysis. If QFD was performed on similar competitive products, much information on product performance and features will be available. However, if it was not performed yet, it would be advised to also perform a competitive analysis with similar products before going to the idea generation phase. This is especially true if the product is being manufactured in a mature industry. Some competitive information can be obtained from trade journals.

In addition to performing competitive performance and feature analysis, a competitive cost analysis can be performed by having engineering, manufacturing, and purchasing specialists analyze the component for its functional purpose. Any special features and their associated costs should be considered for future products. Experienced manufacturing specialists can look at a component and determine what manufacturing processes and materials were used. After establishing the processes and materials used, the cost to manufacture those products can be determined in terms of what it would cost to make that exact product at one's own company. However, it is difficult to determine how much it would cost the competitor to manufacture it. If the purchasing organization has strong relationships with some suppliers, they may be willing to provide assistance at determining costs. The cost and features can be summarized on a spreadsheet as shown in Fig. 12.1. It is important to know the volume of such products because that affects the calculation in amortizing tooling costs over the life of the product and identifies any further economies of scale relating to changeovers and administrative costs. A summary of such competitive analysis can be compiled by completing the information requested in the spreadsheet as shown in Fig. 12.2. A patent search should be performed on those features which will be considered for adaptation with future products and models.

Manufacturer:

Product:

Model number:

Annual sales volume:

Retail selling price:

Estimated manufacturing cost (see below):

Cost Breakdown

Component	Material	Manufacturing operations	Estimated manufacturing cost	Features	Comments

Total: _____

Figure 12.1   Competitive cost analysis breakdown.

Function Analysis and Feature Costing

Function analysis defines the reasons for having a product feature or explains the need that it fulfills. The function description is performed by using two words. The first word is an action verb which describes what function that component or object does. The second word is a noun describing the object which the action verb performs to or with. For example, a hammer has several components. A hammerhead "transmits force" and "drives nails." The rear portion of the hammerhead "removes nails." The handle performs a few functions including "applies leverage" and "absorbs vibration." Foam rubber–coated handles provide the additional secondary function "improves grip" and "provide comfort." This list of functions will later be used to provide a list for possible option elimination, product improvements, or opportunities for design modification.

Manufacturer					
Product					
Model number					
Annual sales					
Retail price					
Manufacturing cost					
Weight					
Key features					
Brief description of target market					

Figure 12.2   Nontechnical competitive analysis summary.

Next to this, the cost of that feature should be listed. This cost can be obtained from the purchasing organization or manufacturing organization depending on who makes or assembles that product. It is recommended to break down the costs into labor, machine processing, and material costs in order to obtain additional insight. A cost analysis for a wine bottle opener (Figure 12.3) is shown in Fig. 12.4.

Innovation Phase—Identifying Design Alternatives

After completing the feature costing and competitive analysis phase, the idea generation phase for identifying alternate design approaches should be implemented. This involves a brainstorming session. The key to any brainstorming session is not to criticize any ideas, no matter how ridiculous or impractical they appear, because free thought associations can help to generate creative problem-solving alternatives. In addition to ideas that reduce cost and improve value, ideas which add features or improve quality and reliability should be solicit-

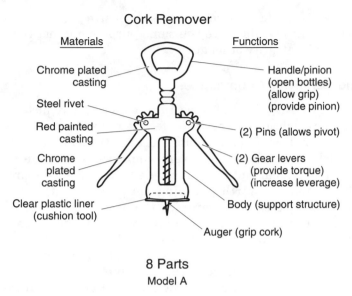

Cork Remover

Materials		Functions
Chrome plated casting		Handle/pinion (open bottles) (allow grip) (provide pinion)
Steel rivet		
Red painted casting		(2) Pins (allows pivot)
Chrome plated casting		(2) Gear levers (provide torque) (increase leverage)
Clear plastic liner (cushion tool)		Body (support structure)
		Auger (grip cork)

8 Parts

Model A

Figure 12.3 Drawing of a "Model A" wine bottle opener. (*Courtesy of Richard G. Bradyhouse, C.V.S. Value Analysis Consultant, Baltimore, Md.*)

	Unit cost	Percentage of total cost	After value analysis	
Material	4.55	51.4%		
Labor	1.20	13.6%		
Machine depreciation	1.25	14.1%		
Plant overhead	0.90	10.2%		
Total manufacturing costs	$7.90	89.3%	$4.70	
Sales, engineering, and administration costs	.95	10.7%	.95	
Total costs	$8.85	100.0%		
Profit margin	$1.40	15.8%	**$2.60**	**$4.60**
Sales price	$10.25		$8.25	$10.25
Annual volume	125,000.00		250,000.00	125,000.00
Annual profits	$175,000.00		$650,000.00	$575,000.00

Figure 12.4 A cost breakdown of a wine bottle opener.

ed. Each alternative should then be discussed to identify the most likely ones to investigate for each product function. For example, a business card holder box that has simulated wood-grained panels glued onto its side for decorative purposes has the function "appeals aesthetically." An alternate way to satisfy this criterion would be to make the whole box shape with a plastic wood grain finish. This would eliminate the extra panel, glue, and assembly operation.

Another alternative would be to see if a less expensive plastic material could be used which would serve the same purpose and not compromise the product's integrity or longevity.

Prioritizing and Identifying Opportunities

Value analysis will yield a host of opportunities for cost reduction. However, not all possibilities will be cost-effective to devote resources to investigate further. Therefore, the team must select the most likely possibilities for follow-up. There are several approaches that can be taken. First, each individual on the team can be told to select the proposals that they think are worth pursuing and write a list. Then, when all lists are completed, they can pick the ones which received the most votes. Variations of this technique will have each team member rate each proposal on a scale of 1 to 10. A 1 indicates that the project has a very low expected value, and 10 has a high expected value. Expected value is the combined product of the probability that the investigation will be successful and the potential value improvement of that project. After all assessments are made by team members, the total scores are added up and the top alternatives with the highest scores (or all scores higher than an agreed-to amount) are subject to further investigation. Another approach is to evaluate the savings potential, have the team members mutually assign a subjective probability of success, multiply the two numbers, and select the most viable alternatives that way.

After this selection process has been completed, a list of the alternatives requiring further investigation should be established and responsibilities assigned. This information should be summarized on a spreadsheet (Fig. 12.5).

Follow-Up and Implementation

After the investigative follow-up has been performed, which included feasibility and cost studies, the team can then select alternatives for implementation. To assist their selection, a list of the proposals that are worth implementing should be listed along with the advantages and disadvantages of each proposal (Fig. 12.6). Frequently a change incorporates benefits but compromises an aspect of a current design approach, so this is extremely important not to overlook. Even if testing proves that a change is feasible, there may be some compromise in performance that should be noted in the final decision-making process. The tooling and engineering development costs are considered in the alternative selection. Typically, changes are selected which have a payback in less than 2 years; however, this figure varies by industry and product.

Product description: Wine bottle opener (premium)
Model name: Model A
Annual volume: 125,000

Item Number	Component name/ part number/ material	Number per unit	Function Verb	Function Noun	Current cost	Alternate design proposal	Unit price savings	Manufacturing equipment cost	Engineering development cost	Person responsible
1	Screw Handle/ 1059/Die cast Al	1	Rotates	Auger	$1.65	Tumble plate	$.15	—	$2K	Norman
2	Housing/3345/Al Die cast w.Rd.Pnt	1	Contains	Parts	$2.00	Change to inj. mold. plastic	$1.05	$65K	$8K	Ivan
3	Gear Levers/ 3129/Cr Plated Zn Diecast	2	Increases	Leverage	$1.55	Change to inj. mold. plastic	$.65	$75K	$8K	Ivan
4	Rivets/0034/ Steel	2	Provide	Fulcrum	$.05	Eliminate, add to levers	$.05	—	$1K	Jane
5	Auger/8135/ Investment Cast	1	Grips	Cork	$1.80	Change to spiraled wire	$.80	$1K	$4K	Karen
6	Liner/5016/ Plastic	1	Cushions	Tool	$.40	Eliminate, if plastic housing is OK	$.35	$1K	—	Felicia
7	Assembly operation	—	Assemble	Parts	$.45	Reduced because of fewer parts	$.15	$10K	$1K	Norman
	Total				$7.90		$3.20	$94K	$23K	

Figure 12.5 A value analysis spreadsheet.

Item number	Proposal	Advantages	Disadvantages
1	Tumble plate	Reduces cost	Finish may not be as nice
2	Change housing from aluminum to plastic	1. Reduces cost 2. Red die pigments in plastic solves paint chipping problem 3. Plastic housing eliminates need for plastic liner insert	1. Plastic will not be as strong as the diecast unit 2. Proper plastic material was selected, but testing is needed to demonstrate adequate* durability (not as good as diecast parts)
3	Change gear lever from die cast to molded plastic	Reduces cost	1. Must be tested to show adequate strength but will not be as good
4	Eliminate rivets	1. Reduces cost 2. Weak point in the design was that pins came loose after extensive use	1. May require a new assembly machine to assure proper assembly of press fit 2. Durability of new fastening needs to be tested. Long term field usage effects needs review
5	Change augur from investment cast to spiraled wire	1. Reduces cost 2. May be easier to screw into cork	1 Cork removal is OK, with slightly higher incidence of removal problems than before
6	Eliminate liner	1. Reduces cost 2. Eliminates complaints about liners falling out	1 Cushioning effect of plastic housing may not be as good as before—this is not significant

*Adequate is defined as sufficient to meet or exceed customer expectations.

Figure 12.6 Assessing the advantages and disadvantages of implementing the final value analysis proposals.

Value Analysis Example: Wine Bottle Opener

In the example illustrated for the wine bottle opener, the information search revealed that the product was marketed to be easy to use and have a long life. Market research revealed that a price cut of 20 percent could double sales. Customers have complained about rivet failures, red paint peeling, and the plastic liner falling out.

Many more ideas would be considered and discussed during the brainstorming session than are shown on the final spreadsheet. Also, as the team is investigating possibilities, some of the ideas will prove not to be feasible. The brainstorming session leads to a new concept in wine bottle openers. It is a low-line model that requires only 2

Wine Bottle Opener

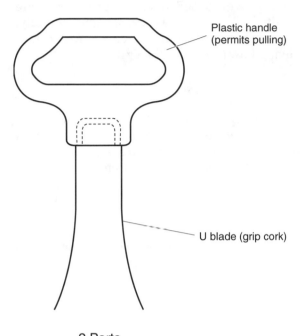

Plastic handle
(permits pulling)

U blade (grip cork)

2 Parts

Proposed model B (insert molded)

Figure 12.7 Drawing of "Model B," a wine bottle opener which appeals to a larger market. (*Courtesy of Richard G. Bradyhouse, C.V.S. Value Analysis Consultant, Baltimore, Md.*)

parts, is portable, and is a lot less expensive to manufacture. This product will be pursued as a new market opportunity (Fig. 12.7).

Following the investigation, testing revealed that the changes would work. Once the value analysis project was completed, the final recommendation was to change several components to plastic and eliminate a few others. A plastic material was discovered which did not compromise the product's design integrity. The strength of the plastic is lower than the metal, but it has more than enough to satisfy the design criteria and customer needs. The tooling and R&D costs will be a combined total of $117,000; however, the cost per unit will be 3.20 lower—a 40 percent reduction. The volume increase at the lower sales price offsets the cost higher profit margin (e.g., the price is elastic). Selling the unit at $10.25 has a variable margin of $4.60, while selling it at $8.25 has a margin of $2.60. This profit reduction is offset by increased sales; hence, profits will be increased at a lower price as is shown in Fig. 12.4. Also, although not shown in the accounting system, the allocation of corporate and plant overhead on a per unit basis is probably overstated because of the volume increase; hence, actual profits will probably be even higher. Finally, the total number of parts was decreased from 8 to 5; this will reduce administrative costs by having fewer parts in the system.

Summary

Value analysis lowers product costs, reduces the number of parts, improves profitability, helps create new product offerings, improves customer satisfaction, reduces warranty, promotes teamwork, and helps give its participants a better appreciation of customer values and design tradeoffs.

References

1. Bradyhouse, Richard, "Case Study of a Wine Bottle Opener," unpublished, September 1992.
2. Demarle, David J., and Shillito, Larry M., "Value Engineering," in Salvendy, Gavriel, (ed.), *Handbook of Industrial Engineering,* Wiley, New York, 1982, sec. 7.3.

Bibliography

Bradyhouse, Richard G., "Better Knowledge Needed of VA, J-I-T Concepts," Modern Purchasing, October 1985.
Bradyhouse, Richard G., "Value Engineering in Today's Rapidly Changing World," Value World, April/May/June 1990.
Miles, Lawrence D., *Techniques of Value Analysis and Engineering,* McGraw-Hill, New York, 1961.

13

Marketing Strategies: Advertising, Promotion, and Packaging

Marketing a product requires a business assessment of the markets, market size, target markets, competition, and pricing. It is essential to perform this analysis up front because it can help avoid costly marketing blunders. There will be times when the cost of obtaining some information through market research will be prohibitive or the time required to obtain such information will result in a delayed introduction for a product, which is believed will be successful and such a delay would greatly reduce sales and profits by having a later product introduction. An effective system to address these issues is outlined and discussed in this chapter. Finally, the method is summarized with a checklist.

Product Marketing Plan

A product marketing plan reviews all aspects of the product's marketing issues. It encompasses the following issues.

Situation analysis

A situation analysis analyzes the basic issues relating to the product. It identifies the customer's current way of coping with a situation or a want or need that has to be addressed. It can also describe how this product will better serve that purpose or address those needs.

Marketing challenges

Discussing market challenges involves the issues and hurdles that are faced with marketing a product. For example, one of the issues that faced Chrysler Corporation in 1983 prior to the introduction of the minivan was uncertainty in consumer acceptance of the product in the marketplace. Chrysler marketers were faced with the difficulty of educating consumers on product advantages of the vehicle, because nothing like it had ever been introduced before.

Opportunities

Listing opportunities, benefits, and advantages of marketing a certain product helps the product development and marketing team to develop effective strategies to market the product. For example, when Apple Computer began marketing the Apple II personal computer in 1979, sales soared because Apple incorporated the spreadsheet software VisiCalc in the package to make it user-friendly. This was a marketing approach that had not been used before in small computers and had a lot of applications with small businesses. Ford recognized a market opportunity in 1986 with the Taurus; they had utilized substantial market research to identify car features which would be pleasing to a driver. Additionally, Ford benefited from entering a market segment which, at that time, did not have strong competition.

Sales strategies and objectives

The sales strategy and objectives should include a discussion of the sales expectations for the product. Although it is difficult to anticipate the sales for the product's life, an estimate of the first year sales should be included. A general strategy for the time sequence for addressing different markets should also be discussed. For example, a report may read as follows:

> The first year may introduce a high-line (premium) product to industrial consumers selling 15,000 units. Then an adaptation of the product will be introduced 6 months later for consumer channels which is expected to sell 40,000 units. As product awareness expands, we anticipate market growth in the industrial channel to be around 30 percent in the industrial channel and 45 percent in the consumer channel. In the third year, increased competition is anticipated, which will reduce our sales from the previous year, but this effect will be partially offset with some product improvements.

It is important to estimate the length of the product life cycle, if possible. Most products generally undergo four phases during their life cycle. Typically, the first phase is the *introduction phase,* where sales are growing but profits are negative because of the research and development as well as advertising costs required. The *growth phase* sees rapid expansion of sales and profits. New competitors enter the market. During the *market maturity phase,* sales have stabilized at their peak and profits are being eroded by competition. During the *decline phase,* sales decline along with profits, competitors discontinue their products, and eventually the product becomes unprofitable and is canceled. This is illustrated in Fig. 13.1. An important concept is to be the first to introduce a product because one may be in a better position to reap the profits from the growth phase, which will cause market penetration and improve profitability in subsequent phases.

The strategy should also indicate whether a *push selling strategy* will be used in which case the distribution chain tries to market the product through efforts with the retail outlet. If a *pull selling* approach will be used, the marketers try to create a demand with promotions, advertising, and word-of-mouth recommendations. This creates a desire for the retailers to sell the product because of strong customer demand.

Brand and product name

Name selection can be a crucial factor in determining the success of a product. Selecting a name for the product produces an image for the

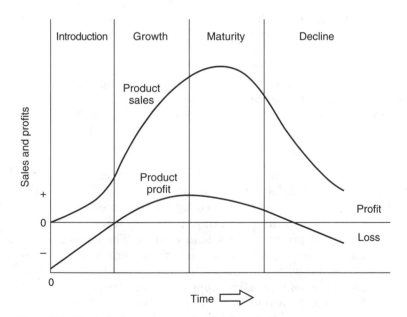

Figure 13.1   Typical phases in a product's life cycle.

consumer. A classic example of how important this is, was illustrated when General Motors successfully marketed the Chevrolet Nova in the United States. However, a similar car with the same name did not sell well in Mexico because, in Spanish, the name Nova means "does not go." For a product as complex as a car, it was amazing that sales could be so greatly affected by its name. A well-chosen name will generally be short, stand out, be easy to pronounce and remember, tell how the product is used, and suggest action. Procter and Gamble chose the name Plax for its prebrushing dental rinse because of its connotation for removing plaque on teeth. Plax fits these criteria because it is easy to pronounce and remember, is distinctive, is only four letters long, and helps to identify what the product is supposed to do (remove plaque). Another well-selected name is Drano, which is used to clear clogged plumbing.

Similar considerations should be given to brand name and logo selection. The connotation of the brand name should be considered when marketing a product to take advantage of a good brand name. In 1992 Black and Decker promoted a new line of professional tools using the brand name "DeWalt." This name was chosen because market research showed that many professional market customers had a high regard for this name, while many professional customers generally associated the Black and Decker name with consumer tools. After making this brand name change, along with changing their existing product color to yellow, sales for the company's professional tools greatly increased, exceeding the companies initial expectations. The 3M Company used the respected "Scotch" brand name to introduce a new line of camera film. Scotch already had a good reputation for making audio tapes and 3M was capitalizing on this to enhance its marketing efforts and gain a competitive marketing advantage. Before utilizing a product or brand name, a name search must be given to assure that no trademark infringements will occur.

Markets and sales estimates

It is important to identify the market segments of the end user. This can be in the form of a brief summary of the markets. A hypothetical report is shown in Fig. 13.2. This product represents an existing product for which some new features and improvements were incorporated from an established product and sales network. The sales territories are separated by five regions. The market segment has two categories: large customers, whose annual sales are over $50 million, and small businesses. This segmentation approach can also be developed for other countries and future years as part of the overall marketing strategy.

Market segment	Location	First year sales goal	Market potential
Large business	Northeast	1,100	4,000
Small business	Northeast	2,200	14,500
Large business	Midwest	3,000	17,200
Small business	Midwest	4,700	21,800
Large business	Southeast	1,800	8,500
Small business	Southeast	2,700	13,700
Large business	West Coast	2,600	12,300
Small business	West Coast	3,400	17,600
Large business	Northwest	800	3,500
Small business	Northwest	1,200	5,200
Total		23,500	18,300

Figure 13.2 A hypothetical market projection summary.

Distribution channel

Determining the type(s) of distribution channel(s) is important because it can have a great impact on sales. Describing the distribution channel(s) will specify the general category of how the product will be distributed. The channel should be selected based on those distribution channels that can best satisfy the target market. Sometimes there will be several distribution channels. For example, some retail customers purchase directly from the factories to eliminate middleperson costs, while others utilize the middleperson to take advantage of their economies of scale for distributing the product; hence both are needed. The area of specialization for a distributor needs to be listed because some deal with specialty shops, while others with retailers. Each distribute in a different market. Industrial suppliers sometimes use a combination depending on their customer.

Target market

Describing the target markets identifies typical customers or occupations. In an industrial application it would identify the job classification such as commercial plumbers, electrical contractors, screw machine product manufacturers, etc. In a consumer application it would include a demographic and psychographic profile. An example would state that

> This product appeals to an average customer, age 40, whose annual income is above $45,000, who is likely a college graduate, in a management level job or a professional field. The product generally appeals to both single men and women; however, it is anticipated that 70 percent of the consumers will be male. The consumer is active in leisure activities such as golf, watching sporting events, camping, movies, dining out, and concerts.

Sometimes a few target markets and market segments can be identified. The way a product is positioned in the market plays a crucial role in the marketing because the creativity used will define the image that a product will generate for its user as well as demonstrate the product attributes. The positioning and image for identical products with different target markets are vital. Arm and Hammer marketed a baking soda product which originally was used for baking. However, they expanded its product scope with new market applications by identifying many uses for its baking soda product including cleaning kitchen surfaces, refrigerator deodorizer, brushing teeth. A fragrance was added, and it became a cat litter box and carpet deodorizer. The Arm and Hammer Division of Church and Dwight Co. brilliantly expanded its market by incorporating only minor changes into its product. Smirnoff vodka is manufactured in the United States. However, it takes advantage of the American perception that Russian vodka is superior in its marketing strategy by using a Russian brand name.

Pricing

A marketing plan should indicate the price at which the product will be sold through the distribution channels, retailers, and customers. It should also specify discounts given for volume purchases. The price at which it will be sold to the end user, after the distribution channel markups, should also be indicated so that sales estimates for the markets can be established.

There are several pricing strategies that can be used. The first is a *standard markup,* at which the product is sold at a specific percentage higher than manufacturing and development costs. This is recommended for competitive bidding in supply and industrial customers. However, when product differentiation or an innovative product exists, other approaches should be employed.

A *skimming strategy* can be employed. With this strategy, high prices are charged initially to achieve large profit margins. The markets that have great demand for this product will be willing to purchase this product at that price. When demand for the product reduces, competition enters the market; or at a predetermined interval, the price is then reduced to generate more sales and appeal to a larger market. A skimming strategy makes sense if

- There are no product substitutes.
- The product is introduced a long time before competitors can manufacture a product to compete in the marketplace.
- Exclusive patent rights have been granted.

- Product demand exceeds production capacity, and it cannot be increased in the near future—and price gouging will not affect the sale of other products.

- The variable profit margin increases with a change in price (the price increase increases the profit margin faster than sales are reduced).

When implementing a skimming strategy, the high profit margins received will attract a lot of competition, so an aggressive product value improvement strategy should be implemented to ward off the competition when it becomes significant.

A third approach is a *market penetration strategy*. A low initial price is charged to obtain a strong market penetration, which will discourage potential competition from entering the market because of reduced profitability. Once a large market share has been obtained, prices are raised, and the company profits from both a reduced cost structure relating to economies of scale and increased sales from having a larger portion of the market. This strategy is a longer term strategy and is recommended if

- The product has a long life cycle.

- There is a lot of potential competition because few barriers to entry exist.

- When the price is reduced, profits increase because the variable profit margin reduction is offset by the increase in sales.

Another approach is a *product line pricing strategy*. In this method, two products are manufactured with slight differences to assure product differentiation. One product is targeted at the mass market. Another one is given a few minor changes such as add-on features, color changes, improved packaging, etc., and is differentiated in its marketing approach to obtain "snob appeal" or have a status associated with that product. The pricing markup more than offsets the cost of the added features. This way both market segments can be addressed, and the profits achieved can be higher than would be achievable otherwise. This is common practice in the cosmetic industry. For example, Cheseboro Ponds marketed the Baby Face women's facial or press powder. Baby Face was targeted for the low-end mass market. They later introduced a similar facial powder which differed insignificantly in terms of performance and cost, and repositioned it as a high-end or upscale product. It was given the brand name Erno Laslo with a more appealing package and was sold in a different distribution chain. The principle purpose of the product was for women's facial powder, but the status appeal allows for higher profit margins to be charged in one market segment.

Competitive comparisons

Competitive comparisons are an essential portion of the marketing strategy because they can identify aspects of other products, packaging, and promotional advertisement which customers find appealing. Comparisons also help identify some of the challenges that must be overcome with the competition when marketing a new product. Comparisons can help identify competitive product advantages with the new product which can be used in advertising and sales promotions. Chrysler Corporation used competitive analysis to promote its Dodge Spirit and Plymouth Acclaim by comparing them to the top-selling Honda Accord. Chrysler's research showed that 117 out of 200 customers preferred the Spirit and Acclaim over the Accord and those products also were roomier. That advertisement helped to educate the customer on the superior aspects of those Chrysler Products.

Market shares between manufacturers are monitored to see if one manufacturer is gaining share. Any significant changes should be investigated to identify new marketing opportunities. Figure 13.3

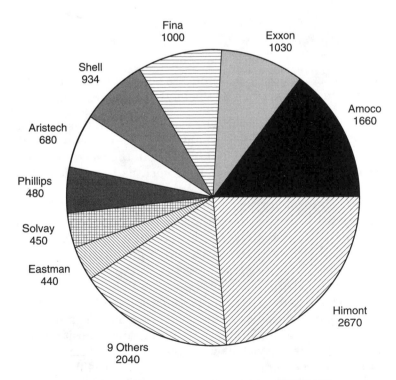

Total value of polypropylene supply = $3,985 MM

Figure 13.3 Pie chart of polypropylene market share. (*Courtesy of Amoco Chemical Company.*)

depicts how Amoco Chemical monitors market shares of poly-propylene with a pie chart to better present the information to its audience.

Identifying user habits and needs

Identifying user habits and needs is essential to pinpoint possible product improvements and advertising themes. Understanding user habits will help the engineering group design for potential abuse and use. Computer workstations are designed for office worker comfort and durability in an office setting. For example, the computer key-board is tested so that it will operate if dropped on the floor or if someone drops an object such as a textbook onto it. A less obvious example would be to observe that stereo speakers are used for rest-ing places for people's drinks at parties; therefore, it might be advan-tageous to design a speaker which will not become stained or dam-aged if a drink is spilled on it. Identifying user needs is also critical. Sometimes these needs are not obvious. Beer marketers frequently identify human companionship needs as a way to market their prod-ucts. Old Milwaukee beer's advertising theme is to have friends doing activities together such as fishing and camping while drinking their beer at a cookout. Some perfume manufacturers try to portray their brand as a product which will make women become attractive to men.

Identify the image to project
and the product message

It is important to identify the image to project and the product mes-sage based on user needs, habits, competitive analysis, and market segment that is being addressed. The image to project depends on the market segment. The General Mills cereal Wheaties uses the theme "Breakfast of Champions" and a successful athlete to promote the product to people who ascribe to be athletic. Nissan ran a series of television advertisements for its luxury car the J30 which displayed a sophisticated, refined customer living a life of wealth to promote the status appeal of its product.

In addition to the image, the product message is also important. The message portrayed by Eveready when marketing their Alkaline Energizer battery is that it lasts a long time. They use a toy rabbit pounding on a drum, while the announcer says it is "still going" (the commercials are attention getters because the audience thinks that it is watching a commercial for another product and realizes that it was fooled when the toy rabbit marches onto the screen).

Advertising, promotion budget, and allocation

The primary purpose of advertising is to increase demand for that product or brand; therefore, the ad or the advertising strategy must ultimately give the consumer a reason to buy the product. It can also be used to increase public awareness of a company; this can be referred to as *image advertising*. The amount of money spent on advertising should be such that for each dollar spent, the variable profit margin will increase more than one dollar, in the long run, as a result of the advertisement or promotion. Obviously, it is difficult to obtain this information, but this type of thinking should predominate the decision-making process for advertising expenditures. The total dollar allocation should be specified with a breakdown of the amount to the various media sources and, if possible, the specific publications and periodicals.

The primary purposes of advertising are to

- Aid introduction of the product to the target market.

- Motivate buyers to make purchase decisions.

- Help buyers confirm purchase decisions after the sales were made to enhance word-of-mouth advertising.

A mnemonic for advertising a product is AIDA for getting *attention* from the audience, holding their *interest,* arouse a *desire* to purchase the product, and obtain *action* to buy the product. Attention-getting themes may include a shocking or noticeable statement or picture. A common example is to include an attractive woman or man in the advertising theme. Interest in an ad can be maintained by addressing an interest in the product theme which the target would find appealing. Arousing desire can be obtained by showing how a product satisfies a customer's needs. For example, cosmetics are marketed by showing how they will make someone look beautiful, which will improve their social life. Obtaining action is getting people to buy the product. An example of this would be to tell the audience to buy the product "while supplies last," which would motive the audience to take action quickly. Another approach is to list a toll-free number to call to place an order. This allows the consumer to make a purchase with little effort.

The creative aspect of advertising cannot be overlooked and can be essential at successfully selling a product. *Pioneering advertising* develops the primary demand for a new product by showing potential customers how a new product satisfies a need. *Direct advertising* is used to obtain an immediate purchase, while *indirect advertising* is used to display product advantages. *Comparative advertising* is used to compare the product to competitive brands in a direct A to B comparison. The risk with this approach is that the competitive product receives free media exposure.

The objectives and advertising strategy should be identified. Frequently, an advertising agency will assist with these issues and recommend the media to utilize. Sometimes there are phases of advertising to introduce products. One phase might include a *brand awareness phase* which tries to strengthen customer perception of a brand. Then a *new product introduction phase* will introduce the consumer to the new product. Then a *brand association phase* will be started to tie the new product to the brand name to solidify its image. Finally, an *arousal phase* will be implemented to motivate a consumer to purchase the product.

Part of the advertising strategy is to utilize the media to help introduce and sell the product through product reviews, press releases, and interviews for interest stories. Some strategies for working with the media will be discussed later. The media can include magazines, television, radio, trade journals, and billboards. Each should have a specific audience and purpose for selecting it.

When innovative or novel products are being introduced, the manufacturer must help educate the consumer about the product benefits and create a "product want." If this is not done properly, a technically superior product can be a flop in the marketplace.

The product marketing plan should be updated if new information warrants adjustments and changes.

Advertising to Sell the Product

The famous advertisement for a hamburger chain in which an elderly woman (Clara Peller) exclaimed "Where's the beef?" got one's attention, aroused interest, and created a desire to buy a hamburger with a lot of beef, and perhaps may have spurred some action to buy such a hamburger. The award-winning advertisement received a lot of publicity and was very popular to the point of being a fad, e.g., thousands of T-shirts were sold which displayed the slogan. However, it was ineffective for its sponsor, because the advertisement overshadowed the fact that it was advertising Wendy's hamburgers. While many consumers could joyously recall Clara Peller saying "Where's the beef?," they could not identify that this was an endorsement for Wendy's hamburgers. Therefore, a memorable advertising theme must effectively tie into the product that is being advertised.

Promotions

Promotional strategies need to be developed for the budget allocated. They can be in the form of point-of-use displays, product demonstrations, coupons, and contests. Demonstrations can help introduce a product, and a well-performed demonstration can increase sales. Therefore, training the display personnel for the presentation techniques is of paramount importance. For competitive demonstrations, any related apparatus must be coordinated to assure that it is available. These displays can emphasize points that were determined to be important from field trials and focus groups. Promotions are often very effective motivators to improve sales when used in conjunction with advertisements more than if used alone.

Trade shows and expositions also provide excellent opportunities to promote one's product. The shows and expositions should be thoroughly reviewed to determine which ones will effectively help promote the product.

Contests can also provide exposure and help promote a product. Free giveaways and similar promotions have also been used successfully to stimulate sales.

The advertising and promotion agencies must be supplied with information showing the product's strengths, competitive advantages, competitive analysis, and information regarding market segments, target markets, and both customer demographics and psychographics. This information will help agencies advertise the product more successfully because they will be better able to design an ad which appeals to the target markets.

Preparing product demonstrations, videos, and other displays will greatly assist these efforts. The promotions should promote and reinforce a few key themes that prospective customers will remember about the product and can share with their associates and friends who were unable to attend the show.

Packaging design

When purchasing products in department stores, the packages on the shelf frequently promote the product's key advantages and features. Therefore, the packaging design is an important consideration for products in consumer channels. In industrial channels, packaging design is usually of less significance other than to assure the product is protected from damage. The package should be designed with several considerations in mind. One would be that the product promotes the desired theme. Children are attracted to animals, so many children's cereals use a cartoon animal to promote their product. For example, Trix cereal, by General Mills, uses a white cartoon rabbit who tries to eat the cereal but cannot because a kid says "silly rabbit, Trix are for kids." Nine Lives cat food successfully used a "finicky cat named Morris" to market the product. Morris was used in television commercials and was photographed on the box of the product. Similar to the advertising message with media channels, it can have a photo or a drawing which promotes a theme to the target market. It can have one with an emotional appeal aimed at either traditional or modern values. For example, some Coca Cola glass bottles have the traditional shape to emphasize the classic Coke flavor and some people save them as collectors' items. On the other hand, prepared microwavable food boxes will try to emphasize a more modern theme.

The package should emphasize the product's key selling point. For example, food manufacturers state on their packages "reduced sodium," "no cholesterol," "all natural," and "reduced calorie" with their food products, if it is appropriate, to emphasize the health aspects of their products to their customers. These selling points are designed so that they can easily be read at about 7 ft away. The design should clearly project the image and the key selling points of the product. Once those objectives are achieved, additional material and information may be counterproductive and reduce the effectiveness of the product. Those consumers who require additional information can be satisfied by making that information available on the side of the box, so they can read it by pulling it off the shelf. The color of the box can also grab the customer's attention and help a product stand out from other packages on the shelf. A final consideration is to make the package easy to open and close, and yet maintain product integrity (where appropriate). Tubs of margarine fit this criterion well and are more effective than sticks; however, some consumers prefer the sticks, so this should not be the only consideration.

A few packaging designs should be proposed and then evaluated with members of the target market. Those that are received most favorably should be reviewed to see how the best ideas can be incorporated for a better package. The final package design should be retested before it receives final approval. Figure 13.4 shows some packaging designs. Figure 13.4*a* is a photo of the box used to market a Toro Air Rake. It has a drawing of the part which shows how the unit can be easily held in one's hand. It also shows key selling points in the form of a bullet list on the box. Figure 13.4*b* is a photo of a White-Westinghouse room air conditioner. It has a photo of the unit and some simple selling points on the left making statements such as easy to use, easy to install, quiet and efficient. Also included are six more specific selling points on the right. A Skilsaw package is shown in Fig. 13.4*c*. This is a circular saw manufactured by Skil, a division of Emerson Electric. A circular saw is a powertool that is heavily used by carpenters and tradespeople. Carpenters who have good experiences with their circular saw frequently have a preference for buying other professional tools from that same manufacturer. Skil was the manu-

Figure 13.4 Assorted photos of packaging used to market products.

Figure 13.4 (*a*)(*upper left*) A Toro 600 Air Rake. (*b*) (*upper right*) A White-Westinghouse Continental Series compact room air conditioner. (*c*) (*lower left*) A Skil professional circular saw, also known as a "Skilsaw." (*d*) (*lower right*) Compact Kitchen by little tikes.

facturer who introduced the circular saw. As a result, carpenters call a circular saw a "Skilsaw." This is a desirable situation for a product to have. Other products which have this attribute include Scotch brand transparent adhesive tape, Post-it brand self-stick removable notes, and Kleenex brand facial tissues. The word "brand" is added by the manufacturers to prevent the name from being a generic description of the product so that the manufacturer does not lose the rights to the product. Figure 13.4*c* is a Compact Kitchen by little tikes. The photo shows a picture of the product next to a young girl. A key selling point is the girl's smile as she plays with the product. Beneath the logo is a selling point aimed at parents: "toys that last."

Selling emphasis

The selling emphasis must be identified up front in order to maximize the effectiveness of the sales force. The emphasis will be a guide to the sales force which tells them what percentage of their time they should allocate toward different markets. If the sales force discovers that they can obtain more sales by allocating resources differently, this should be discussed with the marketing group to modify the strategy. However, it is possible that certain markets are being targeted early in order to obtain a larger customer base in the long run. If this is part of the strategy, it must be communicated to the sales force.

Communication and Timing

The information regarding target markets, demographics, competitive advantages, product selling points or features, product and promotional themes, marketing strategies, and introduction dates need to be shared with both the advertising agencies and the sales force. Advertising is often coordinated with the sales force so that they can use the advertising efforts in their sales pitch, i.e., salespersons may tell retailers that their product will receive "national media exposure" (or whatever media exposure the product will receive). Sometimes advertising can be used to bait local retailers to commit to large purchase orders by having them involved in the advertisement. For example, when selling a new product, at the end of the advertisement the announcer may state "available at your local K-Mart," Sears, or Wal-Mart, etc.

The timing of the advertising and promotion strategies must be coordinated with the product development schedule to assure a successful new product introduction. Additionally, the timing must take seasonal demand variations into consideration. For example, leather gloves sell in the autumn and winter. Therefore, manufacturers advertise during those times and would be wasting their time marketing those products during summertime.

Free Publicity

The media can be effectively utilized to obtain free publicity. Some of the key strategies for this are to first announce a press release for the new product. The press release should be issued between 8:30 and 9:00 a.m. before the reporters are busy and will have time to review them. The press release should be succinctly written and answer the questions who, what, why, how, when, and where. It should indicate who or which company is manufacturing the product, what the product is, why it is being sold (e.g., its selling points and key product features), how it will be used, when it will be on sale, and where it will be sold or marketed. All press releases should be followed up with a phone call to clarify any points and answer the reporters' questions. If the company needs to hold a press conference, the company should notify the editors so that they can assign the appropriate personnel to report on the conference. It is ideal to announce it one week in advance and schedule it in the morning when the reporters are not too busy. It is recommended to remind the reporters of the conference one day in advance. The press conference will be most effective if there is a one- or two-page handout and the presentation has visual aids.

Summary

Developing a comprehensive marketing strategy will enhance the success of the new product's sales. The customer demographic and psychographic patterns along with competitive product advantages and key product features should be utilized to name the product, project a product image, advertise, and package the product. The sales force and distribution channel must be selected and must be made aware of this information.

Bibliography

Dalrymple, Douglas J., and Parsons, Leonard J., *Marketing Management Strategy and Cases,* 4th ed., Wiley, New York, 1986.

Feeney, Ann, "How to deal with Colorado's Business Media," *Colorado Business Magazine,* April 1988, p. 20.

Mossberg, Warren S., "Latest Formula in Spreadsheets Is Ease of Use," *Wall Street Journal,* May 28, 1992, p. B1.

Northwood, Warren, "Press Conferences: Getting Your Point Across," *Colorado Business Magazine,* January 1986, p. 28.

Smith, Ward, "Business and the Media: Sometimes Partners, Sometimes Adversaries," *Vital Speeches of the Day,* September 17, 1985, p. 49.

Trachtenberg, Jeff, "Words Still Matter," *Forbes Magazine,* May 4, 1987, p. 142.

Twedt, Dik Warren, "How Much Value Can Be Added Through Packaging," *Journal of Marketing,* 32 (January 1968), pp. 58–61

14

Performing Corrective Action

"Train, train, train; until you die"

—TOM PETERS

When the product does not meet its customer requirements for durability, manufacturing process capability, cost, and appeal, or encounters product process failures, verification failures, customer complaints, poor sales, and an inability to keep up with delivery schedules, warranties, etc., corrective action must be performed.

A Seven-Step Corrective Action Process

A general approach to solving problems involves a seven-step plan of action. Those seven steps are

1. *Describe the problem* using the facts that are reported. Indicate the magnitude of the problem. Additional research may be needed to obtain all the information required to properly address the issue.

2. *Define the root cause* of the problem. This is the source of the problem, and by eliminating this cause the problem will be corrected.

3. *Establish an interim action* to either contain the problem or minimize the adverse effects to be encountered.

4. *Develop a permanent* fix to the problem. This is usually a long-term solution which specifically addresses the root cause of the problem.

5. *Verify* that the corrective action was successful. In a manufacturing problem this can be done by statistically qualifying the process. With an engineering issue, this can be achieved by perfor-

mance testing, Weibull analysis, stress analysis, etc. Marketing issues can be done through market research techniques.

6. *Specify the controls needed to prevent* this problem from happening again. This also includes updating the documentation as appropriate. In a manufacturing environment, updating might include incorporating SPC into the process or scheduling preventative maintenance on the machine. The documentation might be the manufacturing control plan or the preventative maintenance log. In product development, it may require modifying test requirements and procedures. In market research, it could require new research methodology and revisions to the focus group guidelines and research questionnaires.

7. *Prevent a similar problem from happening* with other products by either improving the management system or incorporating similar controls from step 6 into similar product lines of systems. For example, suppose that a furniture manufacturer discovers that its customers are complaining that armrests are breaking on their couches. After investigation, the company discovers that armrests break because people sit on them. The management first has to decide if it is worth the extra cost to design the arm rest to accommodate a 275-lb person sitting on it. Suppose they decide that for their customer base, it would be worthwhile. They go ahead and modify the design accordingly and also verify that it works. The final step of the solution would be to review all couches and chairs and see if they should incorporate a similar design criterion as would be determined by each market.

Figure 14.1 is an example of an eight-step corrective action process used by Champion Laboratories to correct a problem with an oil filter. The sequence of steps is slightly different from the process described above, but it covers the same topics. The verification step is combined in step 5, "corrective actions."

Program Status Reviews

A variation of the seven-step corrective action process can be used to monitor product development issues. The management should call regularly scheduled meetings, perhaps weekly, monthly or whatever is appropriate for the circumstance, and review all issues of concern. Engineering management should review all engineering and lab test failures. Manufacturing management should review all tooling delivery dates and process qualification issues. All manufacturing processes that do not meet quality standards, or do not meet cycle time requirements and perform required tasks, should be identified. Then the responsible individual is assigned to perform a five-step corrective action report.

Concern No:	Concern Title:		Date Opened:	Champion
CONAC	Customer complaint of filter with non–conforming seam		2–20–92	Deb Seals

(2) Concern Description:	Lines	Product Name:
	100 (A)	Oil Filter
Filter spun on chuck allowing a deformed seam.	Date(s)	Date(s)
	1–24–92	

(1) Team Members/Activity/Phone
Al Yellig Plant Manager
Ron Berger Tool Design
Mike Summerfield Prod. Foreman
Patty Massie Sealer Operator
Cary Moudy QA Analyst
Mike Gruca QC Manager

(3) Containment Actions:	% Effected	Effective Date Mfg. Retail
100% all warehoused componet parts and finished inventory.	100%	2–20–92 | 1–24–92 | | 2–06–92 |

(4) Root Cause(s): Definition:	% Contrib/Cause
	100%
Tooling chucks have both fine knurl and coarse knurl sealing diameters.	

(5) Corrective Actions:	% Effective
Eliminate all Fine knurled chucks from production floor.	100%

(6) Implementation of Permanent Corrective Actions:	Effective Date Mfg. Retail
Remove fine knurled chucks from production floor.	2–20–92 |

(7) Actions to Prevent Recurrence:

Print changed to construct coarse knurl type chucks only.

Reported By:	Last Change/Status:	Concurrence: Supervisor	Date
Cary L. Moudy	*Closed* 3-17-92	*Cary T. Moudy*	3–17–92

(8) Congratulate your team.

Figure 14.1 A 7-point corrective action plan used to correct a defect with an oil filter. (*Courtesy of Champion Laboratories, Inc.*)

The five-step process could be as follows:

1. Problem definition

2. Root cause

3. Corrective action

4. Verification

5. Prevention

If this type of product or process is similar to another product/process in the works, then the information should be applied to those products and shared with those product development groups. Also, assure that documentation was updated as is appropriate.

This approach to program management will assure that the problems receive proper attention and are addressed in a timely manner.

Some basic problem skills that are used to aid problem-solving efforts include brainstorming, grouping, prioritizing, Pareto charts, cause-and-effect analysis, histograms, and developing checklists.

Brainstorming

Brainstorming is a method used with a team of people to promote a free flow of ideas. The goal is to generate a quantity of solutions or possible causes of problems. Brainstorming generates creative solutions to problem solving. Not all of the ideas that are presented will be realistic. However, when using this method, one "unrealistic" idea can trigger a thought which can lead to an innovative yet pragmatic solution.

The way to perform a brainstorming session is as follows:

1. Review the following guidelines for all participants:

- *All ideas are acceptable.* There is to be absolutely no criticism of any idea, no matter how "dumb" or "unrealistic" it appears.

- *The wilder, the better.* Wild and crazy ideas can generate creative, pragmatic ideas with the participants.

- *Quantity over quality.* The purpose is to generate many ideas and stimulate free thought; later the list can be reduced and grouped.

- *Building and combining is to be encouraged.* Modifying existing thoughts can generate more refined solutions.

2. *Define the problem* for which causes or solutions are being sought.

3. *Call upon each group member* in the room to give an idea and then continue until either ideas are exhausted or time constraints

dictate. As each idea is stated, list it on a board or a flip chart for everyone to see. All ideas should be visible to the participants during this process. After the session, this information should be typed and distributed to group members. At a later time, new ideas can be added and analyzed more critically. There are two commonly used approaches. One involves consensus decision making, the other involves grouping.

Consensus decision making

With consensus decision making, the goal is to obtain a general agreement among group members. This can be done by having everyone separately list their top 10 or 20 recommended solutions from the brainstorming list. This information can be summarized with the top 10 or 20 remaining. A discussion of the items can occur. Then, if desired, the process can be repeated until the list is reduced to a manageable level for investigation.

Grouping

Grouping is a method of combining the list of information into one key topic or phrase. Frequently, lists of 50 or more items can be summarized into fewer than 10 general topics because of the similarities between ideas. This is very useful to focus their problem-solving efforts and reduce the list to a manageable level. It is imperative that

Collect data (list customer complaints) *Phase 1*	Group into categories (list in similar groups) *Phase 2*	Summarize categories (identify general group categories) *Phase 3*
Heavy to lift	Vibrates excessively	
Vibrates excessively	Noisy	
Hard to use	Unpleasant sound	Noise and vibration
Cumbersome to carry	Clatters	harshness
Hard for a new person	Hard to keep in hands	
Noisy		
Unpleasant sound		
Too complex to use		
Hard to move	Heavy to lift	
Clatters	Cumbersome to carry	Heavy and bulky
Requires a lot of training	Hard to move	
Hard to keep in hands	Bulky	
Bulky	Hard to use	
	Hard for a new person	Not user-friendly
	Too complex to use	
	Requires a lot of training	

Figure 14.2 Grouping customer complaints for a consumer product.

all people have equal input in this process. A dominant personality can cause this method to be counterproductive.

Figure 14.2 is an example of a grouping technique used to group and classify customer complaints so that corrective efforts can be more focused. In the first group, the complaints are all listed. In the second phase the information has been rearranged to keep similar complaints together. During phase 3 the groups of similar complaints have been summarized in only a few words.

Cause-and-Effect Diagram

Another problem solving technique utilizes the cause-and-effect diagram. This is also called the fishbone diagram because of its resemblance to the skeletal structure of a fish. In Japan it is referred to as the Ishakawa chart after its founder, who is a renowned quality guru. The chart analyzes a situation by identifying the causes. It can be prepared in the following manner using a group problem-solving method:

1. Determine the problem at hand (this is also called the effect). Place it on the middle right of the page.
2. Draw the "backbone" connected to the effect.
3. Draw the categories of the causes as separate offshoots. Frequently these categories are divided into four groups: manpower, materials, machinery, and methods.
4. List the causes of the problem as they fit into each category.
5. Identify the causes which most probably have the biggest impact on the problem. This is usually done after the team members have studied the diagram for a while.

Based on this information a corrective action plan can be developed.

Figure 14.3 is a cause-and-effect diagram used by Champion Labs to identify the causes of an occasional nonconforming Angleus Sealer. It was successfully used to help identify the root cause and resolve the problem.

The cause-and-effect diagram is an excellent problem-solving technique for both complex problems and problems that need to be solved by someone who is inexperienced or unfamiliar with a system that involves several interactive effects.

The Pareto Chart

The Pareto chart was devised by Vilfredo Pareto, an Italian sociologist and economist.[1] The Pareto principle is that a relatively small

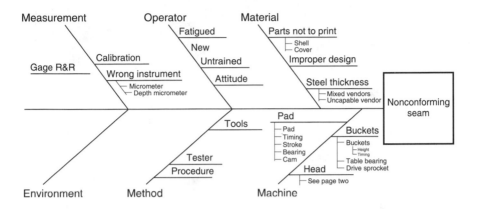

Figure 14.3 Cause-and-effect diagram used to solve an oil filter sealing issue. (*Courtesy of Champion Laboratories, Inc.*)

number of factors account for a disproportionately large amount of the total effect. It has also been known as the 80-20 rule, which signifies that approximately 80 percent of the effect is accounted for in 20 percent of the causes. Joseph M. Juran frequently refers to allocating a majority of resources to address "the vital few."

The Pareto principle is a valuable one to apply to resources to solve problems and perform corrective action. Pareto charts can be made as follows:

1. Identify the problem and how it should be classified.

2. Collect the data; compute the totals and percentages.

3. Rank in order from lowest to highest.

4. Plot the data in order from lowest to highest in the form of a histogram.

Sometimes the cumulative percentage contribution data are plotted above the bar graph. A Pareto chart is shown in Fig. 14.4. The chart shows data collected by Reinz Wisconsin Gasket's manufacturing operation to show both how many and what types of customer complaints they have received over the past year. Their definition of customer includes final inspection (the figures were changed and the actual data were exaggerated for illustration purposes).

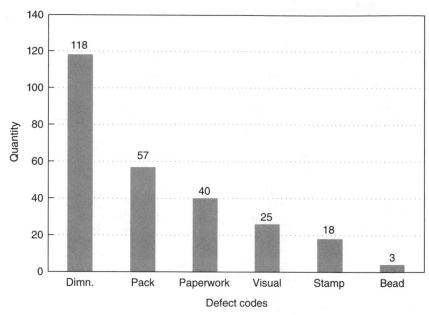

Figure 14.4 A Pareto chart of customer complaints. (*Courtesy of Reinz Wisconsin Gasket.*)

The Check Sheet

The purpose of a check sheet is to

- *Help collect and report data* in an organized manner when performing an investigation or analysis.

- *Identify procedures* to undergo for tasks such as experimentation, testing, inspection, maintenance, safety precaution, etc.

A check sheet might be used to collect scrap data by defect category at a molding press for flash, short shots, and sink marks. Other examples would be to inform an inspector of the calibration procedure to use before measuring a shaft diameter with an LVDT column gage or a procedure for a lab technician to follow when preparing a unit to run a durability test on a unit to assure testing consistency. It will also reduce the chance that the test lab's time will be wasted because of negligence due to an improperly prepared test unit. Checklists are useful to organize test plans and test procedures. Employees who use this technique collect more consistent test data.

Experimental Designs

A simply designed experiment can be conducted using a 2 by 2 matrix and using t or F tests to analyze the differences in a manufacturing

Machine rate	Machine type 1	σ	Machine type 2	σ	F test
Slow	Experiment 1		Experiment 2		
Medium	Experiment 3		Experiment 4		
F test	▬▬▬▬▬		▬▬▬▬▬		▬▬▬

Figure 14.5 A basic 2×2 designed experiment matrix which utilizes the F statistic to test for significance.

process measuring 32 pieces at each level in order to establish 97 percent confidence with the results. Figure 14.5 is a full factorial experiment which tests two types of machines and two rates of processing slow and medium. Thirty-two pieces will be measured and the standard deviation calculated. Once these data are collected, an F test will be performed to see if there is a significant difference in the capabilities of the two machines and the manufacturing rates.

Performing more complex tests such as fractional factorials (the Taguchi method) is beyond the scope of this book, but one can obtain information about this method from the American Supplier Institute.

Stratification

Stratification analysis is a technique in which one simply breaks down the data to a lower level and analyzes it. For example, suppose a manufacturing assembly line is encountering difficulty performing an assembly operation press-fitting a shaft. An analysis of the process capability of the parts as received revealed a wide dispersion of the data and a C_{pk} of 0.87. However, further investigation revealed a bimodal distribution which invalidated the assumptions used to calculated the product's C_{pk}. Further investigation revealed that the shafts were ground on three separate machines. Each machine's process capability was studied. The findings revealed that two machines were capable, but the other machine had extreme variation and needed to be rebuilt. By analyzing the problem at a lower level, the problem could be solved. The corrective action in this instance also included improved process controls and a better preventative maintenance program.

Frequent investigations in stratified data reveal inconsistent raw material sources, several machines performing one function, inappropriate goal setting, and monitoring by management, etc.

Scatter Plots

The scatter diagram is a way to identify a relationship between two variables by plotting them on an x-y graph. The independent variable is displayed on the horizontal or x-axis and the dependent variable is listed on the vertical or y-axis. The dependent variable is the item affected by changes in the independent variable due to a causal relationship. Figure 14.6 is an example of a few scatter diagrams. The top, Fig. 14.6a, shows a positive correlation between the variable X and Y. This means that as X increases, so should Y. Figure 14.6b (middle) shows a negative correlation, e.g., as X increases, Y decreases. Finally, Fig. 14.6c shows no correlation between X and Y. Scatter plots are useful for identifying possible relationships between variables; however, one has to identify a reason for that relationship in order to eliminate chance occurrences. For example, some financial analysts believe that there is a correlation between long-term stock prices and women's skirt height above the knees. Although a correlation of significance may be proved, there is not a direct relationship between the two variables.

Histograms

A histogram is an excellent technique that can be used to collect and analyze data. It can reveal whether a distribution is normal, skewed, or bimodal. A *bimodal distribution* is one that has two peaks and can reveal a lot about a manufacturing process. In Fig. 14.7a it reveals a bimodal distribution for a hole. The process had a drilling and a reaming operation. Further investigation revealed that the undersized hole problem was due to the occasional malfunction of a switch during the reaming operation. Figure 14.7b is a computerized histogram from a cold-forming operation for a hexagonal nut and washer assembly. The histogram is reporting data collected about a characteristic called the total indicated runout (T.I.R.), which is a unilateral specification. A unilateral specification is a one-sided specification, e.g., 0.012 inches maximum. For such a specification, the desired T.I.R. value is zero, but it is unrealistic to expect such precision, so there are efforts to reduce variation (less runout is better). However, these data show how the population is distributed from this process.

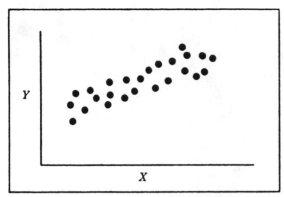

(a) Scatter diagram: Positive correlation

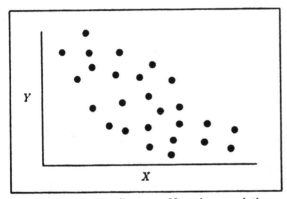

(b) Scatter diagram: Negative correlation

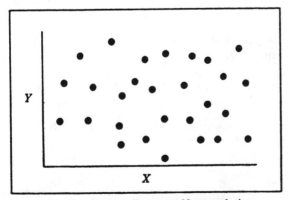

(c) Scatter diagram: No correlation

Figure 14.6   Scatter plots. (*Reprint permission from AT&T.*)

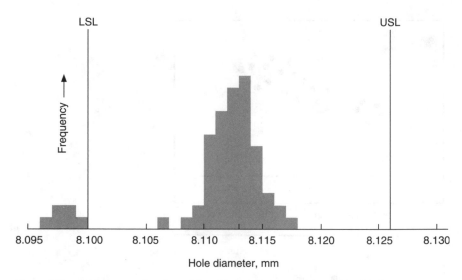

Figure 14.7a A histogram showing a bimodal distribution for a machined hole.

Conducting Meetings

In order to conduct group problem solving and perform corrective action, one must effectively lead meetings. It is best to

1. Start with a *published agenda*. The agenda should be distributed in advance and list all invitees and topics to be discussed. The last item on the agenda can be designated "other" to allow all meeting participants the opportunity to discuss any items related to the subjects that they feel are important.

2. *Stick to the agenda*. During the meeting, if the discussion wanders off to new topics, one may politely ask whether "This item can be discussed at the end of the meeting, so that we can proceed with the agenda as listed." However, this requires judgment, and different approaches should be used depending upon the circumstances.

3. *Summarize the discussion* after each item on the agenda is covered. After reviewing the information, ask for feedback to determine if the summary was correct and if any important information needs to be added.

4. *Assign responsibilities and timing*. All items requiring action or follow-up should have a person assigned to follow it up along with a completion date. The meeting coordinator should ask the members who will address the item. This approach improves the commitment of the meeting participants by having it assigned on a more voluntary basis.

```
                    SPECIALTY FORMING, INC
```

Customer: CHRYSLER	Cust. code: 6501269	Date of Report: 10/12/92
Description: FLANGE HEX/WASHER	Characteristic: T.I.R. .012	II: CHECK 5 PCS. AN HR, RECORD 1 PC/SPC CHART, THE OTHER 4 PCS/IN-PROCESS INSP.
Part #: JN 4029-C.F.	Revision: (REL)8-13-84	SHEET. USE MANDRAL & INDICATOR GAGE.

Special Instructions: RECORD ALL TOOL CHANGES/ADJUSTMENTS, & M.O. CHANGES.[.000, .001, .001] [.000, .001]

TRACEABILITY	SPECIFICATION	DISTRIBUTION	CAPABILITY		PREDICTION
Container # :	TOL: UNILAT.	SD: 0.00113	6SD/TOL(Cr): *UNILAT*	ZU: 7.828	% ABOVE USL : 0.00
Sample # :	USL: .012	+3SD: 0.00653	TOL/6SD(Cp): *UNILAT*	ZL: *UNILAT*	% BELOW LSL : 0.00
Inspect Date:	TARGET: UNILAT.	MEAN: 0.00312	SD Type Cp: *UNILAT*	ZU/3: 2.609	% OUT OF SPEC: 0.00
Inspector :	LSL: UNILAT.	-3SD:-0.00028	RMS Cpk: 2.609	ZL/3: *UNILAT*	% IN SPEC :100.00

HISTOGRAM

```
Reading  Freq Theoretical freq. if normal
 0.0260 |  0|  0.0|
 0.0250 |  0|  0.0|
 0.0240 |  0|  0.0|
 0.0230 |  0|  0.0|
 0.0220 |  0|  0.0|
 0.0210 |  0|  0.0|
 0.0200 |  0|  0.0|
 0.0190 |  0|  0.0|
 0.0180 |  0|  0.0|
 0.0170 |  0|  0.0|
 0.0160 |  0|  0.0|
 0.0150 |  0|  0.0|
 0.0140 |  0|  0.0|
 0.0130 |  0|  0.0|
 0.0120 |  0|  0.0|-------------------------------------------------------------USL
 0.0110 |  0|  0.0|
 0.0100 |  0|  0.0|
 0.0090 |  0|  0.0|
 0.0080 |  0|  0.0|
 0.0070 |  1|  0.6|#=============================================== +3 SIGMA
 0.0060 |  8|  7.7|####
 0.0050 | 34| 42.5|##################
 0.0040 |115|108.0|#####################################################
 0.0030 |138|142.1|###############################################################======= MEAN
 0.0020 |102| 91.2|##########################################################
 0.0010 | 28| 28.5|#############
 0.0000 |  0|  4.9|================================================== -3 SIGMA
          ::::           # out of spec.  Coef. of Skewness  Momental Skewness  Coef. of Excess  Kurtosis  Chi-squared
Samples:  426               0                0.219              0.110             -0.154          2.946       8.7
```

DATA

Audit Date:	0.0040 0.0040 0.0040 0.0040 0.0050 0.0030 0.0030 0.0020 0.0020 0.0020 0.0020 0.0030 0.0040 0.0050
Audit Shift:	0.0030 0.0030 0.0040 0.0030 0.0030 0.0040 0.0030 0.0030 0.0030 0.0020 0.0010 0.0010 0.0020 0.0030
Audit Time:	0.0040 0.0040 0.0030 0.0030 0.0040 0.0030 0.0030 0.0020 0.0030 0.0030 0.0030 0.0040 0.0010 0.0030
Audited by:	0.0020 0.0030 0.0030 0.0020 0.0020 0.0040 0.0030 0.0020 0.0040 0.0030 0.0040 0.0040 0.0040 0.0040
Label Check:	0.0030 0.0030 0.0030 0.0020 0.0010 0.0030 0.0020 0.0010 0.0020 0.0030 0.0020 0.0020 0.0040 0.0040
Disposition: _____	0.0020 0.0030 0.0030 0.0030 0.0030 0.0030 0.0030 0.0010 0.0020 0.0030 0.0020 0.0020 0.0030 0.0040
	0.0060 0.0020 0.0040 0.0060 0.0040 0.0030 0.0040 0.0050 0.0040 0.0020 0.0040 0.0040 0.0040 0.0040

Samples were taken from subgroups: # 1 (3-18 1:00) through # 426 (9-11 7:00)

Figure 14.7b A computerized histogram for a unilateral specification, total indicated runout for a cold-formed hexagonal nut. (*Courtesy of Specialty Forming, Inc., Tiffin, OH.*)

5. *Review all of the key points and action assignments* at the end of the meeting so that it is fresh in their minds and any misunderstandings can be rectified.

6. *Publish and distribute the minutes.* This is very important to assure a common understanding and follow-up.

The meeting leader should be supportive of each member and solicit input from silent members when possible. Sometimes these people will have a contrary viewpoint. This is an invaluable asset that should not be disregarded. Complementing people for good ideas helps to encourage participation and support of the meeting objectives. Leaders should try to be unbiased and not utilize their authority to influence the decision-making process. That person should try to solicit input from the participants and not dominate the discussion.

Figure 14.8 is a example of an advanced quality planning checklist, which was updated after a meeting was conducted. After the meeting is conducted, an update is distributed showing due dates, persons responsible, and percentage complete. At the bottom of the checklist, areas of concern are summarized, with corrective action responsibilities, and timing assigned. This also is a good highlight for manage-

Advanced Quality Planning Checklist			
Customer: XYZ Motors Part Number: L9831C4	Part Name: Gasket-Cylinder Head		
	Team Member(s) Responsible	**Due Date**	**Percent Complete**
Customer Engineering	B. Grede	4/05/89	100%
Consuming Plant's Input	Grede/Johnson	4/20/89	100%
Quality History and Previous Statistical Studies	R. Johnson	5/07/89	100%
Design FMEA	B. Grede	6/01/89	100%
Process Flow Diagram	Evans/Johnson	6/15/89	100%
Process FMEA	R. Johnson	7/07/89	100%
Tooling Designed and Built	J. Evans	9/02/89	100%
Packaging Designed and Fabricated	A. Woods	1/15/90	50%
Manufacturing Control Plan	Johnson/Evans	9/02/89	100%
Process Inspection Sheets	R. Johnson	10/15/89	100%
Process and Gage Verification	R. Johnson	12/15/89	95%
Samples Due	R. Johnson	1/15/90	85%

Summary of Major Issues		Date: 12/09/89
Issue	**Team Member(s)**	**Due Date**
1. The flange over body dimension obtained at operation 50 is not well-centered and has a C_{pk} of 1.18. This needs correction.	J. Evans	1/07/90
2. Visual inspection demonstrated a high number of dings in the fire ring material. This must be corrected to reduce scrap.	Evans/Johnson	1/12/90
3. The samples are due January 15.	R. Johnson	1/15/90

Figure 14.8 An advanced quality planning checklist along with a meeting summary notes for follow-up regarding an engine cylinder head gasket. (*Reprinted with permission from Quality Progress Magazine, an ASQC publication.*)

ment's attention. Before the next meeting is called, a checklist from the previous meeting should be distributed with a meeting notice to allow meeting participants to prepare for items requiring updates for the next meeting.

Resolving Warranty Issues

Warranty meetings can be held in which all significant warranty problems are listed. The tasks for improvement are prioritized and assigned for follow-up using a seven-step corrective action analysis. In some industries where a manufacturing plant also has testing facilities, it is useful to have the plant receive the responsibility for warranty resolution. A plant should then have a warranty budget and a small staff assigned to correct these problems. The plant's manufacturing and engineering organizations will be more cooperative, because they both report to the plant manager. The plant manager would have the incentive to show profits by meeting both production schedules and shipping quality products which do not compromise customer satisfaction. If substantial redesign efforts are needed, the corporate engineering staff can provide additional support. A dotted line reporting relationships should exist between the plant's product engineering and the corporate engineering organization. This will allow all proposed changes to be reviewed by the corporate engineering group so that problems not anticipated by the plant's product engineers can be identified by corporate engineering before an engineering change is instituted. Also it will encourage the plant's product engineers to consult with corporate engineering to resolve warranty concerns. It also will include corporate engineering in a communication loop regarding warranty problems so that product improvements can be included in future design efforts. When a manufacturing plant has warranty responsibility, conflicts between quality, design, and manufacturing can be resolved by a lower level of management. If the quality, engineering, and manufacturing departments' supervision reports to a plant manager, a more cooperative problem-solving atmosphere can result than between the plant management and corporate engineering.

Continuous Improvement Planning

After a specification freeze and an introduction of a new product some resources should be devoted to improving it by either addressing customer complaints, adding new features, or reducing the cost that it takes to achieve a product function or feature without compromising product durability or integrity. These improvement opportunities should be established by determining resource limitations and by using the Pareto principle to prioritize projects. Interdisciplinary team meetings should involve engineering, marketing, manufacturing, warranty (customer complaints), and suppliers in order to maximize customer satisfaction at later product iterations.

Reference

Chrysler Corporation, *Quality Circles—Leaders' Manual,* Corporate Educational Services, Detroit, Mich., p. xiii–3.

Bibliography

David, F. N., "Tables of the Correlation Coefficient," London Biometrika Office, 1938.
Gevirtz, Charles, "The Fundamentals of Advanced Quality Planning," *Quality Progress,* April 1991, Milwaukee, Wis., pp. 49–51.
Mazda Motor Manufacturing (USA) Corporation, *Seven Tools of QC,* Flat Rock, Mich., 1986.

Index

ABOUT THE AUTHOR

Charles Gevirtz is a senior product contract engineer at Chrysler Corporation. Previously, he was a quality commodity manager with Black and Decker Corporation and an applications engineer for O'Brien Energy Systems. He is a professionally licensed engineer and a Certified Quality Engineer with the American Society for Quality Control. He has worked with more than 100 manufacturing facilities at improving their total quality programs. Mr. Gevirtz has a master's in mechanical engineering design from Cornell University and an M.B.A. in marketing from Wayne State University.